SMALL
PUDDLES

THE TRIUMPHANT STORY OF
YALE'S WORST OARSMAN. *EVER.*

MICHAEL P. DANZIGER

FOURTH BOAT BOOKS

BOSTON

First Print Edition, April 2017
ISBN: 978-0-9982852-1-4

WWW.SMALLPUDDLESBOOK.COM

FACEBOOK.COM/SMALLPUDDLES

TO VOGEL.

I wouldn't have done any of it
without you.

Yes, I was a matador, and a very bad one.
But at least I was one.

— A FORGOTTEN BULLFIGHTER

———————

The key to my appreciation of the football experience, and
similarly of college life in general, is my belief that determined effort,
in the face of difficult challenges is worthwhile regardless of success
when it contributes to the good of a group – the team, the college,
the community – and when it adds to my development as a person
well fitted for a useful life.

— ROOSEVELT THOMPSON, YALE 1984,

RHODES SCHOLAR

———————

Nothing in the world can take the place of persistence. Talent will
not; nothing is more common than unsuccessful men with talent...
Persistence and determination alone are omnipotent.

— CALVIN COOLIDGE

PROLOGUE

"Congratulations, Mike."

"Thanks, Zig," Earlier that day, Mike Hard and his teammates from the U.S. National Team had won the lightweight fours event at the Head of the Charles. It had been Mike's fourth victory at America's premiere rowing event, and he was annoyingly blasé about his accomplishment. "It's great to win, but I thought our margin was going to be bigger." Then his voice got more excited. "Hey Zig, a few rowers are having a party in Somerville. Would you like to go?"

"Sounds great," I said.

An hour later we opened the door on a large living room with about thirty people milling about. Mike and I headed over to a refrigerator on the porch and grabbed a couple of beers. He then introduced me to some of his buddies.

These weren't just "a few rowers" as Mike had described

them. That would be like hanging out with Michael Jordan, Larry Bird, and Magic Johnson, and calling them "a few ball players." Almost without exception, everyone at the party was a winner at the Head of the Charles, and many were finalists in the previous summer's World Championships in Bled, Yugoslavia.

I was perhaps the only one at the party whose rowing feats didn't warrant induction into crew's pantheon, as I had rowed in neither the Head nor the World Championships. But the people seemed nice, and the beer was cold, so I felt right at home.

I soon found myself talking to a slight German man wearing a cowboy hat; his somewhat misguided attempt to assimilate himself into American culture. His name was Alvin and he struggled with his English, but spoke it well enough.

"How did you do in the race today?" I asked Alvin.

"I came second, so this was not too disappointing. It is the first time I have been rowing for such a long race in a single."

"Did you used to row sweeps?" I asked.

"Yes. But two years ago I switch to the single. I trained very hard. My goal was to become fastest in Germany and do well in the Worlds in Bled."

"How did you do?"

Alvin was very matter of fact. "Because I learn quickly in the single, I was fortunate to win that time, in 1988."

I couldn't believe I was talking to a World Champion oarsman.

"You won the World Championships!?!" I gushed.

He nodded. "How did you do in Bled?"

He thought I was on the U.S. National Team. I hated to let him down. "I didn't row in Bled. I haven't rowed since I was in university."

Alvin narrowed his eyes and looked at me with a mixture

of disappointment and suspicion. We talked for another minute or so, then he politely excused himself to leave. He wanted to talk to some real oarsmen.

As Alvin left, a drunken prep came up to me. "Champion for a day!" He shouted. "I'm the champion."

He wore a Yale rowing shirt. I didn't recognize the champion from my time at Yale, so I assumed he had won the shirt in a race against Yale.

"Where'd you go to school?" I asked him.

"Penn," he said. "This is Pete Nordell's shirt. I got so many of these Yale shirts that I use 'em to clean my car engine."

"I guess it's the next best thing to getting into Yale."

"How many Penn shirts you got?" the Quaker asked.

"Not a one."

"Ha! Were you a heavy?"

"No, I rowed lightweight."

This was hard for the guy to believe since I was nearly half a foot taller than he was.

"You row with Hard?"

"Same time, different boat."

"So," the champion said, summing things up, "you never beat Penn, you're a lightweight, and you didn't even make the varsity."

"You got it."

"So ... you suck."

With that, my new friend hoisted his glass, announced to anyone who would listen that he was the champion, and left me, as Alvin had, to join some others who he deemed more worthy of his association.

Mike Hard had heard the exchange. "That's just Matt. He gets this way when he's drunk. Actually, he's a pretty cool guy most of the time." Later that evening, the party moved to a room that was filled with rowing memorabilia. Lining the walls were posters from many regattas and championships, along with oversized photos of oarsmen whom I recognized in the room. An MIT oar hung from the ceiling. This room was a shrine to the sport of crew.

On the other side of the room, Hard, Alvin, Matt, and several other oarsmen gathered and talked. It was getting late, and people were beginning to leave. Several of the oarsmen raised their glasses.

"To the next stroke!" One of them hollered. They all began to drink. Again. Before he took a sip, Hard turned to me and saluted me with his beer bottle. I locked eyes with one of Yale's best rowers and raised my cup.

ONE

I pushed open the door to the room I shared with Jon Diamond in a basement suite of Vanderbilt Hall and looked around. It had only been three days since we moved in, and already the room was beginning to resemble the sty which The Banner, Yale's yearbook, would choose as 1981's most revolting room on campus.

A four-gallon tub of ice cream, which we had heisted from the dining hall two nights before but never eaten, was now a light brown puddle in the middle of the room. A once half-full (an optimist would say it was half-empty) spittoon left by some football players as a reminder of their stay in our suite, lay toppled near my bed. The smell was vile, I was told, but my olfactory sense had mercifully ditched me moments after my arrival in New Haven. Strewn across the floor were piles of clothes, piles of books, piles of garbage, and buffer piles to keep all the piles in proper order. Both our mattresses were bare, though J.D. displayed some vestige of civility by having a pillowcase on his pillow.

I negotiated the treacherous path to my bed and sat down.

I glanced around our sewer. The walls were bare, save for a letter I had neatly tacked to the wall nearest my bed. It was a Yale Crew letter. Not the blue, felt varsity letter that the varsity athletic department would confer upon me in gratitude for leading the sons of Eli to many triumphs over our valiant Crimson foes.

No, this was a letter inviting—actually, beseeching is a better word—me to join the Yale Crew. Penned by Rick Elser, Yale's Freshman Lightweight Crew coach, I had read the letter so many times in the three weeks, it had long since been committed to memory. But I would read it again, in much the same manner that a soldier at war rereads letters from his wife or girlfriend. Rick's letter welcomed me to Yale, and briefly described the Crew program. The first year, he explained, all the freshmen rowed together. From sophomore year on, I would be rowing with the varsity squad.

"But I have never seen a boat before, let alone rowed in one," I thought, the first time I read his letter.

Rick's next paragraph quickly soothed my fears. "Crew is a

sport that you can learn in the first two years, and then excel at in your third and fourth years."

Excel. Yes, that was precisely what I planned on doing. I would fulfill Rick's prophecy. I would excel in my third and fourth years. Who knows? Maybe I would learn so quickly that I would accelerate the excelling process and master the sport by my second year.

The reason I was bound to excel was simple. Rick's own words said it best: "You are the ideal size and weight for Lightweight Crew." This was too much for me to stand. At a shade under six foot four and with a measly 152 pounds spread over my long frame, I was thrilled, surprised, and frankly quite relieved, to hear that I was the "ideal size and weight" for anything. Boy, was I lucky I found Yale Lightweight Crew. Of course, Yale Crew would find out that the converse was also true.

I never dreamed that I'd receive a recruiting letter. Granted, Rick Elser was no Barry Switzer, and he didn't seduce me with promises of sports cars, willing cheerleaders, and lots of spending money. Nor did I get follow-up phone calls and the occasional visit to my house. No, Rick probably knew that along with being "the ideal size and weight for crew," I was a one-letter kind of athlete.

But I felt sought after. That made being a freshman at Yale a less daunting experience. Two of the other three guys who shared our suite were John Basher and Stephen Anderer, both all-state football players heavily recruited by Carm Cozza to do battle for the Bulldogs in the Yale Bowl. Neither John nor Stephen was timid. Though as lost as any of the other 1,297 members of our class, these guys would swagger, rather than slink, around their strange new environment. I was eight inches taller, and nearly sixty pounds lighter than Bash (never John), but our strides were derived from the same attitude.

An hour earlier, this very stride, along with a map tucked in the front of my course catalogue — which I discreetly carried like a talisman around campus for the first three weeks — delivered me to the Beinecke Courtyard, one of the most impressive spots at Yale.

As I walked across the Cross Campus lawn, a row of elm trees welcomed me to Beinecke. Immediately I was struck by an enormous white building that reminded me of a Greek temple, except that this one was not a crumbled ruin. It was Commons, the freshman dining hall. Inside this imposing marble structure, over 1,200 hungry freshmen would gather for their meals.

Outside stood a monument to the alumni who had surrendered their lives in World War I. On it was carved the words:

Nine Doric (perhaps Ionic; I always get them confused) columns rose some thirty feet in the air. Yet their girth, coupled with the enormous triangular entablature that rested on top of the columns, made them appear squat. Inside the entablature were carved the names of some of the battlefields, like Argonne, Ypres, and Chateau-Thierry, on which these young men made the ultimate sacrifice. The building was instantly inspiring.

Forming a right angle with Commons on its left was the Beinecke Rare Book and Manuscript Library. Unlike Commons, this building reminded me of nothing I had ever seen. A cube-shaped, windowless building, so white that it appeared translucent, as if constructed from Egyptian alabaster. Dozens of identically sized cubes were indented into the facade of Beinecke in such a way that light and shadow mingled in a unique relationship inside each cube.

Housed inside were some of the most treasured books and manuscripts in the world, including one of the Gutenberg Bibles, and the papers from the Zenger trial. Yale so cherished these possessions that in the event of a fire, the security system would suck all the oxygen out of the library, immediately extinguishing the flames. Of course, the concurrent result of this book-saving system was that any and all people in the library would suffocate and perish. I learned this on my orientation tour of Yale and thought it offered an interesting glimpse at the administration's priorities.

On the other side of the courtyard was an Alexander Calder stabile. This colorful sculpture provided a change from the monochromatic scheme of the rest of the courtyard. As the wind blew, the stabile moved almost imperceptibly. Yet its movement changed the otherwise static courtyard.

Directly to my right was Woodbridge Hall. Here Bart Giamatti, Yale's President, worked. Everyday he made decisions that, like Calder's stabile, changed the college in important, if subtle ways.

If he had been looking out of his window at the courtyard on August 29, 1981, he would have seen a crew shell, held in slings. And perhaps he saw me striding towards it.

I approached the sleek blue fiberglass boat, and was quickly greeted by a thin man, just shorter than myself. He, sported a mustache above his wide grin.

"What's your name?" he asked me.

"Mike Danziger."

"Well, Mike, have you ever rowed crew?"

I shook my head. "No sir. Not yet."

"Not yet," he repeated, smiling broadly. "I'm Dave Vogel, and I coach the varsity Lightweights. I'd like to see you at the meeting tonight. It's at 7:30 in Linsly-Chittenden Hall. Know where that is?"

I patted my trusty Blue Book. "I'll find it by 7:30."

"See you then, Mike."

"Yes sir."

I turned to leave and heard Dave's voice again. "By the way, cut the 'sir' shit; you're in college now."

I thought I was being polite, but Coach Vogel made me feel like a chump. I certainly didn't call him sir out of any respect I had gained for him in the previous 45 seconds. Nor was I trying to kiss his ass. Calling an adult "sir" was instinct developed in me by my fifth grade English teacher. A giant of a man with a fu-manchu mustache, Mr. D'Angelo possessed an eighth degree black belt and an explosive temper. I always assumed he'd shred me with his bare hands if I referred to him as anything other than "sir." Standing before Coach Vogel, I'd rather have risked myself at the lethal hand of Mr. D'Angelo than have the varsity Lightweight coach think I was a chump. I nodded sheepishly, consulted my map, and headed off in a deliberate manner in the exact opposite direction from my intended destination at Vanderbilt Hall.

Back in my room, I gazed at the letter above my bed. I

couldn't wait for 7:30 to arrive. Not only was I "ideal" according to Coach Elser, but hadn't Coach Vogel all but begged me to show up at the meeting?

The door swung open and J.D. slalomed through the debris and threw himself on his bed. "What's up tonight, Zig?"

"I'm going to the crew meeting in Linsly-Chit." I had been at Yale a scant three days, and already I was on a nickname basis with some of the buildings.

J.D. rolled over and stretched. "I was thinking maybe I'd see what it's all about. Why don't we head on over together?"

"Sounds good to me."

TWO

J.D. and I filed into the lecture hall along with almost 200 prospective oarsmen and oarswomen. We took our places in wooden chairs with wraparound desks and surveyed the crowd.

"This isn't exactly the United Nations," J.D. commented.

He was right. Though Yale crows about drawing its student body from all over the world, its boats are filled with a cross section of New England prep school students. The crowd was a real mixed bag. There were people from schools as different as Andover and St. Paul's. Quite remarkable! Just about every guy in the room had preppy good looks, and was wearing his school t-shirt.

I felt a little out of place. Collegiate, my alma mater, is a day- prep school. But I had applied to, and been rejected by, every single school whose representatives surrounded me. Now we were all together at Yale.

Though the path from Collegiate School, where I had spent 12 wonderful years, to Yale was hardly lightly trodden, I still found myself stunned to be here. Did I belong? Was I an imposter? Would my four years here matter to me—or to

Yale for that matter? To understand how I ended up at Yale it's helpful to know two men who loomed large in my life: Bruce Breimer and Dick Danziger.

———————

Bruce Breimer, or Boss, as everyone called him, had been helping students from my school navigate the college process for nearly two decades, and he was, by consensus, and orders of magnitude, the best at what he did, anywhere. He got the name Boss from Boss Tweed, the scandalous New York labor leader of the early 1900s, about whom he taught in an urban history class. But the moniker really described him. He was the Boss. Tough, demanding, always obeyed. And more than that, he was the hardest working, most informed person in his field. Students trusted his instincts, which were born from years of success. Likewise, colleges knew Boss was an honest broker. If he told Bill Fitzsimmons, the Dean of Admissions at Harvard, that a Collegiate boy who maybe didn't fit the admissions profile on paper, but would be great at Harvard, sure enough that boy would be going to Harvard.

Boss was blunt and honest, and didn't suffer fools or have any use for nuance. When you walked into his office, you better be ready to answer direct questions about your academic interests, potential use to the college community, and what you hope to accomplish in the next four years. If you didn't flinch, met his gaze with your own, and had a real sense of who you were and what you might want in a college, it would be intense, but time well spent.

Otherwise, the meeting would be quick, chilly, and you'd miss a chance to really engage with a brilliant man.

Boys feared the Boss not because he was loud and direct, though that was a bit unnerving. What was really frightening was that Boss made you look at yourself honestly and he dared you to remove the easiest and most used excuse a teenager had in his arsenal: that you weren't really trying your hardest. For many of us, we could shrug off disappointing results or unmet standards by saying that we hadn't given it our all. To leave it all on the field and still come up short because you weren't good enough took a brand of courage I sure didn't begin to know anything about. Likeability and an odd take on life, along with the ability to get words on paper without filtering them through too much self-consciousness got me 90% there. The other 10% would either never happen or Boss would pull it out.

In the fall of my senior year at Collegiate, I stared at the door to Boss' office, wondering when it would open and be my turn to get scrutinized.

The door opened and I could hear Matthew Brody speaking.

"I'm sorry, Boss. I didn't look at the essay section of the application."

Boss wasn't in a forgiving mood, "Sorry doesn't walk the dog, Matthew. I don't want to hear a sniveling apology. I have a better idea. Why don't you not apologize, not make excuses for once. Instead, why don't you give a shit. I do, and I'm not the one who's going to be going to college. This was a waste of my time." Mathew shuffled out of Boss's office sheepishly as I stood to walk in.

I am easily intimidated, but even if I wasn't I'd have been on my heels. Boss is average height, but his frame carries a lot of extra weight. His heft adds to his persona. He didn't rise from his seat as I walked in. He didn't need to.

"Hi Boss"

"Zig," he says, waving me in without a smile.

I sat down in the chair and looked at him across of heap of papers he had yet to grade and recommendations he was writing.

"Have you gotten anywhere on this thing, Zig? Can you see yourself at any of these schools?"

"I think I'd like to go to Yale," I said, tentatively. "If I could ever get in, that is."

"Great fit," he agreed. "The residential college system is made for you. Small within big. And it's intellectual without being effete. I could see you really getting into some of the history seminars and also writing for the literary magazine. Zig, it's not for everyone, and it's really tough to get into. Just because you'd love it, doesn't mean you have a prayer of getting in. But yes, I think Yale would be good for you. And of course, I think you'd be great for Yale. You know why I think Yale would be good for you?"

My palms went up. Shoulder shrug. Boss continued. "Because it's hard, demanding. You have to work there. A place like Brown, much less structure, fewer requirements. It's up to the students. And frankly, you aren't a self-starter. You'd float around for four years at Brown. At Yale, it's hard work. And you can do hard work...if it's demanded of you."

Boss, pulled out my dossier: Transcript, extracurriculars, teacher comments... a glimpse of who I am.

"Your grades are terrific. So are those of everyone who applies to Yale. And we love you here and will support you. But my support doesn't mean shit if you aren't great. It's called credibility. The deciding factors will be SAT scores and your essay. You have to figure out something really interesting to write about."

Boss looked at me over his glasses, then continued on.

"Have you given thought to what you want to focus on

in your essay? This is your chance to introduce yourself to the folks in admissions. Look, everyone has good grades and at least 1450 boards. That's a given. Two thirds of these really qualified kids won't get in. The ones who get in, make their case in the essay."

"Boss," I said, knowing my answer wasn't what he wanted to hear. "I am really stuck. I am happy, optimistic, and want to be a vital part of whatever campus I go to. Why shouldn't I be? My family has plenty of money, I haven't wanted for a thing, and I've spent 12 years here, and loved every second. There's no grit. No defining moments. No overcoming odds. I'm lucky and I know it."

Boss looked at me. "Are you kidding? Don't bullshit me. You and I both know that you aren't the typical pampered kid that most associate with this school. You look it, but you aren't"

"I'm not?"

"Hell no Zig! The fact that you are sane, let alone happy, is a miracle." He looked at me. Again nothing. Vacant stare.

"You grew up in a family of wealth. Fine. But you also grew up in a house with perhaps the biggest tyrant I've ever come across. Ever. In all my years. Your dad is a maniac." Then Boss' voice softened and he looked at me almost sympathetically. "And you are kind, open minded, gentle and want to help the very people your dad disdains, the vulnerable. Don't think I haven't noticed you spending time with the homeless across the street at the Hotel Belclaire. I've seen you tutoring kids of all stripes from the younger grades. I've seen all of that, you know? And that is the antithesis of your father."

"My dad's okay," I said. "Just a bit of a temper sometimes."

In some ways, Boss and my Dad were similar. They shared a lack of discipline at mealtime (and in between) that left them overweight, and neither was a stranger to bombast. The difference was that when Dad raised his voice, it was to force me to become more like him, or at least more like the way he wanted me to turn out; when Boss turned it up, it was to dare me to become better, to try harder, and to not be an underachiever. He dared me to be Michael Danziger, whomever that might be.

"Save it, Zig. Don't apologize for him. It isn't your job and he doesn't deserve it. He is a lunatic. A bully. Really unsettling to be around. I mean it. He's a fucking parody of himself. You live with him, and revere him somehow. And you have been able to sift the good inside of him that is buried under a very dangerous shell. I've never seen anything like it."

"So you want me to write about my Dad and how he has influenced me? How he taught me right and wrong by doing both?"

"Well, yes." Boss leaned forward, jabbing a number two pencil at me. "That's exactly what you need to do. Now get out and do it." He flicked the back of his fingers in my direction, which I took to mean I was dismissed.

THREE

N ow that Boss mentioned it, my dad was a gold mine of material. Bombastic, snobbish, yes a bully, and doctrinaire to the extreme. There were two ways things "were done" according to my father: his way and the wrong way.

To know about how my father treated me, it might help to know about television in our home. I can remember watching *Petticoat Junction*, a subtly sexy comedy about country folk in a small town whose lives revolved around the comings and goings of the train station. I loved the show, the catchy theme song, and I think I had the beginnings of my first crush on one of the young women with two names: Bobbie Sue or Betty Jo. Not sure which.

Anyway, I was watching *Petticoat Junction* in the living room when my father walked in. He didn't tread lightly, so I sensed his presence right away, but my eyes were still trained on the 19-inch Motorola color television we had gotten months ago. He walked right up to the TV and slammed his thick palm on the power button. The screen went black, then there was dying flash of color from a spot in the center of the screen. Then nothing.

"How come you did that?" I asked.

"That's it," my father declared. "No more television."

"No more TV, tonight?" I asked, disappointed.

"Ever." he said.

"Ever?"

"That's right, ever. Unless the Mets make the World Series. You can watch a bit on weekends with me. But basically, ever."

"Why not?" I wondered, really bewildered by this random, but gigantic, piece of news.

"Because that's the rule." He turned and walked away.

Of course, since television was now forbidden, it became my obsession and I watched all the clandestine TV I could.

We lived in an apartment and the doorman would blast the doorbell three times from the lobby when my mother and father were about to get in the elevator from a night out. I'd turn off the TV, fluff the pillows on the coach, and even wipe the static off the screen, in case he touched it.

I memorized every *Brady Bunch* episode, lusted after the women in *Love, American Style*, and grew up with the *Little Rascals*. Whenever my folks were away, I was planted in front of the TV. It was the forbidden fruit and I had to taste it.

If I had been allowed to watch television, I am certain I would have watched a small fraction of what I watched since it was verboten. That's kind of how it goes with ludicrous rules.

There was one time I could watch television, not including

limited weekend time and a two-week period in 1973 when the Mets lost to the A's in the World Series. Because the remote control hadn't been invented yet, my father would sometimes have me kneel next to the television with my hand on the dial. He would tell me to go clockwise or counterclockwise, and how many clicks.

There were only half a dozen or so channels, so it wasn't such hard work. But still. Kind of absurd — without the kind of. I'd sit there for an hour or so. Left two. Right three. Sometimes, he'd tell me "do a lap" which meant a slow sampling of all the channels. Though I wasn't remotely aware that my services would be replaced by a piece of plastic in a few years, I did my job well and even enjoyed it when I lingered a bit on a show I wanted to see, before being barked at to keep the lap going.

This went on in one fashion or another for a decade. The fall of my senior year, just around the time I had been urged to explore my relationship with my father, his parents were killed in a car accident on the Taconic as they headed to Vassar, where my kind and loving grandmother was an alumna.

A few weeks after the funeral, my Dad and his brother were getting their parent's house ready to sell. As part of the sad process, Dad announced that each of the four grandchildren could go into the house and take something that either had particular meaning or that we thought might be of value someday. As the oldest by three minutes over my sister, I was allowed to pick first. The advantages of primogeniture were never so clear. My grandparents were not super rich, but they lived a more than comfortable life, and in doing so acquired the accoutrement of wealth. My twin sister, when it was her turn, nabbed the Chippendale furniture. My cousin David claimed the silver setting that served a dozen. And my youngest cousin Becky, then a seventh grader, decided that what she wanted most was the crystal chandelier.

But I went first! I entered the old Victorian house and went straight for what I prized most, and carried it out in my arms. What I had was a grey box with some dials on the front, flat and rectangular, ten inches in length, maybe seven inches across and just a few inches tall. An arm swung out on the bottom so the box could be propped up. A power chord at the rear finished the picture.

As I left, cradling my inheritance against my chest, my father looked at me.

"That's it? A radio?"

"This is what I want," I said, meeting his incredulity with my certainty. "There is nothing else in this house I want."

My dad looked puzzled, certain that I had blown my chance to feather my future nest with something really valuable.

"Suit yourself," he said, and then he told my sister it was her turn to choose.

That night, I put the grey box on my night table and plugged the cord into the wall. I turned the dial to 1010 WINS news and listened to the familiar voice assure me that if I gave him 22 minutes, he'd give me the world.

Seemed like a fair trade, but I had other ideas. On top of the box was a button, light grey, and about half an inch square. I pressed the button and the front of the box lifted up on its rear hinge revealing a three-and-a-half inch black and white television! I flipped the switch from radio to TV, and turned the dial slightly to left. Channel four flickered to life in my bedroom. I was watching my own television in my own room.

I am not sure I had ever been happier. To this day, though not a "thing" person, that radio/television is my most prized possession. It sits on my desk, a reminder.

So it was my father, this towering figure, this overbearing presence who ruled by fiat and by keeping me on my toes, who I feared, revered, and whose approval I somehow sought above all, about whom Boss wanted me to write. Beneath layer upon layer of bombast, snobbery, bully, and brute lay a man who had supple intellect, a deep sense of justice, and passions that ranged from opera to the arcane Japanese tea ceremony. He was a passable lawyer in his father's firm, but had he not thought so little of the field, he would have been a fantastic teacher.

There was a problem about writing about my father. Well,

there were two. The first was that I would have to be able to hold and present both sides of this complicated man with whom I had an even more complicated relationship. How could I describe his fearsome side and then show how much I adored him? It would be hard to put into words, but I'd been living it for 17 years so there had to be a way.

The other problem was more practical. Surely my father would want to see my application essay, so I really needed to write two essays: the essay Boss suggested, and a dummy essay to show Dad.

Both Boss and my father were brutal editors, requiring nearly a dozen drafts, challenging every assumption and making sure each word was right, and each point well-supported. And though I'd write two essays, one would be sent to admissions officers; the other would end up in a trash can.

For the next month, I worked on my two essays. For the one going to college admissions, Boss wanted me to be sympathetic but not apologetic for my father's temper, bias, and doctrinaire view of the world. But he didn't want me to describe a cartoon character either. What I was trying to do was show that I was able to see though his bombast and glean the values that he held dear, and that were dear. It was hard to do, and for several drafts, I didn't come close.

"You got it, Z," Boss finally told me. "This works. It more than works. This shows that you are tough, insightful, sophisticated, and willing to look beyond the surface to find the core. It's searing but really fair. It's good. Very good."

I left his office feeling proud that I'd met the standard of a very demanding man. But not the only demanding man whose standard I had to meet. My other essay was on "The Virtues of Effort" in which I profiled efforts that were valuable, just for having taken place, regardless of outcome. The athlete who dove for every loose ball but sat on the bench, farthest from the coach; medical research that makes progress but doesn't cure the disease; and my own struggles in classes that were just beyond my level but in which I tested myself daily.

My father, predictably, thought my examples were either lousy, clichéd, or didn't support my thesis at all, which he found clichéd to begin with. On a mid-December weekday, I walked into his study and handed him my eighth draft. He skimmed the sections he had seen before and had approved and nodded at some of my improvements and additions. He held his pen poised above the paper as he read — this alone shows a side of Dad I cherish; he cares, really cares and wants me to do my best — but it never touched one of the three sheets.

He looked up and me and nodded. "I don't think you can do much better than this. It's fine. Type it up one more time and it's ready to send off."

I took the paper and walked out of his study. As I turned into the hallway that led to my bedroom, I crumpled the essay into a ball. When I got into my room I launched the ball of paper into the air towards my trashcan. It hit the front rim and fell onto the floor. I reached down to pick it up and put in the rebound. Then I had another idea. I went over to my desk with the essay, laid it on the desk and smoothed it out a bit.

I opened my desk drawer and took out the manila folder

that held the essay I had written for Boss about my father. Then I grabbed a stapler and attached the second essay to the first. Across the bottom of the third crumpled page I wrote, "This is the essay I showed my old man."

I guess that did the trick.

FOUR

At the front of the room, during the first week of my "bright college years with pleasure rife," stood five men. I recognized only Coach Vogel. A rugged man with silverish hair and a gentle face raised his hand and began to speak.

"I'm Tony Johnson," he began, "And I coach the Varsity Heavyweights." He then introduced the other men. There was Coach Vogel; Nat Case, the Women's coach; Rick Ricci, coach of the Freshmen Heavyweights; and finally Rick Elser, my pen pal, who was short, slight of build and had matted-down wiry hair.

Coach Johnson continued with his deep, soft voice and easy smile. "I assume you all received our letters." Wait just a minute! I wasn't the only person in the room who received a chummy note from the coach? The magic of word processing, and its ability to shatter the illusions of a teenager, hadn't touched me until this moment. I later found out that every male between 5'7" and 6'4" and under 170 pounds received one of Rick's "recruiting" letters. I wondered how many of the recipients had pinned the letter to their walls and committed the words to memory. I decided that I was probably alone in that group.

I snapped out of my disillusioned state to see Coach Johnson pulling down a movie screen. "I realize this film is a few years out-of-date, and might seem a bit campy," he apologized, "but it may be helpful for those of you who aren't familiar with crew." A hand gesture darkened the room and caused a projector to start spinning.

The movie was called *Symphony in Motion*. It opened with boats gliding across a mirror lake. The boats had one, two, sometimes eight oarsmen in them. I was surprised that in some boats, each oarsman pulled one oar. I thought oarsmen always had an oar in each hand. All the while, there were strains of soothing orchestral music in the background.

The second "movement" took us to George Pocock's boat shop somewhere in Washington State. This man, portrayed as an artisan, turned trees into sleek racing shells before our eyes.

More rowing on the lake, and then we were taken indoors to watch a man practicing on a rowing machine. The machine had an oar on one side, a sliding seat, and dials facing the man working out. As this scene flashed across the screen, many of the people in the room booed. Some giggled nervously. I looked over at the coaches. They were smiling at each other. J.D. turned towards me and shrugged.

The crescendo came as boats glided across the lake to the harmonious strains of an orchestra.

Up came the lights, and Coach Johnson and his colleagues grabbed our attention by holding up t-shirts. There were about twenty different shirts all told, each a different color. Some had sashes that traversed the shirts diagonally. Others had crossed oars. Still others were more simply designed.

"These shirts," Coach Johnson stated, in a more commanding voice, "Are what we row for. When we win, our opponents surrender their racing shirts to us. In turn, we must relinquish our shirts if we lose a race.

"This is the racing shirt of the rival we most like to beat on the water." He held aloft a crimson shirt with an H on the right breast. On cue, the entire room hissed in unison.

Here we were, at school for less than a week. We hadn't the foggiest idea what it meant to be a "Yalie." But we were certain of one thing: We wanted to beat Harvard.

Again I looked towards the front of the auditorium at the coaches. More smiles.

Finally, Coach Johnson held up a blue shirt with white piping at the neck and arms, a white sash across it, and a Y on the right breast. "If, at the end of the season, you have this shirt in your collection, it means that you have won either the Sprints or The Race. So this is the most important shirt of all."

At that moment, I coveted that blue shirt more than any object ever in my life. Even more than the radio.

The last five minutes of the meeting, the coaches entertained questions about the program. Several hands shot up.

"Where is the gym?"

"What river do we row on?"

"Do we really have to get up at five every morning?"

Coach Vogel answered this question. "No one likes getting up before dawn. I certainly don't. You can practice at 5am anytime you like. The rest of us will be working out in the afternoons." One myth shot down. I was relieved.

"When are cuts made?"

Coach Johnson fielded this question. "I think you'll find that cuts really aren't necessary in our program. The process is very much self-selective. Those who don't quit, won't get cut."

I thought to myself, "I can do that. I can not quit."

"It's not as simple as you might imagine. At Yale, we practice eight minutes for every minutes of racing that very few ever know about." Coach Johnson added. I felt as if he were speaking directly to me. "Less than one in ten of you will be rowing by senior year." A sobering thought indeed.

J.D. and I walked out together. And in the gloaming on Old Campus we vowed solemnly that we would never, under any circumstance, quit. I wondered how many similar oaths were taken on the freshmen quad.

The next day, I headed over to Payne Whitney Gymnasium to attend my first crew practice. I took the path between Morse and Stiles, the two modern colleges, and there it towered: The "cathedral of sweat," as we all came to know it.

Payne Whitney is an impressive sight, but the impression I got certainly wasn't of an athletic arena. What loomed in front of me was a nine-story Gothic tower, whose base ran almost the length of a city block. The Yale catalogue described Payne Whitney as the "largest indoor athletic facility in the free world."

I imagined that the Russians had some place even bigger, where they would haul little three and four-year-old Russian kids off to if the toddler displayed a glimmer of athletic potential. These children would be housed away from their family and friends for their entire childhoods and taught archery, or gymnastics, or whatever. Then they would emerge from the largest indoor athletic facility in the entire world and win lots of gold medals for Mother Russia. No wonder these comrades never smiled on the victory stand. If I were trapped in an athletic dungeon and didn't ever get to play tag or spin the bottle or watch ESPN, I'd be relieved that the whole ordeal was over.

Snapped out of my reverie, I entered through the heavy wooden doors of this penultimate gymnasium and waved to a guard in a booth as I walked by.

"Just a second, pal," he said. "Where's your pass? Gotta have a pass to get by me."

"That's all right, I'm an oarsmen. I'm just on my way to the tanks." I said this with surprising authority considering I had no idea what, or where, the tanks were.

He responded with an even greater level of authority and not a small touch of ridicule. "Everyone's an oarsmen at first. You'll get a pass just like all the other oarsmen."

I was deflated. "Where do I get my pass?

"Right over there." He pointed to a line of at least fifty students.

I thanked him and began to walk towards the line. He shouted after me, "I hope you're still an oarsman next year." I couldn't tell if he was sincere or sarcastic.

An hour later, I found myself, pass in hand, in the basement of the gym, where the tanks were. I pulled open a blue door and found myself in a giant room unlike any I had ever been in before. Under a 30-foot ceiling lay a deep, narrow room filled with the means and machinery of rowing. On the left side of the room were mats, benches and barbells strewn about. In the back corner, I recognized the rowing machines from the movie which had drawn sneers from the crowd. There were four of them, and they seemed benign enough to me. On the right was what I took to be the tank. In the middle of the tank, there were eight seats, one behind another, with oarlocks on either side. Five-foot wide pools of water ran down both sides of the seats. Mirrors around the tank, I assumed, let the oarsmen (I really liked the sound of that word, "oarsmen." It sounds rugged, somehow Norse) could check out their technique. The room was dank, redolent of mildew, sweat, and chlorine. The fetid odor reminded me of my dorm room.

I heard a noise from another room. I passed through a side door into an identical room. Guys surrounded the tank, watching somebody row. I recognized Rick Elser standing on a walkway, eye-level with the oarsman. I joined the rest of the group and listened in.

"You're watching Steve Gavin row," Rick informed us. Steve betrayed no emotion. He simply began to row, very slowly and carefully. "He is the Captain of the Varsity Lightweights. Notice how the stroke is really quite simple. There are four components to the stroke. The catch." Steve rolled his seat forward, reached out with his arms, and stuck the oar in the water. "The drive." Steve pulled his oar through the stagnant water. "The finish." Steve raised the oar out of the water. "And the recovery." Steve then rolled his seat forward to take another stroke.

"Catch, drive, finish, recovery… catch, drive, finish, recovery." Rick repeated these words over and over, as Steve dutifully provided the visuals. "If you can master these seemingly simple steps, you can help Yale Lightweight Crew win races."

Then Rick stepped down, turned a dial, and the water on either side of Steve started rushing by him like an indoor river. Rick got back up on the platform and smiled as we gaped in surprise and excitement. I bet the Ruskies didn't have one of these in their dungeon. This looked like fun, not drudgery.

I stood among the other guys, towering over almost all

the rest, who were also "the ideal size and weight" (still smarting from that one) and repeated in my head the formula for crew success again and again. Catch, Drive, Finish, Recovery. I would never forget these four steps. And just to make sure, I devised, right then and there, amongst the other pretenders to rowing greatness, a mnemonic device to help me remember the four critical components: Captain Danziger Fine Rower. I wanted to use "Oarsman" but I couldn't come up with a synonym for "recovery" that began with O. Plus, I wanted to stick with Rick's words.

It occurred to me that if I could learn to do what Steve was doing, perfect the movements, and never quit, there was no reason I couldn't be rowing in front of a bunch of freshmen in three years as Rick chanted the familiar litany, "Catch. Drive. Finish. Recovery."

When an audience leaves a musical, some exit the theater singing a memorable number from the show. In much the same way, I found myself leaving the tanks repeating Rick's words.

Just outside, a man appeared in front of me. I recognized him immediately. His words confirmed my recollection. "I'm Rick Ricci," he said. "And I coach the freshmen heavyweights."

"Pleased to meet you," I said.

"What's your name?" I told Coach Ricci who I was and he replied, "How tall are you, Mike?"

"Six four." I rounded up.

"Why are you trying out for the lightweights?"

"Well, I got this letter asking me to try out."

I was about to explain, as if he couldn't tell, that I was the "ideal size and weight for lightweight crew," when he said, "With your height, I think you are more suited for heavyweight crew."

How, I wondered, could I be more suited? Was there a loftier superlative than 'ideal'?

"How much do you weigh, Mike?"

"About 155."

"How would you like to weigh 175 or 180 come spring?" Rick queried. Had I just stepped out of the gym and into a Charles Atlas ad in the back of a comic book?

"That'd be great," I practically gushed. No one would kick sand in this guy's face again.

Rick nodded. "I'll tell you what. You row with the heavyweights, and I will put you on a weight explosion program. You'll be bigger by the spring rowing season," he assured me.

How quickly Rick Elser's letter vanished from my mind. My loyalty to the lightweights couldn't compete with Rick Ricci's Dynamic Tension, or whatever method he had that would make A Man Out of Mike. Somehow, the lightweight program would have to manage without me. From now on, I was a heavyweight.

I shook Coach Ricci's hand. "When do I start practicing?"

The coach smiled. "Tomorrow at three."

Whereas I had been the tallest lightweight, I was average height amongst the frosh heavies, as we were known. In fact, there were a few guys on the team who positively dwarfed me, Paul Fost and Colin Cooke being the behemoths of the squad. Both guys were over 6'7" and very strong. Of the forty or so guys trying out for the two boats that would row in the spring, everyone knew that Paul and Colin would be sitting somewhere in the first boat. More significantly, Paul and Colin were quietly certain of this.

For the next couple of weeks, we practiced in the tanks, trying to act out the four elements of rowing that Rick Elser had preached. What Steve Gavin had made look so simple was in fact the opposite. Even if any of us individually could have duplicated Steve's motions, the task of all eight of us performing the sequence was far beyond our limited capacity. We didn't remotely resemble the boats we had witnessed moving across the screen in "Symphony in Motion." Our motions were more a cacophony, eight distinct splashes indicating the differences in our strokes. While I was Finishing, Chris Wilkinson might be Recovering, Chris Duncan could be Driving, and Paul Fost was liable to be at the Catch. Driving towards the finish while the man behind me was readying himself for the catch was particularly perilous, as I would drive my kidney into a waiting oar handle. Operant conditioning (i.e. fear of pain), was as much responsible for our improved timing as was practice.

One day, I looked in the mirror at the side of the tank to check my form and what did I behold? A small lump on the back of my arm, above the elbow. Was it? Could it be? Yes, it was the debut of the first muscle I had developed thanks to crew: a larger tricep. I was elated.

When I got back to the suite, I proudly flexed in front of Stephen.

"Not bad," he charitably observed. "You're getting to be a regular giant." He then pushed his right hand down, locking his elbow. A horseshoe of a muscle emerged under the flesh on his arm. I nodded in admiration. I had something to shoot for.

FIVE

rew practice was the only aspect of life at Yale that I was sure about. Five days a week I would show up at the gym for practice. Other than that set activity, I found myself at sea, especially when it came to navigating my way through the seemingly limitless paths that lay in front of me. The Blue Book, aside from having a map of the campus in it, contained course descriptions for thousands of courses. Looking through this ledger, I found myself feeling like a man drinking from a waterfall. There was so much there that I feared I might not get a drop. My involvement with crew resolved this problem for me.

One day in the locker room before practice, I was getting into my shorts and t-shirt when I overheard some of the guys on the varsity discussing what courses they wanted to take. One of them had a unique system: He only took courses that had a nickname. He rattled off lots of them: Touchie Feelie, Clapping for Credit, Rocks for Jocks, Nuts for Sluts, Hand Holding for Credit, Heroes for Zeros were among his course selections. He even took a class called Moons for Goons, an astronomy course.

"You learn anything in that class?" he was asked.

"You bet I did," he bragged. "I found out that there are stars that are gigantic, but they are so far away from Earth that you can't even see them." Everyone cracked up.

This master of the Blue Book even announced that he had completed his distribution requirements using his simple and fool proof system.

I was sold. I quickly went home and made my selections. On my schedule were a world history course called Plato to NATO, and an ancient philosophy course with the moniker Greeks for Geeks.

I also chose an art history survey course, and an English class which I didn't find satisfactory. To be more accurate, it was the English class that did not find me satisfactory.

About two weeks into the term, I looked at my syllabus and panicked. Our first paper, on "Young Goodman Brown," a short story by Nathaniel Hawthorne, was overdue?? The class met on Tuesdays and Thursdays, but the syllabus said the paper was due the previous Friday. Surely this was a typo? I called my professor, whose name my memory has mercifully blotted out. A female voice answered the phone. I recognized it as the same voice that had informed the class that papers were to be typed, with 22 lines per page, 1¾" margin at the top and bottom of each page, and a 1¼" margin on either side. Due dates were firm, not subject to negotiation, she had warned the sixteen freshmen who sat at attention as she relayed the requirements.

I considered hanging up the phone at her first utterance, but I screwed up my courage and timidly began to speak. "This is Michael Danziger..." There was no response on the other end. She had no idea who Michael Danziger was, and I guessed she wasn't dying to find out. I'd give her a clue. "I'm in your

English class. The one that meets on Tuesdays and Thursdays from 9 to 10:15."

"Well Mr. Danziger," Professor Hard-ass replied, "you've interrupted my Sunday supper. What is it?" Terrific. She was clearly not in a charitable mood. I shouldn't have called during dinner. But I did think she ought to know about the typo in the syllabus.

"Pardon me," I began. "I'm just calling because I think there is a mistake on the syllabus."

"The syllabus is correct," she informed me in an indignant tone.

"Well it says here that our paper was due last Friday, and our class doesn't even meet on Fridays. Didn't you mean to put Tuesday?"

"It says Friday because that is when I wanted the papers. Everyone else, Mr. Danziger, handed the paper in to my office on time on Friday, as specified in the course outline."

Well done. My very first written assignment, and I screwed it up. "Well, I'll be sure to get it in first thing on Monday," I promised.

"You do remember my policy with late papers, don't you?"

Now she was just making sport of this scatter-brained freshman. Of course I hadn't remembered her policy. "No, I'm afraid I can't recall it."

"I take a grade off the paper for every hour it is late."

"I see." I was totally deflated. "Sorry to interrupt your dinner, professor."

"Good bye, Mr. Danziger," she said, making sure I knew that she hadn't forgotten my name.

As soon as she hung up, I rushed to my typewriter and started cranking out the paper. I had read that Hawthorne story at Collegiate, and remembered some of the themes of lost faith, allusions, and puritan culture. I threw it all into the paper, added some Hamburger Helper so it would meet the length requirement, and made sure my margins were just as they were supposed to be. I proofread the paper, and was surprised that it was actually pretty decent.

The next morning, I bolted out of bed at eight o'clock and rushed my paper over to my professor's office in the Hall of Graduate Studies. I attached a kiss-ass note of apology, and noted that the paper was under her door at 8:15.

The next day I strolled into class and took my seat. My paper was waiting for me, face down. I turned it over and flipped to the last page to check the grade. A note explained the most amazing grade I had ever received.

———————

"As I explained, your grade on this paper was diminished one full grade for every hour it was late. I trust your word that you handed the assignment in at 8:15am. According to my calculations, your paper was 65 hours tardy. To calculate a grade I had to go through the alphabet two and a half times before arriving at your grade. As for the paper, it is focused and well-written, but lacks cogency because you do not always define your terms. For instance, what does 'faith' mean to you? More examples would have bolstered your arguments."

I looked at the grade: ZZO+ After class I approached the professor. "About this grade," I began.

"Yes?" she said. I could tell she wasn't about to budge.

"I don't mean to seem like a grade grubber, professor, but

I really think this deserved a ZZN-. Would you be willing to reconsider?"

A smile passed her lips for the first time since I had known her. "I might reconsider if I thought it would help you out, Michael." Her voice was softer when she called me by my first name. She looked at me like a puppy that had shit on the rug one too many times. She liked me, but couldn't keep me in her class.

"There aren't enough papers," she continued "to get you back into the alphabet even if you were to write nothing but straight A papers from here on in, and I don't doubt that you could. I think it would be best if you considered dropping this course."

"I think you're right."

"Good luck, Michael."

"Thank you."

The next day, I found myself in a select group, even among Yale's elite intelligentsia. I was one of nine Freshman not taking English. Instead, I enrolled in a bartending course. Mom and Dad were just thrilled when their scholar called home with this news. Dad muttered something about my tuition expenses being analogous to buying a nice car and driving it off a cliff.

When Rick (it took me about three weeks to realize that Yale athletes call their coaches by first name) decided we had finally displayed a certain minimum level of skill in the tanks, he announced that we would start rowing on the water.

We all jogged about a mile down Chapel Street towards the Yale Bowl until we reached the lagoon, where the freshmen squad practice in the fall. It is a protected channel of almost 2,000 meters, just over a mile. Next to the dock was what looked like a large garage. Rick opened the doors and we all peered in. The space was dark and musty, but we could see large wooden boats on several racks. The boats looked sleek and fast; I couldn't wait to jump in.

Rick divided the sixteen oarsmen and two coxswains into two boats. I was assigned to the two seat and would be rowing on the port side (I had written "port" and "starboard" on my left and right sneakers just to keep things straight). Since we'd be moving backwards, however, port was only left for the coxswain. I had to quickly reverse-learn the words I had given each sneaker.

The guys I'd be rowing with lined up next to a boat on a shoulder-height rack. Rick's voice caromed loudly off the steel walls. "Hands on the boat! Ready to lift on two! One, two, lift!" He had to be kidding. This "sleek" racing shell weighed a ton. I almost crumpled under the weight of my one-eighth's responsibility.

Again Rick's voice boomed, "Over your heads in two!"

Unbelievably, we managed to get this beast over our heads. I wobbled like a weight-lifter under a barbell, waiting for the judges to give the sign to spike the bar onto the floor. As commanded, we lowered the boat onto our shoulders, four of us on each side. The short walk to the dock was excruciating. The gunwale dug into my shoulder and nearly brought me to my knees.

It dawned on me why so many people quit this sport: they couldn't bear lugging such an enormous vessel around on their shoulders. I sympathized utterly, entertaining thoughts of packing it in right there and letting the other seven guys deal with the ship for the next four years.

We managed to get the boat down to the dock's edge,

where Rick instructed us to lower it carefully into the water. After dumping the boat into the lagoon, we grabbed some oars from the boathouse, put them in their oarlocks, and got into the boat. We shoved off from the dock and drifted to the middle of the lagoon, and Rick pulled up next to us in his coaching launch.

I was ready to go. Enough of this tank shit; time to do some real rowing. Turned out, not yet. Rick raised his blue cardboard megaphone to his mouth and delivered the news: "The main difference between rowing in the tanks and rowing on the water is balance. In the tanks, you are sitting on solid ground. In the water, balancing the boat, or keeping it set, is very difficult. So, for the first few days, we will be rowing in pairs and fours. When I feel you are ready, only then will you row all eight."

I was under the impression that we were going to be making a little symphony in motion. Instead, we would be limited to duets.

"Bow pair," Rick bellowed, even though he was about two feet away, "ready to row at the catch." Jeff and I pulled ourselves up the slides. "Ready all row!"

With quartz timing, Jeff and I dug our oars into the water and executed a perfect stroke. The only problem was that the boat hardly moved an inch. With the freighter we were in and seven passengers along for the ride, we had to budge almost sixteen hundred pounds of dead weight. Yeah, this was just like rowing in the tanks.

A week or so of rowing in pairs and fours, and finally we began to row all eight. The balance was incredibly precarious. If all oars weren't on the water at the same time, our shell teetered in the water like a bicycle right after Dad took the training wheels off. The boat would slam from side to side, sending knuckles crashing into gunwales and anguished cries of pain and frustration into the air.

As bad as this was for us neophytes, it must have been way worse for the experienced oarsmen. Colin Cooke, for instance, had rowed for years at Seattle's Lakeside High School. He was stoic, but had to be seething inside. John Raegrant, who rowed on a Canadian junior team was less patient. "Set the motherfucking boat!" he would scream whenever we fell to one side or the other —which was always.

After practice, he would grumble non-stop about how things were so much better where he used to row. I wondered why he didn't just quit if he thought we sucked so badly. And sure enough, one day he did. Rick called his name at practice and there was no response. He was gone, and I'd almost never see him, and certainly never talk to him, again.

I learned that's the way it was in crew. When someone quit, they just seemed to drop out of my life. We'd go from seeing each other every day, and talking about practice over dinner, to nothing, no contact at all. I began to find out that oarsmen formed a unique and tight fraternal order, and when somebody defected they were all but forgotten.

By mid-October, there were a little more than three boats of oarsmen left from the original six. Guys quit for all sorts of reasons. Some wanted to concentrate more on class work; others didn't like Rick; some couldn't abide by the commitment of practice five days a week — and Rick said we'd start practicing on Saturdays come November; and there were others who discovered they just didn't like crew.

Whatever the reason, attrition was taking its toll, just as Tony had said it would. Every time someone quit, I had mixed emotions. On the one hand, I felt bad that the guy wouldn't be around anymore — unless, of course, the guy was an asshole, in which case I was psyched the whole way around — but I also felt a sense of accomplishment. I had stuck it out when others had not.

One Friday, Rick took us out to watch the varsity row on the Housatonic River in Derby, Connecticut. The boathouse at Derby is a 20-minute ride from campus, and I was underwhelmed when we finally arrived at the building that Yale rowing called home, a square, squat stucco structure. I was expecting something grand: a great big house with turrets and a shingle roof perhaps. The crew had occupied an august structure, like the one I had pictured, on the banks of New Haven Harbor but when the harbor traffic got too great after WWI, the varsity crews had moved to Derby.

Inside the building, the locker room was spare. Small, partitioned stalls against the wall with hooks for clothing, that was about it. There were no chalk boards or goofy posters that coaches sometimes put up, like the one with a little poodle kicking the crap out of a huge Doberman ("It's not the size of the dog in the fight; it's the size of the fight in the dog.")

Instead, the most striking thing about the room was a large, framed, black-and-white photo of an exhausted bunch of oarsmen at the end a race. The eight men in the shell had nothing left to give. They were spent. A couple of them leaned out of the boat, looking as if they were about to puke. One had his foot out of the shell, dunked in the water. The rest were just sprawled out all over the place. As exhausted as they were, they all looked equally satisfied.

"Great shot, huh?" Someone I had never seen before interrupted my inspection of this image of exhaustion and elation.

"It sure is, did they row for Yale?"

"Yup. They were the crew from 1956. That shot was taken

right after they won…" he paused for emphasis, "…the Olympic gold medal in Melbourne."

"Wow," was all I could muster, and the stranger disappeared from my side as quickly as he had materialized.

Around the locker room, the varsity guys joked around before practice. There were the typical sounds of towels snapping against bare asses, and a group of oarsmen gathered around one who was embroidering a story about his conquest of a girl (or was it three?) whom he had met at the Calhoun Happy Hour the night before. He drew admiration as much for his skill as a raconteur as he did for his tales of conquest. What intrigued me was that his licentious tale was peppered with crew phrases like, "She gripped the oar a little too tight, but her stroke rating was right on the money." And, "I called for a power ten to get her timing right… Of course, I could have gone all night, but she told me to way enough and paddle home."

Tony poked his head in to the locker room, "The boats are set. Let's get on 'em." In a flash, the upperclassmen were off the benches and on their way down to the docks.

SIX

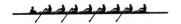

Watching the varsity row was inspiring. I was in a launch with Rick, Colin, and Chris Duncan, trailing behind three boats that were racing in the traditional Friday three mile choose-up race. Two things struck me immediately: the level of their concentration, and their perfect timing. Every oarsmen was focused, riveted, on the task at hand. Their eyes were fixed straight ahead, never wavering. The only voices I heard were those of the coxswains. The sound in our boats resembled a floor fight in the senate, with everyone recommending something different that might help the shell move faster. The coxswain was often little more than a mediator in the ongoing debate.

Not a half an hour ago, these varsity oarsmen were carrying on like a bunch of frat boys the night after hazing. As soon as they got into the shells, their demeanor completely changed. Rowing was serious to them. Good oarsmen don't fuck around in boats.

Along with the focus, I was struck by the timing in the

shells. At the Catch, four mini-geysers popped up simultaneously on each side of the boats, as the oartips disappeared into the Housatonic. A moment later, the oars would reappear as one, and start their journey back to another perfectly timed Catch.

There was clearly a relationship between the timing and the high level of concentration in the boats. Until we Freshmen settled down inside our boats, we'd never row like the varsity.

"See those puddles, guys?" It was Rick's voice over the roar of the outboard. "The guys who are doing something in there are throwing out huge puddles with each stroke. The guys who are making small puddles won't be around for long. Look at Jens' puddles." He pointed to the man rowing in the stroke seat of the lead boat, a wasted gesture since everyone knew who Jens was. He was Jens Molbak, a blond giant of an oarsman. He was probably the best oarsman at Yale, and he was only a sophomore.

I looked at his puddles. They were whirlpools that maintained their shape long after the other puddles on his side of the boat vanished.

Rick narrated for a couple of strokes. There was admiration in his voice. "He just sticks that oar in, digs a hole in the water, and powers it through all the way to the finish."

If Jens had been around in '56, there was no doubt in my mind that he would have been in the picture that hung in the boathouse. As it was, he'd have to settle for destroying sixteen of his teammates in a choose-up race.

Once the boats were out of the water and on the racks, the guys shifted back into frat mode. There was even a keg on the dock to ease the transition from determined oarsman to party boy.

Two weeks later, I was surprised to find myself rowing in

a three mile race at Derby. It was a race against Dartmouth and the Coast Guard Academy. The format was known as a "head race", where the boats line up one behind the other, and take off at fifteen second intervals. The time in which it took each boat to cover the three-mile course determined the winner. The lightweights, my former teammates, and the women's crew were racing that day as well.

Before the race, Rick told us to think of it as more of a practice or a scrimmage. The real races were in the spring. Then he reached into a box and pulled out some t-shirts. "Wear these," he said, throwing each of us one of the white shirts with a blue Y '85 on the right breast.

Team uniforms! I was thrilled. I was now officially a Yale oarsman.

We walked down the stairs looking like a unit. Even the boat didn't seem so heavy as we lowered it with care into the water. We shoved off the dock and paddled to the starting line. I was ready to make some Jensian puddles of my own. None of us was prepared for the effort required of a three mile race. Since we had never gone farther than a mile before, fatigue set in, and whatever style and timing we had was gone after about five minutes of rowing.

Aside from watching the varsity practice two weeks ago, we also hadn't ever been on the river. I had no idea where we were. Wes Boyd turned his red head around and said breathlessly, "Hey Mike, I'm beat. I got shit housed with a buddy of mine from Dartmouth last night. Got in just in time to turn off my alarm. How much longer do we have until we can stop this nonsense?"

Breathless, I replied, "I don't know Wes. I think we've got something like two miles or so left. I think I remember that park over there from when the varsity was racing. But I'm not sure."

Other guys in the boats were also grumbling about how tired they were when Jay Grossman, the cox, spoke up. "Quiet in the boat," he yelled through the megaphone that was strapped to his head. "I'm the only one who talks here. Everyone else shut up and row."

"Eat shit." It was Wes.

"I heard that, Boyd," Jay said in a good-natured tone.

Just as we had a lot to learn as oarsmen, Jay could have stood a little improvement in the coxing department. His job, as I understood it, was to steer the boat, keep the oarsmen apprised of their position in the race course and relative to other boats, and encourage our effort. His attempt to motivate came through phrases like, "You're dying guys! You're not even half way done and you're dead in the water." And, "We just took a power ten, and Coast Guard gained three seats on us. Let's see a little effort." Not exactly the carrot in front of the horse, but he was a beginner just like we were. Mercifully, the race ended. We pulled our boat out of the water, placed it back in the rack and waited anxiously for the race official to announce the results.

We finished last. Last among the ten heavyweight entries. Last among all the lightweight boats. And last out of all the women's boats. Oarsmen have a term for our position in the order of finish: DFL. That stands for Dead Fucking Last.

Rick put a happy face on our abysmal showing. He told us that we had to look to the spring. That's where the real racing took place. We didn't want to peak too soon, he warned us. There was little chance of that happening.

Our second, and last, head race of the fall was on Princeton's Lake Carnegie. (Lake Carnegie was built from the largesse of steel stud Andrew Carnegie. The administrators wanted their scrillionaire alum to give a couple of buildings, maybe a library while he was at it. Nope. He decided what the university really needed was a lake. So he built it. Carnegie sounded like a great guy.) Our trailers, loaded with our boats, arrived Friday night. Early Saturday morning, we headed down to unload and rig the boats.

When I got down to the parking lot, I saw a sight which spoke volumes about the rivalries that develop between schools that row against one another. There was Rick Elser rigging one of his team's shells. He was wearing a Princeton racing shirt that he had won as cox the year before. To add insult to insult, Rick was cleaning grease off the riggers with yet another of his Princeton racing shirts. What balls! Wes came bounding up beside me. "Check out Elser, rubbing it in Princeton's face. Think he has another one to wipe his ass?" I joined Wes in laughing at the thought.

We rowed much better this day, and finished somewhere in the middle of the pack. We certainly didn't put in any jeopardy our spring season by peaking too early, but we didn't humiliate ourselves either. Everyone on the team was excited by our progress.

The only thing to dampen our mood that afternoon was a 501 yard passing performance by Princeton's quarterback Bob Holly, which ended Yale's undefeated football season.

The next week was The Week. The Game. Harvard versus Yale. Everything was The Something. The Party, The Tailgate, The Rivalry. My best friend John Solomon came down from Harvard for The Weekend, and we drank, got in fire extinguisher fights, and cut down each other's school at every turn. The Game itself was almost inconsequential, a cold blur which interrupted two and a half days of partying. We won, and I sang lustily as our band played "Bright College Years" at the end of The Game. As the Yale half of the packed Yale Bowl waved white handkerchiefs in victory, I began to feel a part of the school, with all its tradition, ritual, and spirit, for the first time.

Upon returning from a five-day break, during which I feasted and gave thanks with my family, our class received some awful news. One of our classmates, John Angell, had died over the Harvard-Yale weekend. Apparently he had far too much to drink, passed out, and died of alcohol poisoning during the night. The drinking age in Connecticut was 18 in 1981, and kegs of beer and punches mixed with every type of alcohol, including 180 proof grain alcohol, were in abundance all over Old Campus. It absolutely never occurred to me that anything bad could come of drinking. Maybe I'd puke or have a terrible hangover, but that was something I'd get over. John's death was, in every way, a sobering experience.

There was a memorial service for John in a church near campus. I had to be there. Although I never knew John Angell, and likely would never have met him in our four years at Yale, he was my classmate, and I felt a loss. If one of the 45 boys I graduated with from Collegiate had died, the entire class would have shown up for his memorial. I assumed that all 1,299 members of our class at Yale would be at John's memorial.

I was shocked to see that no more than 75 classmates filled the chapel to remember John and mourn his loss. As I stood and listened to people talk about John, I learned something about my class at Yale. I learned that though we would all turn our tassels together in May of 1985, that was the only act we would ever commit as one. Apart from attending the same college, we had very little in common. Precious few of my classmates would ever know me; even less would care about me. That bothered me, but made me grateful that I had crew. There would always be the guys in my boat with whom I would share a goal and an experience. The sense of belonging was comforting.

SEVEN

The return from Thanksgiving vacation signaled the end of the fall season, and ushered in winter training. Rick gathered us together in the heavyweight tanks before our first winter practice, and explained what we could expect in the following four months.

"Alright," he began, "fall rowing is fun. We began the process of learning how to row, we got a chance to row on the water, and compete in a couple of head races." He paused so we could all reflect on what we had already accomplished. Fun isn't a word I would have used, unless I was in the habit of choosing my words randomly. But I wasn't about to raise my hand and disagree. In fact, the fall wasn't so much fun at all. It was hard work, and it was rewarding. But fun? Hardly.

"The winter," Rick continued, "is a whole new ball game. We will practice at least two hours a day, six days a week, right here in Payne Whitney. You won't even see a boat until March. Sometimes it's hard to see the light at the end of the tunnel. However, the effort we put into winter training will translate directly into shirts in the spring. Get into your workout gear and let's get started."

As promised, indoor practice was hell. Not even Rick would have used the word "fun" to describe winter workouts. Winter practices actually lasted about two and a half hours, but they seemed longer. I'd walk into Payne Whitney around three o'clock every afternoon, and the sky would be slate-gray and by the time I emerged it was to darkness. Practice varied from day to day, but I learned to count on a session in the tanks with about fifteen to twenty minutes of full power rowing, five or six trips up the stairs to the top of Payne Whitney, some weight lifting, and perhaps an ergometer test.

The ergometer test, or "the erg," as everyone called it, was the bane of my existence from November through the beginning of March. This was the machine that elicited boos and whistles when it appeared on the screen during "Symphony in Motion." I quickly learned why. After a couple of sessions on the erg, its mere mention called up feelings of fear and intimidation.

There were four ergs in the corner of the women's tanks, two port and two starboard. Each erg had a rolling seat, foot stretchers, and an oar handle on one side or the other. The oar handles were attached to metal flywheels which were parallel to the floor and just under the foot stretchers. Right in front of the foot stretchers were two dials: a small tachometer which registered the number of revolutions of the flywheel, and a timer like the ones I had seen in darkrooms before; it's hands went counter clockwise, very slowly.

It is impossible to understand what an erg is like unless you have been on one, and once you've experienced time on one, just as impossible to forget. For me, a typical erg (there really is no such thing as a "typical" erg, since each one is unique with regard to the effort it demands, the feelings it evokes, and the pain that results) begins hours before I enter the gym.

As soon as Rick notified us that there was going to be an erg test, about every two weeks, I would start to psyche myself for the occasion. In lectures, it might have seemed as if I were taking copious notes, scribbling down every pearl of wisdom which the professor had to offer. In fact, I was writing down projected splits for the erg (each minute, the cox will inform the oarsman how many revolutions the flywheel has made in the previous minute. That is a split. The aggregate of all the splits is the final score). I planned to go out high, around a 640, settle into something around 560 for the body of the piece, and then go balls out for the last two minutes, bringing my splits up around 600. The best laid plans of mice and oarsmen...

I would arrive at the gym about an hour before I was scheduled to pull my erg and change into my workout gear, and take a pre-erg-dump. Then I would slowly make my way through the maze of hallways from the lockers to the tanks. I might encounter some guys on their way back from the erg. Wes, normally buoyant, looks down. The erg must have really kicked the shit out of him today. "How'd it go?" I ask. He just shakes his head and walks by. None of them ever looked very good, but at least it was over for them.

When I arrived at the tanks, I would be greeted by erg sounds: the clank of the oar handle at the catch; the whiiizzzz of the flywheel; the clank of the oar handle again. All the while, there is cheering. Those who have yet to pull are gathered around exhorting their team-mate in the battle against the erg. The only ones who aren't cheering are the guys who have most recently finished their erg. They are easy to spot. They're the ones who are sprawled out on the mats, gasping, bodies heaving, totally exhausted.

Knowing that I'm up next and seeing how much it hurts, is torture. I don't know why I watched other people struggle, but it was part of my preparation for my own ordeal.

The erg was frightening because it is the truth. It let everyone know how hard you had been working, and how strong you were. There is no way to finesse an erg, no way to charm a good score out of it. The erg was coldly objective, and considered no variables. In a sport many consider to be the ultimate team endeavor, the erg loomed in stark contrast as distinctly individual, even lonely. No one could help you once you strapped yourself into the foot stretchers and began to pull on the oar handle. The truth is painful. And we faced it all too often on the ergometer.

"Zig, you're up. Let's go." Jay, the grim reaper, called me. "We're already way behind, so get on it."

I would walk over slowly, tie my feet in and start taking a few warm up strokes. What makes the wheel hard to spin is that a weight is placed in a basket and hung off the flywheel. The more weight, the more difficult the wheel is to keep moving. Today's erg is a ten-minute piece with four and a half pounds in the basket.

"Ready, Zig?" Jay asks. I have no choice so I nod. Jay would set the clock to ten minutes thirty seconds. I would have thirty seconds to get the wheel spinning as fast as I could without any weight. At ten minutes to go, Jay will add the four and a half pounds.

My eyes are glued to the dial. The tach has increments of 10, and goes up to 80. Each number indicates ten rotations of the wheel. Burying the dial at 80 is called "pinning the erg." Without any weight on the wheel, I am pinning it, and bracing myself for the weight.

As soon as the hand passes the ten-minute mark the weight

was added. "There's the weight. You're on it Zig. Let's see how well you can do."

For the first 15 seconds or so, the wheel is spinning so fast that the weight is barely noticeable. After about 30 seconds, I start to feel it. The needle is no longer pinned. It is at 72, and I'm feeling really strong.

"That's it Zig. Working well. Let's settle into something we can maintain throughout the body of the piece." Jay is warning me not to "fly and die," a term for starting out with really high splits, and then dropping precipitously.

My first split is 720. A bit higher than what I had projected during Scully's lecture about Michelangelo's influence on Raphael, but I feel terrific.

"You are rowing at a 34, Zig man. Relax on the recovery. Take your time. Plenty of time to spin that wheel." I felt fine. The needle is in between 60 and 70. I'm concentrating on getting the oar moving right at the catch. Gotta drive those legs down. The oar handle slams into my ribs at the finish, sending the needle up just a bit. This is my day. Watch out Chris Duncan. Your 5,870 is going down today, courtesy of Zig, Master of the Erg!

"That second minute was a 640. You're entering the body of the piece. Let's take a ten to relax and set a pace that will take us all the way through." Fuck relaxing! I'm way too strong to relax. I'll take your ten, but I'm taking a ten to get that needle back up to 70, where it belongs when I'm on this machine. I drove harder and slammed the oar even harder into my ribs. My rating comes up a bit. Then I look at the needle. What's it doing under 60? My ten drove the needle the wrong way.

"Zig, you're shooting your slide. Legs, buddy, legs. Power the oar with the legs." My legs start to tingle a little bit. My lungs are burning. I'm gasping. Oh man, I was getting tired and I hadn't even finished the third minute. Don't think about that, or you'll quit. No never. Don't so much as think about quitting. That was never an option. My legs are simmering with lactic acid, but quitting was for pussies. My mind is racing. Jeff quit last week. So ashamed he hasn't shown up since.

I hope I never see that quitter again.

The oar just gets heavier and heavier. The slower the wheel turns, the harder the oar is to pull. Colin would suggest keeping the needle around 700. That way it's easier to pull. Easy for you to say, you behemoth. He got off on the sound of the wheel spinning. For me, I am now experiencing what Sisyphus went through. The rock must have been easy to shove up the hill at first. But once he lost momentum, forget it, it was impossible to keep it from slipping down. The needle was my Sisyphean rock. I couldn't let it fall on me.

"570, Zig. Three down. Here comes the body of the piece. Head up. Concentrate. Breath easy, stud. Stay with me." Why don't you get on the erg, you little asshole. See how it feels. Don't you dare tell me to stay with you. You're not anywhere near me. Let's go clock, speed up. This minute is taking forever.

I close my eyes with six minutes and thirty five seconds to go. I would row this way for a while. After what seems like about a minute I would open my eyes. The clock is toying with me, sending me into a time warp. Only 27 seconds have elapsed. Don't think about how much time is left. Just think about the next stroke. You can always take another stroke. Each stroke is one less you'll ever have to do on this ghastly erg.

"Okay, Zig. That last spilt was a 510, up ten from the one

before. Three minutes to go. You can do anything for three minutes. Send those legs down."

Three minutes to go? Where have the middle three gone? Swallowed up by the dastardly erg monster, never to be seen again. Three left. I can do it. Hey needle, where do you think you're going? No way pal. Don't even think of dipping below 50. That's out. Not happening. Not today. I'll take a silent, personal, Zig-against-the-erg ten every minute as the hand passes the thirty second point. On this one!

"That's it, Zig. Way to battle. Coming up on two minutes. Let's rock and roll! You can do it. Bring up the rating. Sprint it home! That's right, leave it all on the machine. Don't get off the erg with anything left to give."

Jay is really helping me. His enthusiasm has kept me from losing hope. These last ten are for Jay.

"Two more… and paddle. Way to be, Zig. Row it out. Okay, that last split was a 530, giving you a 5,127. You let it slip a bit during the middle. Gotta work on staying tough through the body of the piece. Well done."

"Alright, Paul, you're on, large man. Let's hustle."

I would get up and collapse. The mat is blue and reeks of sweat, but there wasn't a place I'd rather be. The erg is over, and I survived. 5,127. Almost 200 spins better than last time. I was still nowhere near Colin's 6,970, or even Chris Duncan's 5,870, but it was only December and I was improving.

My hand was killing me. I looked at it, the palm raw and bloody. The oar handle tore the skin right off. I stared with equal amounts of pain and pride at my stigmata. I made it through another erg.

Next I was off to run the stairs and hit the tanks for a session of three six minute pieces at full power. Our first race was still four months away. To dwell on all the ergs, trips to the top of the gym, and pieces in the tank that I still had ahead of me would be suicidal. I'd quit in an instant. Instead, I would approach and accomplish each task as it presented itself.

EIGHT

While I toiled somewhere around the bottom third of the freshmen heavyweights, J.D. ruled supreme over the lightweights. Incredibly strong and fit, he looked forward to, rather than feared, each test that Rick Elser put before the team. On the erg, only Jigger Hermann was even close to J.D. As for the other tests, J.D. competed only against himself. He did almost a dozen more pull-ups than his nearest rival. The results were equally impressive in the two mile run, sit-ups, and a competition Elser devised called the medicine ball race. J.D. especially thrived on this one. In this torturous test of strength and stamina, the guys had to run around an indoor track with a medicine ball in their arms for four minutes.

J.D. was in so much better shape than anyone else on the freshmen lightweights, that it was a foregone conclusion that the other guys would be fighting it out for the seven remaining seats in the first boat. J.D.'s performance in the fall and winter had already secured him a place in the top shell.

The only obstacle to J.D.'s success was his weight. At 165

pounds, he was ten pounds over the freshmen maximum of 155. There were several oarsmen who weighed as much as J.D. did in the winter. But I knew there was a problem. While the other guys were out filling themselves with beer and gulping down huge slices of pizza at Naples every night, J.D. had to struggle just to stay within range of his springtime target of 155.

When J.D. got to Yale, it wasn't unusual for him to heap mounds of food on his plate, go up for seconds and thirds, and then pick off of my plate. He simply loved the taste of food, lots of food.

One evening in mid-January, I came back from dinner to find J.D. sitting on his bed, digging his fingers into a can of Del Monte asparagus. "What was for dinner, Zig?"

"Nothing great. Some chicken drowned in sauce. You didn't miss much." Of course he had missed much. J.D. had missed the opportunity to eat all he wanted with his friends in the dining hall. He looked at me and I could clearly see the battle going on within him. As much as he liked crew, and being the very best, J.D. had to decide whether or not it was worth starving for.

His new restrictive diet effected J.D.'s mood. Where he had once been easy going, now he was tense and cranky. He'd snap at me if I asked him to proofread a paper of mine. This from the guy who gladly wrote and revised my, as well as about six other classmates', high school term papers, while struggling to compose his own. The way of life that his new eating regime forced him into was no good for J.D. nor anyone around him.

A week after finishing off his asparagus, J.D. informed a stunned Rick Elser that he was quitting. It was the right decision. Rowing crew certainly wasn't worth the misery that making weight would surely have entailed. Rick tried feebly to talk

J.D. into sticking with it, but J.D. remained strong in his resolve.

Though scores of other lightweights had quit earlier in the year, J.D.'s departure sent shock waves through the freshman lightweight community. No one could believe that J.D., the one person sure to be in the first boat, was never going to row in a race. Even Jigger, stoic Jigger, who now carried the mantle as best freshman lightweight, was surprised.

For a couple of weeks, Elser would ask me half-heartedly if there was any chance that J.D. might come back. Vogel was also concerned. I didn't realize that the varsity coach even knew who any of the freshmen were. But word of J.D.'s epic feats had travelled through the ranks. Nope, I informed Vogel, J.D. was a goner. In a week he was happily tipping the scales in the mid 170's.

Meanwhile, my weight was headed in the opposite direction. I had stuck to the Rick Ricci Weight Explosion Program, watching my intake of protein and complex carbohydrates. Power milkshakes were part of my daily regimen. After almost five months of this gluttony, I stepped on the scale only to find that I had gone from a paltry 155, to 153. I just couldn't gain weight. I was thirty pounds lighter than the team average, and my scores on the erg were not improving to the point that I could see myself making the first heavyweight boat. Maybe I was meant to be a lightweight after all.

I decided to break the news to Rick after practice one day.

"Rick, listen, I really appreciate your taking an interest in me, and inviting me to row with the heavies. But, I just don't think I'm strong enough right now to be of any use to the squad. Maybe I'd be better off on the lightweights." I hated to dash his hopes, but this is what was best for me.

"See you, then," he replied, masking his disappointment completely. "Good luck as a lightweight." I had prepared a rebuttal to his Elserian pleas to stay with the team, but found I didn't need to use them since no such solicitation was forthcoming.

I called home to tell Dad of my plans to switch teams. "So you're quitting," he declared. "I didn't think you'd quit. Certainly not this early on, anyway."

I tried to explain. "Dad, it's just like switching weight classes in wrestling. I'm not off the team; I'm just performing at a different weight classification."

Even though fiber optics were still a thing of the future, Dad's disapproval came through loud and clear. "Sounds like quitting one team and joining another before you've found out how you can do on the first. Not unlike trading English for bartending."

Obviously Dad's disappointment was tied up with my decision to swap the bards for mixology. I didn't want to explain, and it was abundantly clear that Dad wasn't interested in listening.

"Well, I'm a lightweight now, Dad."

"Guess so."

"I love you."

"I hear you."

I hung up knowing that he'd understand eventually. Dad and I seldom start off seeing an issue from the same angle. Maybe this stems from the fact that we are both sophists (a term I learned in "Greeks for Geeks") at heart and love a good debate. However, I knew that the issue of my moving from heavyweight to lightweight crew would be one in which Dad would finally yield. And I would relish the moment when I could shove my rightness in his face.

The transition from heavy to lightweight wasn't difficult at all. I knew most of the guys on the team through J.D., and though I wasn't the legend that he was, my erg scores, and my times on the stairs were more competitive than they had been among the heavyweights.

Rick Elser seemed like less of a task master than Ricci was. It wasn't that the workouts were easier with Elser, they weren't. He was just mellower about them. He didn't scream and yell. When someone would ask if he had to run stairs, Rick would typically respond by saying that running stairs was optional. He was, however, quick to point out with a wry smile; so was rowing in the spring. That oarsman found himself heading to the stairs immediately.

There was one area in which I found myself wanting as a lightweight, and that was in rowing style. Elser had been a coxswain and was accustomed to determining what was right or wrong with each person's stroke. As a result, his squad rowed very well in the tanks. Their timing and stroke work was far better than that of the heavyweights.

A familiar sound echoing off walls of the tanks was Elser saying, "Danziger, you're late... Danziger, you're early... Danziger, don't hang it up at the catch."

I have always thrived on being the center of attention. In some ways, I seek and require the spotlight. But this was one instance in which I would've gladly deflected the attention to someone else. Rick's words became frustrating after a while. Not because of their monotonous repetition, but because they were true.

I had a lot of catching up to do, and the spring trip to Florida, where crew selections were made, was only a few weeks away.

NINE

For J.D., there was life after crew. He maintained his stratospheric grade point average, and became involved in New Haven's Big Brother/Little Brother Program. I wasn't surprised when J.D. brought an eight-year-old named Andre Turpin to the dining hall for brunch one Sunday. J.D.'s capacity for charity was as large as his appetite.

One day, J.D. asked me to give him a lift to pick up Andre, who lived about two miles from Yale's ivy cocoon in one of New Haven's grimmer neighborhoods. We pulled up to the tenement where Andre lived, and sure enough he came bounding out of his door and down the stairs and hopped into the car.

"Are we going to play football today J.D.? I've got a cold-blooded spiral."

"If that's what you want to do. How about saying hi to Zig."

I wasn't his hero, J.D. was, so he shot me a perfunctory, "Oh, hi Zig."

"Hi Andre."

I looked out the window and saw a little boy sitting on the curb. He must have been at least a couple of years younger than Andre. He looked sad.

"Who's that?" I asked.

"Oh, that's Jaymie," Andre answered. "He's my brother."

"I'll be right back," I said, and got out of the car. I walked over to Andre's brother and tapped his baseball cap. He shot me a look that informed me to keep my hands off his stuff.

"What's your name?" I asked.

"Jaymie." His eyes were sad and wondrous. "What's yours?"

"Hi Jaymie, I'm Michael, but everyone calls me Zig. What are you doing today?"

He looked at me like I was some kind of moron. What did I think he was going to do: play a chucker of polo and then head over to the club for some mixed doubles? He was going to sit on the curb, was what he was going to do. I felt like an asshole.

"What I meant was would you like to come and hang out with me and J.D. and Andre?"

"You bet!" Jaymie's excitement immediately replaced his suspicion of this idiot honky.

"Go ask your mom if it's alright." I wasn't being presumptuous, I knew he had a mom. It was Dad who jumped ship. Jaymie scampered up the stairs, pushed open the plywood door to his house, and disappeared.

He returned moments later with his mother in tow. She looked me over and asked, "You sure you want to look after Jaymie this afternoon?"

"Yes, Mrs. Turpin. That is, if it's alright with you."

Mrs. Turpin let me wait for her response. Then she begrudgingly said, "I suppose it's alright with me. You just make sure you have him back for dinner, and be sure he minds himself."

I was relieved that she found me an acceptable playmate for her son. "You bet I will, Mrs. Turpin. I'll see you around six."

She smiled for the first time. It was a pretty, loving smile. "That'll be just fine."

The ride back to Yale was a riot. J.D. and Andre sat up front, and Jaymie and I were in the back. J.D. moved the power windows up and down, from the control on the door, which amazed Jaymie, who was convinced J.D. possessed telekinetic powers.

Of course, Andre knew this trick but didn't let on. In fact he was an accomplice. He would say, "I'm thinking about that back window, the one by Zig," and he'd close his eyes really tight. Magic: the window would either rise or descend. This would send Jaymie into frenzied giggles. He'd look at me, and I'd shrug, equally amazed by the powers of the Amazing Andre.

For the rest of the afternoon, Jaymie kept talking about those incredible windows. He was disappointed when Andre failed to move the windows in our room. It wasn't that he couldn't do it, Andre explained, he just didn't feel like it.

After Andre's demonstration of his latest gift, the "cold-blooded spiral," Jaymie and I split off from the other two and wandered around campus.

"You're tall, Zig," Jaymie announced, staring up at me from my waist. "Do you play basketball?"

"Nope." I said. Then I qualified my response. "Well, not real well."

Jaymie looked disappointed. Of all the 6'4" guys in the world, he had to be hanging out with a white one who couldn't even play hoops. "Well then," he asked, "what do you play?"

"I row crew."

His response was predictable, and not at all different from the ones I had gotten from my friends back home when I told them I was an oarsman. He sort of knit his brow, and looked really confused. "Come on," I said, hoisting him onto my shoulders. "I'll show you."

We made our way to the Payne Whitney gym and walked past the guard, who now gave me a familiar wave.

Before showing Jaymie the tanks, we checked out some of

the other stuff that the largest indoor athletic facility in the free world had to offer. We shot some hoops, looked at the pool on the sixth floor (the largest above ground swimming pool in the world, commie or otherwise), and tried out some of the Nautilus machines. Jaymie even sat on a mock polo pony and slung the mallet at a ball which rolled back to him on the sloped floor.

At last it was time for the unveiling of the tanks. The room was as alien to Jaymie as it had been to me five months earlier. After Jaymie got used to the size of the room, and had a good look around, I got into the tank with him. "This is like a boat, only without the boat," I explained most unsatisfactorily. "We practice rowing here, and then later on, when it's warmer, we row on the river."

"You mean the New Haven Harbor?" Jaymie asked.

"No, the Housatonic River." This was also greeted by a vacant stare. "I'll take you there later, " I promised. "It's not too far away, and you'll get to ride in a motor boat."

Jaymie smiled broadly at this thought. Cruising around in a speed boat sounded like a lot more fun that watching some tall guy who can't even play ball sit in a tub and row.

I demonstrated the rudiments of rowing, and felt like Steve Gavin must have felt when he demonstrated the Catch, Drive, Finish, Recovery sequence in September. The only difference was that while my eyes were riveted to Gavin's every movement, Jaymie couldn't give a shit, and just wanted to leave.

So that's just what we did. As we exited the huge arched doorway of Payne Whitney, Jaymie asked me a terrific question.

"Zig," he wondered, "why do you row? It seems like a dumb sport to me."

I stopped and looked at him. After a good long pause, I said, "Jaymie, I guess the reason I row is that I like the people who do it. They are my friends."

I stopped and looked at Jaymie. He was listening very intently for a five-year-old. I wasn't sure if he was just being polite. I assumed he wasn't, so I continued. "And it is a challenge, too. Lots of guys try to row, but almost all of them end up quitting. It gives me a good feeling to know I haven't quit. They keep on quitting, and I keep on getting better. Maybe someday I'll be the best."

Jaymie was no longer paying attention. Neither crew, nor my interest in it held any concern for him. I understood that. My rowing didn't concern many people at all. But I was sure glad he asked that question.

The ride back to the Turpin's was another highlight. Jaymie still didn't know the secret of the windows, but we bestowed magical powers on him. He would say, in a Merlin-like voice, "Andre's window...up!" And presto, the window would obey his command.

We made plans to meet again the next weekend, thanked each other and said good-bye. It had been a great day.

TEN

A few days later, I was working out in the tanks when Lincoln Benet turned to me and said, almost in a whisper, "Hey Zig, there go Hard and Morley. They're gods."

"Gods?" I repeated.

"Yeah. They're awesome," said Lincoln with reverence.

In football, if a player reaches the highest level of talent, fans sometimes refer to him as a superstar. The same goes for athletes in other sports. Every once in a while, an athlete's deeds on the field or court transcend sport and he will be elevated to the status of legend.

In crew it is different. Great oarsmen are referred to as gods. And not by fans, for there are very few crew fans; most of the people who come out to watch races are ex-rowers themselves, or somehow related to one of the people in the boat. No, the ones who deify oarsmen are fellow oarsmen. I never heard my roommate Stephen call John Rogan, the golden-armed quarterback of the varsity football team, a god. The closest Stephen came to that was saying that Rogan could "really bring it."

Football players, I found, were not in the practice of worshipping one another.

Crew is the last sport in which I would have thought that a participant could be called a god. After all, the best oarsman blends in completely with the rest of the boat. This is not a sport in which the individual shines during competition. There are no rim-rattling slam dunks, no home runs.

On the contrary, in crew, the only truly spectacular individual feat an oarsman can accomplish during a race is a called a crab. And that's not like a homer. That's a fuck-up. A crab occurs when the oar goes too deep into the water and the oarsman can't get his blade out in time. This slows the momentum of the boat. A really big crab will almost stop the boat dead in the water. A monster crab, the most sensational individual feat, which every oarsman fears, will launch the perpetrator out of the boat and dump him ignominiously into the water. This is the only way a guy can really distinguish himself during a race. It stands to reason that oarsmen would prefer to blend in and avoid such singular attention being paid them.

Nonetheless, great oarsmen were called gods by their teammates. The reason the guys on the crew so idolized those who were the best, I discovered, was twofold. For starters, no one outside the crew community was about to genuflect in the presence of an accomplished oarsman. Maybe this adulation was a way of justifying all the unrecognized work that oarsmen typically endure. By heaping praise on certain fellows, we were indirectly paying homage to all oarsmen.

Another possible explanation is that since the racing season is so short relative to our practice time (Rick Elser once figured out that for every eighteen hours of practice, we would compete for a minute), practice becomes what the sport is really about to the oarsmen. Those who consistently put up the highest erg scores, run the stairs the fastest, and kick the shit out of anyone they seat race are seen as gods. Crew at Yale becomes such a part of life that one's self worth can become linked with how well he does in crew. By these standards, no one ranked above Hard and Morley.

Whether I was a believer or not, Hard and Morley were gods. Hard and Morley. No first names needed. It wasn't until late fall of my sophomore year that I knew them as Mike and Andrew. And it was a while after that before I ever mustered the courage to talk to either of them.

Neither had rowed before coming to Yale, yet even before racing season in their second year of rowing, both had set up permanent residency on Mount Olympus.

It was on the erg that Hard and Morley achieved full apotheosis. As sophomores, their scores were so superior to the rest of the squad's that they competed only with themselves for the top score. Everyone else battled it out for third. The two of them went to Harvard for the National Team ergometer test and, to no one's surprise, tied each other for the top score in the country.

As Dave once said, "Ergs don't lie." If not, then what the erg was telling us about Hard and Morley was that they were tougher and pulled harder than any lightweight at Yale, or in the country, for that matter. What the ergs told the coaches from the other schools, especially Harvard, who had witnessed Hard and Morley, was that Yale's boats would be equipped with the heaviest artillery for the next three years.

As similar as their scores were, Hard and Morley could not have been more different. Mike Hard was a blonde-haired, blue-eyed Adonis. At 5'10" and 160 pounds, he was solidly built and very handsome. Hard hailed from Tucson, which might account for his laid back nature. He had an easy smile and an even temperament. It seemed that any girl who saw him became infatuated with him. When Dave called a meeting to try to figure out a way to raise money for the spring trip to Tampa, several guys suggested we raffle off Hard. His girlfriend, as was only fitting, was Chris Wolfe, a woman most considered to be the best-looking at Yale.

I knew Chris Wolfe at Yale. Well, that's a bit of an overstatement. I knew of Chris Wolfe. How couldn't I? For one thing, she was Hard's girlfriend, which made her special just because of that. More than that she was beautiful. It seemed like every class or so at Yale had one woman who was prettier and more desirable than all the others. THAT GIRL. Chris was that girl. Tall, nearly 5'10, with beautiful shoulder length dark hair, set against stunning blue eyes and a wonderfully warm smile. Just gorgeous. Iconic. Out of my league? You bet. Out of my fucking galaxy. I didn't have a prayer of hanging with the likes of Chris Wolfe but I saw her around a bunch because she was Hard's girlfriend. Talk about king and queen of the prom!

Fact is, I didn't spend much time wondering what it would be like to be with Chris Wolfe, or trying to come up with some scenario where she and I would fall into an embrace. It was so out of the realm of possibility that my chances of hooking up with Chris Wolfe seemed a twinge less likely than getting road head from Catherine Deneuve while driving to an orgy with

Charlie's Angels, Marsha Brady and Laurie Partridge. That's how iconic and out of reach she was to me.

Did Chris Wolfe know who I was? Tough call. If she did, it was to wonder who that gangly guy tagging along with Hard was. Unrequited didn't begin to describe our relationship. I think for my feelings to be unrequited, she would have had to know I existed, understood my feelings for her, and then consciously decided that she didn't share them. I yearned for the moment where my feelings would reach the unrequited stage. Until then, they remained unknown and irrelevant.

Allow me to digress, because for one night, Chris Wolfe knew who I was. It wasn't at Yale. I didn't have a prayer of spending time with Chris there. Nope, I had to wait a year. I spent a year at Oxford (this is not a coy way of implying I was both a Rhodes Scholar and too modest to come right out and say it; I was decidedly NOT a Rhodes, nor a Scholar) studying 15th Century Italian Art and Architecture. While many take "gap years" between high school and college, I took a year to transition between college and my adult life, and I did it at Oxford.

While I was at Oxford, Chris Wolfe was in Paris, working in I.M. Pei's office, designing the pyramid in front of the Louvre. Cool job for a cool woman. Since looks are somewhat relative, Chris may not have felt as stand-out drop dead gorgeous in Paris, where models are a franc a dozen, as she did at Yale, where she was singular. Not to say she wasn't still a stunner, just that she might not have gotten the attention she did at Yale.

She and Hard had broken up junior year, and I guess she wasn't dating anyone in Paris. One weekend, in the fall of 1985, I decided to sojourn to Paris for a couple days, as it was like going from New York to Boston, except you needed a passport. Somehow, I got Chris Wolfe's number at work and called her.

To my amazement, she knew who I was.

"Chris," I said, "It's Zig, from Yale."

"Zig!" she said with real enthusiasm. "How are you? Where are you?"

"I'm in Paris for the weekend," I said.

"I am so glad you are here," she fairly gushed. "There's a restaurant I've always wanted to go to, and you're the one I'm dying to go with." Then she paused. "I'm sorry. Are you busy tonight?"

"No," I said, "I'm not."

"Then is it a date?" This was Chris Wolfe talking to me. A quick check of the date on my watch confirmed it wasn't April 1.

"You bet it is," I said. "Just tell me when and where to be." At eight o'clock, we met outside the restaurant. I had bought a collared shirt and a blazer, because I didn't realize I'd be having dinner with THE Chris Wolfe. She hugged me warmly and we went inside.

The food was great and kept coming. Soup, salad, great steak, and wonderful veggies. All washed down with wine that Chris picked. We talked about Yale, Oxford, Paris, whatever. I felt clever, witty, and she was a dream. Funny, interested, interesting. A great listener. A great laugh. And so pretty. Prettier than I had remembered, and I remembered her being the most stunning girl I'd ever been near in person. I should have been nervous and self-conscious, but she put me at ease. She must have known that she held this iconic place in my life, but she sure didn't act that way. She was solicitous, she asked about me.

Dinner ended and we stood outside the restaurant. I was standing in Paris, a little drunk, with Chris Wolfe.

"What are you going to do the rest of the night?" Chris asked me.

I could have told her that I was going to head right back to my crappy hotel, think of her, rub one out, and go to sleep, since that was my plan. But I didn't. "I'm not sure," I said. "Any ideas?'

"Well," she said, "my dad rented me this nice apartment on Ile St. Louis. I think I've got some champagne, and I know I have some good music. Would you like to join me."

"I'd love to," I said.

Back at Chris' apartment, we sat on the couch and she popped the cork to a bottle of Dom Pérignon.

"Do you know the story of Dom Pérignon?" Chris asked. "You mean Donald Pérignon, the mayor of Champagne?" I guessed.

"It's Dom, not Don," she corrected, gently, "and he was a friar, not a mayor." She poured some champagne into my flute and explained. "Dom Pérignon was a friar in the Epernay region of France — that's where champagne grapes come from — and he accidentally invented the carbonation process for wine. When he tasted white wine that had been carbonated, he exclaimed…'je pense que j'ai gouttez l'etoiles'.…'I think that I have tasted the stars!"

"Wow!" I said, reaching my glass out to hers, "to the stars." We touched glasses. Luther Vandross played in the background. It was magic. Until… at that moment, I could feel the massive dinner. It was well into the launch sequence, and I needed to get to the bathroom and relieve myself. Tout suit, or quickly as they say on Ile St. Louis. So I excused myself and went to the loo.

Big meal, big guy, big turd. I mean a fucking shot put of shit.I took a look in the tiny French toilet and immediately knew I had a situation on my hands. Outside the bathroom was Chris Wolfe, tasting the stars, feeling a bit lonely, and miraculously loving my company.

Inside the bathroom, there was no way this shit was going down the toilet. Not a chance. So I thought of the options. The first was to blame Chris. Go out and tell her that she could at least have had the courtesy to flush. Have some manners, Chris. I dismissed this option quickly. For starters, that would have been rude of me to say. More to the point, nothing like what I was staring at would ever have come out of Chris Wolfe's ass.

Choice two was to flush and pray. The night had been magical and perfect, and if there was a god of perfect dates, he would surely take pity on me and let this shit go down the rickety French toilet without backing up and flooding the bathroom or busting the pipes in the apartment. Risky, but worth a try. No it wasn't. It would never work, and I knew it. So option two was gone.

That left me with my only move. With my left hand, I reached into the toilet and grabbed the shit. As I did this my right hand reached above the toilet and unlatched the window and pushed it open. In a single move, I chucked the shit out of the window onto rue St. Louis, and shut the window. Then I flushed the toilet, washed my hands, and went out to the living room to join Chris Wolfe, who smiled sweetly as I returned to her.

Two decades later, having told the story many times, I decided to share it with Chris Wolfe. (Oh, did I end up capping off the perfect night by making love to Chris Wolfe next to empty bottles of DP while Luther crooned, "Love the One You're With"? Nope. Not sure what happened, but after about a half an hour after I took that massive dump, the magic seeped out of the evening. I think I came to realize just how improbable this night was, and that "what if" would have been way better than anything that may have happened. Chris bade me the sweetest farewell and kissed me softly on both cheeks.) "Zig!"

Chris Wolfe (now Nichols) said when she heard my voice on the phone.

We got caught up, and then I asked her if she remembered that night in Paris, in the fall of 1985.

"Do I?!" she asked. "It was one of the great nights of my life. I remember every instant," which she then began to prove by naming the restaurant, the wine we had, what she ordered, and even that Luther was playing back at her place.

"Do you remember when I got up to go to the bathroom after we toasted the stars?" I asked.

"I don't," she confessed. "But I do recall.."

"That's kind of a big moment," I interrupted. Then I told her what happened in there, the choices I had, and how I flung my shit out of her window that night.

Chris' response was classic. She sighed a little. "Oh, Zig. That's a wonderful story and I think I really needed to hear it."

"Why's that, Chris?" I wondered.

"Because I'm 44, have two girls of my own, and frankly, I don't think there are many guys left who'd throw their shit out the window for me. Thank you, Zig."

"Chris," I said.

"Yes, Zig?"

"If it's any comfort, I'll always throw my shit out the window for you."

"You're sweet."

———

Back to Yale, and Hard vs. Morley. Morley was opposite

to Hard in both looks and demeanor. At 6'3" he was tall and angular. Whereas Hard was low key, Morley was aggressive. He was a wild man. Morley's legacy as a partier was almost on a par with that of his rowing ability. He drank enthusiastically, and could hold as much liquor as anyone I had ever seen. Pounding beer and shots and cups at Mory's Temple Bar with abandon and joy. Morley's spirit was irrepressible, and anyone who was out with him would invariably get caught up in his bacchanalian vortex and end up face down in the gutter while Morley traipsed off to the next bar. As traditional as the mid-winter crew banquet was the sight of Morley being taken away in a cop car for overzealous public behavior.

Ergs don't lie, and they also reveal the personality of the person on the machine. This was certainly the case with Hard and Morley. Hard approached the erg with a calm confidence. He rowed at an even cadence, his face displaying intense concentration, but little pain, not a trace of the fear that creeps on to the countenance of many oarsmen as they wage battle with the erg. When he was through, Hard would check his score and hurry off to the stairs, or wherever his next workout would be. The dreaded erg seemed to physically tax Hard very little, and emotionally even less.

The erg was Morley's mortal enemy. Whenever there was an erg test, Morley would be sure to go last, so he would know what score to shoot for (He wouldn't have to know who's score — it would be Hard's — just what the number was). Then he would strap himself in. What followed was ten minutes of violence. Morley would snarl, growl, and sometimes froth at the mouth, as he launched his assault on the erg. Hard rowed so smoothly, I could hardly tell he was pulling; Morley was obviously pulling. Once, he yanked the oar so hard that the oar handle snapped in half, and Morley went toppling over backwards, landing on his head. Vogel rushed over, his face pale with the thought of losing one of his two strongest oarsmen, only to find Morley laughing at his own absurd strength.

It was something personal between Morley and the tachometer needle. The needle wanted to go down, and there just wasn't any way Morley was going to let that happen.

I can remember standing next to the erg as Morley pulled. I started cheering. "That a way Morley! Keep it up!" All of a sudden, he turned his attention from the needle and focused it on me. "Shut the fuck up!" he screamed. I retreated and Morley returned his focus to the machine. It was his battle, not mine, and he'd wage it alone. Later on, when I went to apologize for interrupting him, Morley said that he hadn't remembered the event at all. Then he apologized and invited me to his kamikaze party, another event I was sure neither of us would be able to recall.

When he was through, Morley would collapse on the mat, totally spent, and remain there for several minutes. The common display of exhaustion was the only similarity between my ergs and Morley's.

There were probably other oarsmen on the team who were as good or better than Hard and Morley, but none had the aura that those two did. If anyone came close, it was Steve Gavin, the captain of the team. Like Hard, he was ridiculously good looking. His ergs, though, were nothing special. But Gavin had a cool about him that could make people forget about his relatively weak erg scores. He was such a smooth guy that "Gavinish" became the adjective synonymous with "cool." Getting laid was Gavinish. Beating Harvard was definitely Gavinish. Making the varsity boat was the most Gavinish thing of all. Gavin made it his junior year, and Morley made it as a sophomore.

Hard hurt his shoulder and had to settle for rowing in an unde-feated, Sprint winning JV boat. He'd make the varsity his final two years. I, however, was not Gavinish.

By the end of February, everyone on the squad was getting tired of indoor workouts. Even ergs weren't as menacing as they had been before. The routine became such drudgery that I was numb to the erg's attendants: anxiety and pain. Rick must have sensed the lull in the team's intensity, so he gathered us together and announced that winter rowing was over. From now on we'd be doing what we had been training for the last four months: rowing on the water. This was great news, and we greeted it with smiles.

My smile quickly turned to a puzzled frown as I left the gym with John Rowley, a guy who roomed across the hall from me in Vanderbilt. "It's freezing," I said. The vapor from my breath punc-tuated my words. "It's got to be 25 degrees out; 30 at the most. How are we supposed to row? Isn't the water going to be frozen?"

"Maybe the current keeps the water from freezing," John answered. "I'm just happy to be through with running stairs and tugging on that erg."

I had to agree. But all the same, the cozy confines of the gym seemed a sensible alternative to the Arctic-like conditions we were sure to face on the Housatonic.

The next day, we loaded ourselves onto the bus for the 20-twenty minute ride out to Derby. I sat next to Ned Double-day, one of the handsome blonde guys from St. Paul's that filled Linsly-Chit at the introductory meeting. St. Paul's is in New Hampshire, and Ned had rowed there, so I figured he probably knew a thing or two about rowing in cold weather.

"Ned," I asked, "do they give us gloves when we get out there, or was I supposed to bring my own?"

Ned looked at me like I had just asked to borrow his only pair of L.L. Bean boots. "Gloves?" he repeated, with a sneer. "For what?"

"For rowing. You know, so your hands don't freeze off."

"Danzigeek," Ned said with disgust.

He and a few other of the fellows called me Danzigeek because I was so tall for a lightweight. At the boathouse, there was a bar which ran across one of the bays. It was so high that almost nobody could touch it without jumping. Anyone who could grab onto the bar while flat-footed was considered a geek. Only the tallest heavyweights were geeks. Colin and Paul were geeks. Jens was most definitely a geek. My arms are kind of long, so when I reached up I could just about pass the geek test if I got up on my tip toes. Nonetheless, I was as close to a geek as any lightweight would ever be. Thus the name, Danzigeek. Most of the guys had stopped calling me that because they sensed I didn't particularly care for the moniker. Not Ned. He kept on calling me Danzigeek for precisely that reason.

"Danzigeek, nobody wears gloves in the boat. First of all, you need to feel the oar in order to feather it properly. Secondly, only a pussy would wear gloves."

That settled that. I wasn't wearing gloves. I didn't care so much about jeopardizing my feathering feel, but I didn't want to be a pussy. That'd be about as un-Gavinish as you got.

We got in the boats and paddled down the river. Rick was ahead of us in his launch, pushing ice floes out of our way. It was bitterly cold. I didn't notice any increased sensitivity to the oar, since I wasn't wearing any gloves. In fact, I didn't notice much of anything at all. My hands were numb. The rest of me was nice and toasty. I had on long underwear, a t-shirt, sweat pants, a hooded sweat shirt, and a wind breaker.

As the practice wore on, and we got into some power pieces, I started to warm up. My head was itching as the sweat began to form on my scalp. Soon, we were peeling off the layers. By the end of practice, I was down to my long underwear and t-shirt. I thought that maybe it had gotten warmer, but a glance over at Rick, who was bundled up and miserable, told me that it was our hard work in the boat that had comforted us from the cold.

Though I was working hard, my rowing was not so good. I was having trouble getting my oar out of the water at the finish on almost every stroke. This was both upsetting the boat's set, and slowing it down. Tim Cotton, another veteran oarsman from St. Paul's, was sitting right in front of me. I heard him say, "Relax Zig, you're doing fine. Think about taking your blade out square. Then feather." That was really nice of Tim. He knew that I was struggling to make the Florida trip. I followed his instructions, and sure enough, my finishes became smoother.

The warm shower water stung my body, and my blistered hands didn't feel a thing. They were still under Mother Nature's anesthesia.

I had forgotten to bring a change of clothes, so I had to get back into my sopping wet rowing gear. I got onto the bus cold and miserable, but I was smiling.

On the dock, Rick had come up to me. "Zig," he said, "You didn't row very well today, but I think we can find some use for you down in Florida. Consider yourself invited." I had made the only cut, albeit unofficial, that Yale Crew has. Now I had to make a boat.

Gavin had been interviewed by the Yale Daily News about a week before we left for Tampa. Every year, I was told, the News did an article on Yale crew and the unheralded oarsmen who labor under obscurity all year in order to row a few rac-es in the spring. That was about as much notoriety as we ever received, not including the times Morley unwittingly focused attention on the crew through his raucous interludes with New Haven's finest.

At any rate, in Gavin's interview, he explained that the trip to Tampa was crucial in that it was down there that boatings were made. More importantly, Gavin stressed, was the team bonding that went on down there. Florida is very intense, and there is huge competition for seats in the top boats. Sometimes these battles yield great team unity, sometimes they sunder the team. It was important, captain Gavin emphasized, that not only does the squad return with fast boats, but that we return as a team.

ELEVEN

The Florida sun was a welcome break from the bleak New Haven winter. We unloaded all the boats from the trailer and then were led to the bunk house that would be home for the next two weeks. The barracks, as we called it, was one large room with about twenty bunk beds. All the freshmen lightweights would be staying in this one room. In addition, half the varsity team would be in there. After a week, they would go to the nearby Holiday Inn and the other half of the varsity would replace them.

Even though the accommodations were not at all luxurious, I was happy with them because it would give me a chance to become better acquainted with some of the guys. Also, I'd get to know a few of the varsity oarsmen who don't ordinarily pay any attention to the lowly frosh.

The University of Tampa was in the middle of Sexual Awareness Week when we arrived. Posters in the cafeteria announced that there was a soft core porn movie being shown after dinner in the auditorium; apparently the students would have their sexual horizons broadened by way of cinema. Most of the guys decided to head in that direction after the meal.

The movie was pretty tame, and so was the crowd. That is until we got a view of the lovely star of the movie bending over to put on some spike heeled shoes. Just then, some guy in the audience yelled out, in specific anatomical terms, exactly what he thought the "actress" should do next. I looked over and it was Vogel making his feelings known. The entire auditorium erupted in laughter.

———

After the movie, we headed off to the barracks. The person in the bunk right next to mine was Mike Hard. He had deigned to come down from his perch on Mount Olympus and stay in the barracks. Before we went to sleep (at about nine o'clock, since wake-up was at five thirty), he stood up, bent over at the waist, and rotated his right arm in a circle. This was part of his rehabilitation for a nagging shoulder injury that threatened his otherwise secure seat in the varsity.

I was asleep for a few minutes when Hard tapped me on the shoulder and woke me up. I opened my eyes and refocused. Hard wanted to speak to me. I didn't think he even knew who I was. It wasn't quite a flaming bush, but I listened intently as he whispered his short message. "Stop snoring," I considered his words, thanked him, and returned to what I hoped would be a quieter slumber.

"Rise and shine!" the coxswain's yelled. "Up and at 'em. We got some rowing to do!" It was the coxswains rousing us before dawn. Even though I had gotten over eight hours of sleep, waking at five thirty just wasn't for me. I tried to sneak a few extra winks, but I saw Hard bounding out of bed. I did the same. Maybe if I acted like a god, I'd become one.

We went outside into pre-dawn darkness. It was surprisingly cold. This was supposed to be Florida, the Sunshine State. The frigid weather seemed totally unacceptable. I put on the sweatshirt that I was sure I wouldn't need and joined the others on the way to the water.

Every morning, Rick would have the boating assignments on a wooden board. Everybody's name was written on a tongue depressor, each one with holes in either end and hanging on two nails that Rick had hammered into the board. We'd find out who was in which boat, gather together, and get the boat on the water.

Once on the water, I quickly found out that Florida practices were unlike any I had gone through in New Haven. Tank sessions at Yale consisted of power pieces that added up to fifteen, maybe twenty, minutes of full power rowing. In Florida, each practice would be comprised of pieces that totaled thirty minutes of power. An entire racing season was little more than a half hour of power, and we'd be doing that every practice, twice a day.

Rick's plan was for us to do shorter pieces in the morning, maybe 10 three-minute pieces, and longer pieces, usually 5 sixes, in the afternoon. Some guys preferred the shorter pieces because they were over quickly, and you could always survive one more two-minute piece. Others favored the longer pieces, simply because there were less of them. I didn't care. Either way, a half an hour was a ton of work, and I couldn't wait for Rick to yell, "Paddle it in."

Every fifth practice or so would be a "skill-and-drill" workout. There wouldn't be so much full pressure, which was a relief. Instead, Rick would focus on the technical aspects of rowing.

He'd have us row with our eyes closed so that we'd get the feel of the boat running out from under us. Or we'd row with our blades square to the water. This helped the boat set up better, because if the boat was set, no blades would hit the water. If the boat wasn't on an even keel, the blades would catch on the way back, and everyone would get splashed. None of the boats I was in had a spectacular set, so the blades-squared routine was particularly unappealing to me. In all though, skill-and-drill was a welcome break from the usual half hour of power.

Rowing in Florida was a painful experience. My hands were shredded. Both palms were riddled with blood blisters and open wounds. Gripping an oar, not to mention pulling on one, was excruciating. The salt water from Tampa Bay splashed on to the oars and burned my open wounds. Even letting go of the oar was painful, as I inevitably was leaving some of my skin on the wooden handle.

An observer might conclude that oarsmen lack the camaraderie of other athletes because we never gave each other high fives or even greeted each other with hearty handshakes. The reason for that was simple: our hands were so beat up that slapping some one five would be an excruciating act of sado-masochism. Touching fingertips was as close to a high-five as we came.

Showering even proved to be a trying experience. The soapy hot water stung like crazy when it ran into my blisters. I alleviated the problem as best I could by keeping my hands away from the water. I shampooed by lathering up my hair with the backs of my hands. Johnson's Baby Shampoo may be "no more tears" if it gets in your eyes, but when that stuff sneaks into an open blister, it stings like a bastard.

By the end of the first week, my hands were so chopped up that I would do anything to stop the pain. One day in the barracks, I overheard some of the varsity guys talking about how the Australians used to heal their blisters by urinating on their hands.

"Bullshit," one of the guys said.

"Swear to god. I read it in Rowing USA."

"So are you going to piss on yourself today?" The first one wondered. "Or can I do it for you?"

"Piss on yourself. My hands aren't that bad yet."

It sounded like an odd treatment for blisters, and these upperclassmen certainly weren't taking it too seriously, but I was desperate and willing to try anything. That night I quietly snuck out of the barracks, checked to make sure the coast was clear, and began to piss all over my bleeding hands. To attempt to describe the pain would only illustrate the poverty of the English language. There are no words that could communicate the searing pain of uric acid as it fell on my raw hands. I pulled my hands away instantly, cursed myself for believing such a remedy might work, and went back to the barracks.

Aside from the blisters and the sunburn (the morning chill quickly yielded to blazing sun), a little known ailment that afflicted almost every oarsman was row-butt. Sitting on wooden seats six hours a day produced bruises and blisters that were probably akin to bed sores that old folks all over Florida endure. No two seats were shaped exactly alike, so each day I'd develop a new sore on my ass. With every stroke, I'd drive myself back onto the seat and wince in agony.

Life in Tampa revolved around three activities: eating, sleeping and rowing. Jim McManus, Matt Burlage, myself, and a few other freshmen lightweights decided to add a fourth discipline to the routine: drinking. Almost every night, a bunch of us headed over to the Rathskeller, the campus bar at the University of Tampa, whose docks and cafeteria we used. There, we'd have a few beers, maybe have a couple more, and try to cajole a few of the Tampettes to show us their dorm rooms. Somehow, we never really impressed these women, and we'd always end up heading back to the barracks.

While a few of us were out drinking one evening, some of the other freshmen decided to commemorate our sojourn to Tampa. It was a tradition for each class to paint a Y with the year of the class on one of the bridges that spanned the Hillsborough River. This was not good enough for the Class of '85 Lightweights. These guys found a 20-foot square ballast hanging off of a bridge. They rigged up a harness and lowered Potter to the ballast. There he hung, suspended precariously thirty feet above the water with gallons of blue and white paint at the ready.

The next morning, I saw their handiwork as we rowed up river. Sure enough, there was a huge white Y with a blue 85 straddling it. Underneath the Y, just so no one thought the heavyweights had been capable of such artistry on a grand scale, was written 150.

Great job, I thought. These guys had really outdone themselves. On closer inspection, though, I noticed something disturbing. In the bottom corner, they had painted their own names: Potter, Ned, and Sloan. Singling themselves out didn't seem right, but somehow I wasn't surprised. Potter and Ned, who hailed from Middlesex and St. Paul's, had acted from day one like they had something going for them that the rest of us didn't. As one member of my class responded, through his rigid jaw when I asked him where he went to high school, "I didn't 'go to high school', I prepped at St. Paul's." I was surprised that Sloan's name was painted up there. Although he came to Yale with Groton's hallowed breeding, he was a regular guy.

While those three memorialized themselves, McManus

and I were happily enjoying ourselves. One night, me and Mac (we were the only two who didn't miss a night at the Rat) were stumbling home when we came across some oars that the varsity heavyweights used. There was real animosity between the lightweights and the heavyweights. For some reason, the heavies looked down on the lightweights. I never knew why. Maybe they thought of us as puny punks trying to compete in a he-man sport. We called the heavyweights names, like fat weights and dumb weights. They didn't have a nickname for us. They didn't need one. They just called us lightweights. It was just there, a mutual and tacit resentment.

Sometimes, the hostility wasn't even that tacit. One morning, a heavyweight cut in front of me in the breakfast line. I tapped him on the shoulder. "No frontsies. That's the American Way," I explained.

He didn't budge. "Why don't you go out and grab some bird seed, lightweight?" A fine suggestion.

"Thanks, but the French toast looks awful good this morning. Maybe I'll grab some seed as a snack before supper."

My colossal buddy didn't even smile. Nor did he relinquish his spot in line. The only thing worse to a heavyweight than a lightweight, was a wise ass fresh lightweight. And that is exactly what I was.

So here were me and Mac, hammered and standing over these heavyweight oars. Mac turned to me and said, "I wouldn't mind getting rid of some of those brews."

I nodded in agreement, and we proceeded to relieve ourselves all over the handles of the heavyweight oars. The next morning, Mac and I got up extra early and hurried over to watch the heavyweights get in the water. It was sweet revenge watching the bully from the breakfast line grab the oar that we had pissed all over the night before.

The only time the entire team, freshmen and varsity, got together as one was at the annual team barbecue. The highlight of the evening were the skits that each class put on. The juniors had, by far, the best one. It wasn't a skit; it was a video they'd made. They had taken out a shell and a launch, and the camera gave us a Dave's eye view of practice. The people in the boat rowed poorly on purpose, and the voice was a parody of Vogel's coaching technique. "You're late!" The voice boomed. "You're early! You're off the fucking team." And on it went. Everyone, including Dave, was howling. I wondered how closely art had imitated life.

That was it for fun and games. The rest of the time was focused on getting boats together for racing season. For the first week of practice, the combination of oarsmen that Rick put out in the water resulted in fairly even boatings. He always made sure that the talented guys, like Jigger, Potter, and Ned, were spread among the novices.

By the second week, however, it became clear that Rick was getting closer and closer to setting first and second boats. The boats weren't so evenly matched anymore, and I didn't think it was a coincidence that my boat was always rowing in the other boat's puddles.

Rick finalized the boatings with three days left in our fortnight in Tampa. I made the second boat. The first boat had all the experienced oarsmen: Jigger, Potter, Ned, Tim Cotton, and Sloan Walker, as well as three other guys who were just faster rowers than I was. Looking back, I was utterly unprepared to do the work that Rick required of me. The long hours on the water, the early wake-ups, were more than I felt I could ask of myself.

Of course, everyone in the second boat had hoped to be

chosen for the first boat, but the corollary to that wasn't that we were upset to be in the second boat. None of us felt that we had been relegated to the loser boat. On the contrary, every single oarsman and the coxswain had the attitude that he was chosen for the second boat. We made the boat. After all, there were forty people who tried out for lightweight crew and didn't even make it to Florida. No doubt about it, we were proud to be in the second boat.

I called home from Tampa with the news. Mom and Dad were both on the phone. "The boats have been set," I announced, "and I'm in the second boat."

"That's great, sweetie!" said Mom. I could tell she was really proud of me.

"Just let us know when and where the first race is," Dad said, his voice brimming with enthusiasm. "And we'll be there to watch."

We came back to New Haven a team. The competition for seats had drawn us together, not torn us apart, and we were ready for the season to finally begin.

After our first day on the water at Derby, Rick announced that the team jackets had arrived. We all gathered around him as he handed out the blue baseball-style jackets with a white Y and gold crossed oars. A sartorial testament to our efforts. For the remainder of the school year, it was easy to pick out the freshmen oarsmen: they were the guys who strode around campus in their team jackets, no matter the weather. We were the ones who labored in notorious obscurity all fall and winter. And now we wanted everyone to know who we were.

TWELVE

The first race of the season was against MIT. I was beyond excited. We drove up to Boston the night before and stayed in the Sonesta Hotel. I felt like I was on a pro team, although I assumed that pros didn't sleep four men to a double room. The first freshman had two to a room. We split up bow four and stern four. I was the five man, so I slept in a room with Phil Palmer, Jim McManus, and Tom Gramaglia. We pulled the mattresses off the box springs and flipped for who got to sleep on which. I lost and ended up with a box spring.

The weather for the race was horrendous. Even though it was April, Boston had just gotten several inches of snow, and the wind was blowing hard. Rick got us together before the race for our final instructions.

"You're ready for this," he said. He was very calm. I was a nervous wreck. "You have worked hard, and if you row like I know you can, you will win. Go out there and pull hard, go fast, and vanquish the opposition."

We accomplished two of his three objectives. We pulled

hard and we won. We did not, however, go fast. Our time of eight minutes and twenty-two seconds was almost two and a half minutes off the course record. So what? We had won and we were ecstatic. Our first race was under our belts and we had some proof that our hard work had paid off.

Mom, Dad, and Katie, my twin sister, and my best friend (even though he went to Harvard) John Solomon, had all braved the elements to see us race. Mom even shot a roll of film of the race to insure that the images of our victory would be around should my grandchildren ever doubt that I had indeed been in the boat that defeated MIT's second freshmen. Unfortunately, it's tough to see which boat is which from the balcony of MIT's boathouse, so when the film got back from the developer, Mom found that what she had was 24 pictures of a women's crew rowing down the Charles. My grandchildren will just have to take my word for it.

We were staying at the Royal Sonesta, and the night before the race Rick gave some strategy talks, and then he said "You know what, I want each of you guys to bring back a souvenir from the Sonesta. We'll have a look at them on the bus and see what everybody gets." I had no idea what he meant, but my basic understanding was that I was going to steal something: a towel, pad of butter, a knife with the RS engraving, a bathrobe, something like that. As we were leaving I still hadn't taken anything, but then I spotted something. I looked at Mike Hard. He nodded, and I grabbed it

We got on the bus, and we were just getting on the Massachusetts Turnpike, off of Storrow Drive, and Dave said "Let's see what everybody's got."

One kid held up a towel. Not bad. Another guy held up a pair of monogrammed bathroom slippers, and a third guy held up an engraved spoon. Then Rick asked, "Anybody else have something for show and tell?"

I raised my hand like the dumbest kid in class who somehow thought he had the correct answer.

"Let's see it Zig", Rick smiled, as I hoisted the entire switchboard from the hotel's front desk over my head like it was the Stanley Cup.

"Love it." Rick said after a pause.

Then he had the driver spin the bus around, and we drove right back to the Royal Sonesta.

"Give that back." Rick ordered, "great fucking spirit." Hard looked at me and then announced, "Um, maybe you didn't have to take the whole switchboard. I didn't think he'd take the switchboard."

Back at Yale the day after the race, my local youth protégé Jaymie joined me for brunch in Branford Dining Hall. (Yale is divided into 12 residential colleges. Each college has its own library, dining hall, squash courts, a quad for playing football, music room, theater, et cetera. Your residential college has everything. You're part of that college, within the university.)

"Jaymie," I told him, "I've got something to give you."

His waffle-filled face lit up expectantly. "What is it, Zig?" I thought I heard him say through more than a mouthful of food and syrup.

I pulled a small plastic watch from my pocket and slid it across the table to Jaymie. The excited look on his face immediately turned to thinly veiled disappointment. What I had thought would be a happy moment had become an awkward one. It hadn't even occurred to me that Jaymie couldn't tell time yet.

"Listen," I said, hoping to salvage the afternoon, "today you're going to learn how to do something new. Like that time you learned how to catch a football."

That recent memory registered a smile on both of our faces, and after a little coaxing, Jaymie agreed to humor me and go along with this new learning enterprise.

We got back to my room and started with the hour hand. Explaining this aspect of telling time didn't exactly stretch my pedagogic skills. "This short hand," I said to Jaymie, "is called the hour hand. We call it the hour hand because whatever number on the dial it is pointing to, well then that's what hour it is."

Jaymie grasped this immediately, as I knew he would. Then he asked a question which I didn't expect. "What if the hour hand isn't pointing to a number, but is in between? Then what hour is it?"

A fine question. Unfortunately, I didn't have an answer of equivalent fineness. So I resorted to an old Dad ploy, a technique he used whenever he didn't have the foggiest idea how to respond to one of my questions.

"We'll get to that later," I promised.

The minute hand was much more difficult. "The long hand counts the minutes, so we call it the minute hand." This Jaymie understood readily. "Now here's the tricky part," I warned Jaymie. "When the long hand—"

"The minute hand," he interjected correctly.

"Yes, the minute hand. Now when that minute hand is on the seven, that means thirty five minutes, not seven minutes. It's very tricky."

Jaymie was only in second grade. He had just started grappling with take-aways. Multiplication and the fives table were several years down the road. This made the minute hand a daunting and frustrating experience.

For the better part of the afternoon, we tried mightily to unravel the mysteries of the minute hand. Finally, we conceded defeat and I took Jaymie home. The watch on his wrist was more like a bracelet with a puzzle on it, which Jaymie looked at suspiciously and constantly, trying to unlock its secret.

I had failed to teach Jaymie how to tell time. There were lots of things I couldn't teach him, but just being with him, even if it was sometimes aggravating for either or both of us, was a welcome break from classes, crew, and many other assorted pressures that Yale served up in abundance on a daily basis.

All the guys in our boat wore our victory-earned MIT rowing shirts to practice the next Monday. As we happily pranced around the dock wearing the skins of our enemy, the guys in the first boat looked on furiously. They had lost by seventeen seconds to MIT's first boat. As Rick explained to them afterwards, "You did row pretty, but you rowed slow." From then on, we called the first boat the "pretty boys." This nickname wasn't given them with any animosity, though it might have been motivated to some degree by jealousy.

Nevertheless, the name seemed appropriate. Six of the

eight oarsmen had prepped at either Groton, Middlesex, Andover, or St. Paul's. They had names like Jigger, Sloan, Ned, and Lincoln. They rowed pretty, as Rick himself stated. And they were, by and large, a handsome lot.

The second boat, on the other hand, for better and for worse, was not pretty. Only one or two of our crew had gone to boarding school, and neither of them had rowed before coming to Yale. Phil, Tom, Steve, and Tony were the common names of our contingent. We didn't row pretty. And to look at us, we were pretty motley.

But we had MIT shirts and the pretty boys didn't.

The next weekend, we had a triangular race with Penn and Columbia on the Harlem River. We were undefeated and confident about our chances to double the length of our winning streak with a single race.

The Columbia crew was traditionally slow, so the real test would be whether we could defeat Penn. Rick told us that we'd win if we rowed as hard as we had the week before.

Rick also told us a story about a Harvard-Columbia race that took place on the Harlem several years prior. Rick had tons of crew stories, and we all liked to gather around him as he shared his vast wealth of crew lore. In the middle of the race the boats went under a bridge about 50 or 60 feet high. During this particular race between Harvard and Columbia, just as the Harvard boat was going under the bridge (we assumed the Columbia boat was far behind, because Rick didn't mention them once in the story, except to say that it was a home race for them), some guy decided to see if manhole covers defer to the laws of gravity. So this guy chucked a one hundred pound piece of steel off the bridge. The manhole cover whizzed by the Harvard boat, and just missed pulverizing the bow man. Harvard won the race, but hasn't rowed on the Harlem since. The guys in our boat decided we would take a manhole cover "power ten" as we went under the bridge.

The start of the race went as planned. We took three fractional strokes and ten at a high rating to get the boat up to speed. Then we lengthened for ten, and finally we settled down to a rating of 33 strokes a minute for the body of the race. The plan was to stay at 33 and take it up for the last 20 if we needed to sprint.

After the settle, Tally Ferguson, our coxswain, informed us that we already had open water between us and Columbia, and we were up two seats on Penn. "Yeah," came a voice from the bow. It was Stephen Grant. "Let's go get 'em, guys!" Tom Gramaglia, the six man, requested that Stephen please "shut the fuck up and row." Stephen obliged.

We maintained our slim margin for the first five hundred meters. Then we took a power ten, and the Quakers drifted a few seats back. At the 1,000 meter mark, Tally called for the manhole cover ten. We responded with some killer strokes that put us more than a boat length up on Penn. I quickly glanced up to see if any projectiles were heading for our boat. The sky was clear, so it was going to be a safe race.

With five hundred meters to go, Penn was fading and we gained even more ground. Victory was ours, and to secure it we took a power ten in preparation for the sprint to the finish line, which was now less than 250 meters away.

Three strokes into the power ten, I feathered my blade underwater, and couldn't get my oar out of the water. I fought the oar as the handle went slamming into my chest. The boat slowed down, and turned to the right, since my oar was now acting as both an anchor as well as a rudder.

Panic rushed through me as the oar came totally out of the water and pinned me flat on my back against Milan Moore's legs. The oar was now over my head and parallel to the boat. Penn was closing fast as we sat still in the water.

"Keep rowing!" Tally yelled above the confusion in the boat. Some people were still rowing, others were not. Milan, behind me; and Tom in front of me helped get my oar back in the boat. By the time we were ready to row again, Penn was up almost half a length. And there were only twenty strokes to go.

Miraculously, we pulled together and began to eat into Penn's margin. From what Tally was telling us, we were gaining a seat on Penn every five strokes. It was going to be an incredibly tight finish.

When Tally told us to paddle, I looked across and saw that I was even with the five man in the Penn boat. They were not celebrating. After a couple of minutes, the official's launch glided to the Penn shell, and one of the men leaned over and said something to the Penn cox. With that, their boat erupted in exhilaration.

We lost by fifteen-hundredths of a second. I was crushed. Crew, I had been told, was the ultimate team sport; no one man can singlehandedly determine the outcome of a race. On this cold spring Saturday, I laid waste to that theory. Our boat was staring victory squarely in the eye, and I blinked.

That race represented over one hundred hours of practice. With one stroke I had spoiled everything. I felt like jumping out of the shell and letting myself dissolve in the toxic sludge we had just rowed on, when Milan Moore slid forward and put his hand on my shoulder. "Mike," he said, still out of breath, "we all know you didn't lose this race. We lost the race. Last week we won, this week we lost. We do it all together."

I was really moved by Milan's words. I'm not sure that right after the race I would have been able to say the same to him if he had caught the crab. But I was grateful for what he said. In a strange way, it is my most special memory of crew.

We paddled to the dock in silence. While we de-rigged the boat and got ready to load it on the trailer, the Penn guys came over for their shirts. I knew that I'd have to give my shirt to Penn's five man, but I had no idea how hard it would be. As I peeled my sweat and water soaked shirt off my body, I thought of how hard I had worked to earn the right to wear the Yale rowing uniform. All those ergs, the two-a-days in Tampa, the countless trips to Derby. And now I had to relinquish this symbol of my effort and dedication.

The idea of competing for shirts is unique to crew. There's the old saying of giving the shirt off of one's back. That means that you would give everything possible, everything you had. As I handed my shirt to a man I had never seen before, and would likely never see again, and stood at the Columbia boathouse bare backed, stripped of my identity (other than loser) as an oarsman, I gained a new appreciation for an aphorism I had considered trite.

The week before, when the first boat lost to MIT, Rick brought out a box of "betting shirts" for the guys to give to the winning squad. The first boat raced in blue shirts with white sashes and white trim around the neck and arms. However, they only bet these shirts against Harvard and Princeton, and even then, only in the Sprints at the end of the season. In all the other races, they bet plain blue shirts, with a Y 150 on the right breast: the shirt that the second boat raced in and wagered. Even if they lost, they got to hold on to their racing shirts. Handing over a clean, crisp shirt could not have been nearly as painful as giving the shirt off their backs.

Then I saw Dad come jogging towards me, his camera flapping against his chest.

"That was some close finish, Zig," he said. "It looked like you had it in the bag until somebody really fouled things up."

"You're looking at the guy," I said.

Dad smiled and looked at me. He looked like the kindest person alive.

"You want to know my proudest sports memory of you?"

I was in no mood for nostalgia. "Save it, Dad."

He continued anyway. "It was your first ski race at Vail. You were in third grade and wanted to race in a slalom. During the race, you wiped out twice, and had to climb ten feet up the hill just to get through one of the gates. But you finished. The man standing next to me on the side of the course saw your struggle and said, 'I don't know who that kid is, but has he ever got guts.' I still remember your time. It was 97 seconds. The winning time was about 34. In a race that is usually decided by hundredths of seconds, you finished more than a minute behind. But you finished, and I was so proud of you. Just like I am today." Then he put his arm around me.

There isn't anyone who can piss me off as much as Dad can. But there also wasn't a soul alive who could have made me feel proud of my effort, in spite of its results. Dad's words did just that.

Dad got a picture of our boat the moment we realized that we had lost. It is a black-and-white photograph, and it was taken from quite a distance, but the image of exhaustion and despair comes through loud and clear. I had it blown up and it hangs on my wall. I call it "Agony of Defeat." Now every time I watch Vinko Bogataj, the Slavic ski jumper, do his memorable face plant during ABC's introduction to The Wide World of Sports, I know how he must feel, and I can even taste the snow.

—————

The next day, I had planned to go to the Peabody Museum and check out the dinosaurs with Jaymie. I just didn't feel like it. I was about to call and tell Jaymie that I was sick, or had a bunch of homework. But I decided lying to a seven-year-old is pretty uncool, so I drove down Dixwell to pick him up.

I walked up the steps to his house, knocked gently on the flimsy door, and pushed it open. Jaymie was waiting impatiently. He looked at his wrist and announced, "You're seven minutes late, Zig." He was wearing a watch now, not a puzzle, and we both smiled broadly.

"What are we doing today?" he asked.

"We're going to look at some dinosaurs."

"Great! Let's go." We hopped in the car, and yesterday's race became a distant memory.

—————

During the next week of practice, preparing for our race against Rutgers, I concentrated solely on my finishes. I wanted them to be nice and clean. Push down, then feather, then drive the oar away with my hands. Down, feather, and away. I had gotten the Catch, Drive, Finish, Recovery bit down. But now I realized that within that sequence, there were lots of other critical progressions with which I had yet to come to grips. The finish, one-fourth of the stroke, became my obsession.

Rick kept after us to lay the power on at the catch, really

drive the oar through the water as soon as the blade is buried. He was right: A quick catch was what made the boat leap out of the water and gain momentum. But I felt I couldn't concentrate on helping the boat go faster until I ceased worrying about stopping the boat altogether.

All the while, the other guys in my boat were really supportive. Not once did anyone so much as rib me about the Penn-Columbia race. Instead, each guy said that he was glad that it hadn't been him that pulled the crab, since it could just as easily have happened to anyone. This display of team unity wasn't just done in front of me for my benefit. I overheard one of the guys on the varsity talking to Rick about the crab. "I'll bet they kicked his ass in the boathouse," the guy said to Rick.

"I thought they would, too," Rick responded. "But they have just accepted it as bad racing luck. Those guys had a decision to make after the race. They could have gotten pissed at Zig for blowing it, which would have splintered the boat, or they could have pulled together. I'm surprised and pleased at the way they've gone about it. And I feel sorry for Rutgers, because the second boat is going to take it out on them come Saturday."

Rick was odd and cynical, and he seemed distant at times, but he really understood the psyche of a crew, and that made him a great coach.

THIRTEEN

ace day came, and we backed our shell into the starting line. Tally had the bow man take a couple of light strokes to get us aimed straight. Then he called the rest of us to come up to three quarters slide and bury our blades. He lowered his hand, which was his signal to the starter that we were ready to row.

The starter spoke. "Both hands are down. Five, four, three, two, one... Êtes-vous prêt? Partez!"" Rick had prepared us for this bout of French at the start of the race. It is the way international races are begun. I hadn't spoken French since I failed out of Monsieur Broquet's class in eighth grade and was banished to Latin for the next three years. Rick probably sensed that I lacked a gift for the language of love and crew racing starts, so he didn't bother teaching me what the starter's words meant. He just told us to start rowing when the guy said "Partez."

And that is just what we did. Tally's voice travelled down the hull of the shell. "Three quarters half three quarters full ten high! One two three thata way five six seven pour it on and lengthen in two one two ten to lengthen one two reach out and grab some water four five six nice and long guys eight settle in two one two settle."

With that we all held our finishes a little bit longer and then relaxed up the slide. When I took my first settling stroke, I realized with a panic that I was completely out of breath. I was so excited during the first twenty strokes of the race, that I just forgot to breathe. As stupid as it sounds, I entirely forgot to breathe.

Luckily, it seemed like the guys in the Rutgers boat had forgotten to pull hard, because we were half a length up on them at the settle. Still, I was hoping I could hold on. I took a couple of deep breaths. My throat was parched and there was a cool burn under my Adam's apple. I concentrated on relaxing, and, of course, on keeping my finishes clean.

There was a huge curve in the last 500 meters, and we were on the outside of it. Would Rutgers be able to make up a length and a half on the inside lane? Tally called for a power ten as we went into the turn, and we really responded. Instead of Rutgers gaining on us in the turn, we widened the margin on the Scarlet Knights.

We crossed the finish line with two lengths of open water between us. When we finally stopped paddling, John Rowley let out a huge yell. It was three-parts exhilaration, and one-part relief. The recipe for my emotion was an inverted version of John's. I had finally put the crab behind me. It would never happen again. I was sure.

That evening, the entire team — varsity and fresh — gathered at Dave's house to watch the video of our sweep of Rutgers. Our race came on the monitor first, since we had led things off that morning. There we were, kicking Rutgers' ass around the last bend with our humongous power ten. I was reliving the excitement, when I heard Rick and Dave's commentary from the launch.

The first voice I heard was Rick's. "Looks like we're going to win one this week," he said proudly as we pulled away from our opponents.

"That is," said Dave, "if Danziger doesn't fuck things up for you."

Everyone in the room went, "Oooooooooh!" and started laughing. I smiled thinly. But I was upset. If I could put the crab behind me, and everyone in my boat could, then why couldn't Dave? After all, I'd be rowing for the guy for the next three years. I didn't want him thinking of me as a total fuck-up who he couldn't trust in one of his top boats.

The boat didn't have much time to celebrate its success, and I didn't have time to brood over Dave's remark, because we had the Harvard-Princeton race to prepare for. The HYP's were upon us. I couldn't believe that our season was almost over. After all, it had just begun three weeks earlier. The HYP's were the final race of the season before the Eastern Sprints.

The upcoming race was important for two reasons. For starters, Harvard and Princeton have always been our biggest rivals, and to have the chance to race them at the same time is a very big deal. I hadn't been at Yale long enough to develop a hatred for the Cantabs or the Tigers. The only guys I knew at these two schools were buddies of mine from high school. But just so I wouldn't be out of step with everyone else on the team and at Yale, I looked upon the undergraduate population of Harvard and Princeton as being, without exception, comprised of a bunch of arrogant assholes.

The second reason it was vital that we won the HYP's was that the winner of that race had a gigantic psychological advantage going into the Sprints. For years, the winner of the Sprints had been either Harvard, Princeton, or Yale, so the HYP's were an accurate presage of what might occur at the Sprints.

We trained well for the race. On Monday and Tuesday, Rick had us doing six and eight minute pieces. During these pieces, Rick would instruct us to raise or lower the stroke rating at two minute intervals. Phil Palmer, the person in charge of setting the cadence for the rest of the boat (the "stroke"), got to the point that when Rick asked for a 33, Phil was right on it. 28? He was right there, like a metronome. The rest of us just tried to follow.

On Wednesday, we rowed through three time trials against the first boat over the race course. Racing against the pretty boys was serious stuff for us. We always wanted to beat them. Taking a piece off of the first boat was cause for celebration in our shell. It wasn't that we didn't like them. Far from it. The guys in the first boat, for the most part, were some of my best friends at Yale. Lincoln and I hung out together all the time, and even Ned and Potter seemed like regular guys. My original antipathy towards them stemmed mostly from the fact that they were getting laid by all the best looking girls in our class, all the girls I didn't even have the courage to talk to.

Our desire to wail on the first boat was akin to sibling rivalry. We respected them and were glad to be on the same team as they were, but we really wanted to kick their asses on the water. We almost never did, except in short pieces in which they weren't concentrating, and we were pumped. Whenever we did beat them, the pretty boys would invariably wake up and thrash us for the rest of the practice. Which was okay, because we had our moment, and we wouldn't let them forget it. I'd be in the shower standing next to Jigger and say, "Gee Jig, you guys really gave us a scare in that first two-minute piece. It looked like you were going to make a move with 30 seconds to go, but I guess your heart was willing but the body wasn't."

"Yup, Zig," Jigger would deadpan. "But it was just a privilege to be on the same river as you guys." I liked Jigger.

On this particular day, we took off down the race course together, and we stayed right with the first boat through the first 20 strokes. We faltered at the settle and they were gone. After 500 meters, I couldn't even hear their cox, Neil Herbsman, yelling into the speaker system that they had rigged up in their boat. We rowed well and finished three and a half lengths of open water behind.

That was the margin of our handicap in the second race. It is so much easier to row from the lead because the trailing boat is always in sight. When they make a move, we could see it, and counter. This was the case in the second piece. We held our lead until the last five hundred. By then, the first boat had drawn to within three quarters of a length of us. Neil would call a power ten, and his boat would respond by gaining a seat, perhaps two. But Tally was smart. Just as they were taking their seventh stroke, he'd call for a ten of our own. That way we could catch them as they inevitably sagged after the effort of the power ten. Our ten would stop their move and even take back some of our lead. Tally screamed encouragement to us during the final duel to the finish line. "That's the way to do it fellas! Now we're really moving! They think they can take us but let's show them who really wants it! The first boat is going down!" His words were directed as much at us as they were at the pretty boys.

What Tally was saying must have worked because we were holding them off. For the last twenty strokes, Tally called for us to boost the rating by two strokes. We did, and after six or seven strokes, he asked for more strokes in the water. Rick's practices the day before were paying off. We were really sprinting! Phil cranked the rating, and the rest of us followed. To our amazement, the pretty boys went nowhere in the final twenty strokes, and we defeated them by half a length.

A sweet victory over the first fresh. We began to paddle to the dock, only to be stopped by Rick's voice. "Not so fast. We have one more piece do go. That was very impressive. Let's see if you can duplicate the performance. The starting margin will be the same."

We had given all we had in that last, frantic effort. The final race was an anticlimax for our boat and tasty revenge for the first boat. They nearly reversed the margin at the start of the piece, beating us by almost three lengths of open water. It was no fun getting shlonged (a term for losing by a huge margin), but that didn't take any of the starch out of the victory in the previous piece.

Thursday and Friday were taper days. We had light workouts and focused on starts and finishing sprints. The work was short and intense. The idea behind the taper was that in the two days before a race, it wasn't a good idea to tire the crew out with a lot of minutes of full pressure. The last two days were polishing days.

On Friday night, John Rowley and I went to see Chariots of Fire to psyche us up for the race. As Abrahams breasted the tape to take the gold at the '24 Olympics, John and I looked at each other and imagined that the next day, we would bust through the finish line just ahead of our worthy but hapless foes.

The first race of the day was the second freshman race. Rick told us to row like we had in the second piece against the pretty boys on Wednesday. He assured us that an effort like that would result in certain shirts. Our race was important, Rick concluded, because it set the tone for the rest of the day.

We arrived at the starting line, and took our place at the stake boat on the inside lane. Being on the inside was a blessing and a curse. It was good because if we were close going into the final turn, it meant that we had a good shot at winning. The downside to being on the inside was that we wouldn't be able to see the other boats. The stagger put each boat several seats ahead of us.

Our lane position wasn't a factor. We never saw the other boats. Harvard and Princeton cruised away from us just as Ernest Hemingway had explained how Robert Cohn's ancestors had lost all their money: "…gradually, and then all of a sudden." Our two rivals duked it out amongst themselves without giving us a thought. We were not in contention for an instant. It got so bad, that Tally stopped telling us how far off the pace we were, and he began to let us know who was winning between Harvard and Princeton. Princeton won, Harvard was second, and we limped in with the bronze.

Though we had lost our race, Yale rightfully claimed overall victory, as our varsity boat edged out the top boats from Harvard and Princeton in what looked like a three-way dead heat.

The two weeks following the HYP's were spent preparing for the final and biggest challenge of the year: the Eastern Sprints. At the end of the regular season, boats representing the 16 schools with the best rowing programs in the East duel it out on Lake Quinsigamond in Worcester, Massachusetts. Next to the Head of the Charles, it is the most important and widely attended rowing event there is. A victory at the Sprints meant bragging rights as the premiere rowing power in the east, and many believed, in the nation. This was a huge deal, make no mistake about it.

Classes had ended, so we were able to practice twice a day. Our boat's motivation was twofold: first, aside from wanting to be able to call ourselves the best second boat around, Tally and six of the other oarsmen had decided not to return to the crew next fall. We would never row together again. Second, we also knew that we would most likely lose touch with each other once crew ceased to be our common cause. Aside from Rowley, who was sticking with crew, none of the other guys were in Branford College. They would spread out all over campus, and to keep up with them would require a measure of commitment that, despite our vows to the contrary, we all knew we wouldn't abide.

We attacked each practice, and our boat speed began to increase. If we wanted to beat Princeton, we had to find twenty seconds in fourteen practices. One way to gauge improvement is by looking at "spacing," or the distance the boat travels between strokes. When a boat is moving quickly, there are six or seven feet separating the bow man's puddle and seven man's puddle on the next stroke. In the HYP's, Rick told us that we had rowed at a 34, but we were rowing in our own puddles. That's like running really fast without moving anywhere.

But we were moving. Our puddles told us that. Each practice, the sets of eight little whirlpools that we threw into the Housatonic grew both in size and in distance from the previous set of eddies.

Not only weren't we rowing in our own puddles anymore, but we weren't rowing in the pretty boys' puddles either. Whereas they had usually dusted us right from the start and kept us in their wake for the rest of the piece, now we were battling the first boat seat for seat from Rick's command to take it to full pressure, to when he told us to paddle.

We were getting faster just in time for the Sprints. After one particularly good piece, Tally said, "Clean out your drawers, guys. You better make room for a whole bunch of racing shirts."

Then Rick pulled his launch over to our boat. Instead of congratulating us on a well-rowed piece, he simply said, "Pull your boat next to the first boat. Rowley, I want you to switch with Sloan." Our spirits, soaring just a moment ago, had been dashed by Rick's command. By this point in the season, we had come to trust one another; we were really clicking. There wasn't one man in the boat who didn't truly believe that if we rowed well we had as good a shot as any boat of winning the Sprints.

By changing one element within our shell, Rick had altered what we believed was a winning equation. Whether Sloan was better or worse than John was not the point; he was different. Even John, who had been right on the bubble between first and second boats when Rick chose them down in Tampa, looked deflated as he stepped out of our wooden shell, and into the sleek carbocraft which was what he had been aiming for all fall and winter.

Sloan was certainly bummed. He had just been yanked from the first boat, and put in a boat which obviously viewed him as an unwanted intruder. "Let's go, studs," he yelled to the rest of us when he finished adjusting his foot stretchers. "Let's kick some ass, really wail on those guys!"

Sloan was trying to pump us up with enthusiasm. Clearly, he wanted us to row well so that he could prove to Rick that he wasn't the guy slowing the first boat down.

Perhaps he wasn't. Who knows whether the first boat's speed had changed since the switch? For whatever reason, we were slower with Sloan in our boat than we had been with John. There were the odd pieces where we would stay close to the first boat, but for the most part, they were smoking us on every piece.

On the Sunday of the Sprints, the top three finishers from each morning heat race for the championship in the afternoon.

We raced on Saturday. Second freshman and third varsity are not considered "official" boats. Only the varsity, the JV, and the first freshman count, whatever that means.

On this Saturday afternoon, six second freshman light-weight boats backed into the barge under a bridge on Lake Quinsigamond, awaiting the starter's command.

I sat at three quarters slide, my back straight, legs tensed, anxiously anticipating the starter's command. We had been aiming for this moment since September. Could the next six minutes and change possibly make up for nine months of toil?

The starter dropped his flag and we were about to find out. We shot off the line at a forty one, four strokes higher than we had ever rowed before. But we were nervous, and ragged, and when we settled, we found ourselves in sixth place.

Tally tried to bring some order to the boat. "Okay, now let's relax and think about being long and strong, we've got a bunch of boats ahead of us, but there's plenty of time to reel them in. Concentrate now as we take a ten for timing. On this one!"

Tally's words were soothing, and we really needed the concentration ten that he called for. We were beginning to develop a sense of rhythm and togetherness without which we would be doomed. The boat felt as though it was moving better through the water. We passed the 500 meter mark still in sixth place, but moving up on Navy.

"Eyes in the boat, goddamnit!" Tally screamed. He had never been this forceful. "I'll tell you where we are. You all just focus on rowing. Thataway, guys. That's what I mean. We're right on Navy, and moving through. I see MIT. We got them before, let's get them again with a BOBHIC ten." BOBHIC was a term Tally had plagiarized from one of the varsity coxswains. It was an acronym for Bend Over Baby, Here It Comes, and we got a huge charge out of hearing Tally use it. The boat obeyed Tally's command and we moved through MIT.

Tally was doing a wonderful job. He'd never cox a boat again, and he had certainly saved his best for last. There were few, if any, wasted words, and what he did say was either informative or inspirational. That's what good coxing is all about. We had complete faith in Tally. Anything he wanted, we'd try our best to give him.

With 750 meters to go, we left Navy and MIT behind, and now were gunning for Penn, who had about half a length on us, and Harvard and Princeton who were almost a length of open water ahead of the pack. We were rowing at 33 strokes a minute. Two and a half minutes to go, and Tally was like

Roger Staubach conducting a two-minute drill against the Redskins. He exuded a calm confidence, and it was a thrill to be rowing for him.

"We're rowing well now, boys. Let's follow Phil and bring it up two strokes in two. Do it in the water, not on the slide. We owe those guys from Penn. Payback begins in two. Now let's get on it! BOHICA!" (Bend Over Here It Comes Again).

We were beginning our sprint 500 meters before we usually did. In a practice race at Derby, there would have been some grumbling in the boat. Tom Gramaglia might have told Tally to eat shit. But today we were obedient and responded to his command. So did our shell. It seemed to leap out of the water, as each stroke ate into Penn's lead. We took a power ten and moved through Penn. Our loss on the Harlem had been avenged.

Only Harvard and Princeton were ahead of us now. A length separated all three boats, with Harvard half a length behind Princeton and just ahead of us. We were rushing up our slides, trying to take as many strokes as possible. There was a noticeable check at the catch, which sent Tally's whole body jerking forward as all of eight of us, 1,240 pounds, slammed the boat in the opposite direction that it was headed. We were sloppy and rough, but rowing strong. Behind me, I heard Milan gasping for breath and groaning at every catch. My own strokes were getting shorter and shorter, as I found myself only three quarters of the way up the slide and having to drop my blade in the water to keep in time with Phil.

"Here we go!" Tally screamed. "Three seats to get Harvard. And those Tigers are dying. Up in two for a sprint to the finish. On this one!"

I knew there was no way I could possibly bring it up another notch, and I was just as sure that no one else in the boat could either. We were rowing as hard and high we could. When Tally called for the rating to come up, not one of us could respond.

Then an amazing thing happened. With 500 meters to go in the race, the last 500 meters that six of the oarsmen would ever experience, we became a crew. The will of the boat surpassed what the eight individual oarsmen had thought was possible, and we achieved the critical mass that eludes all but the finest crews. Somehow, the rating went up in spite of our collective exhaustion.

We found ourselves even with Harvard and moving right through them. Princeton was seven lanes away, but Tally told us they were coming back to us as well.

"Last ten," Tally called. "This is it. Finish strong, you've done a great job!"

We cranked out the last ten strokes, and Tally finally told us to paddle it down. This was the only time we would disobey him. We slumped over our oars and then lay back in exhaustion.

The finish was close. Less than a seat separated us and Princeton. The official's launch took over a minute before going over to Princeton's boat to inform them that they were the 1982 second freshman lightweight Sprint champions. Just as they were too spent to celebrate fully, we were more tired than we were disappointed.

We paddled back to the docks. The first boat was there to pull us in. "Nice rowing," Ned said, grabbing my oar. "You guys had an unbelievable sprint."

I thanked him and felt water splashing over my right shoulder. It came from the Princeton coxswain being thrown into the water by his oarsmen. Soon, all nine of them were in the water, celebrating.

They had beaten us by less than a seat. We needed to gain 21 seconds on them from the HYP's and we could only come up with 20. If the race had been 20 meters longer, I'd be in the water. On the other hand, we had rowed far better than we had ever expected, and that answered the question I had asked myself right before the race began. Would the next six minutes be worth nine months of effort? You bet it was.

For the second time in three weeks, I peeled off my racing shirt and handed it to a nameless five man on the Princeton team. Maybe next year, he'd be handing me his. The eight other men in my boat were more reluctant to relinquish their jerseys. They'd never wear a Yale rowing shirt again.

The Sprints on Sunday began as an anticlimax for me. For starters, I wasn't involved in any of the races. The lightweights didn't do as well as we had hoped. The first freshmen came in third again to Princeton and Harvard. The JV cruised to its second victory in a row, clobbering the field from the start, while the varsity rowed what appeared to be a lackluster race, finishing third.

One bright spot for Yale was the second freshman heavies, who surprised everyone (who cared) and won. I knew all the guys because I had rowed with them until my secession in January. They hadn't done particularly well during the regular season, and it was great to see them win the Sprints. Coach Ricci had eaten a lot of shit because neither of his squads were so hot, so it was nice to see him finish well.

Race results aside, the atmosphere was thrilling. There were scores of boats and trailers, and hundreds of oarsmen milling about. I felt a bond with each of them. We were tied together by a common effort. All of us had worked hard for an entire school year to arrive at this moment. This was every oarsman's day in the spotlight, and each man, be he a winner or a loser, was proud of himself, and, by association, the other oarsmen.

There was lots of shirt swapping going on after the races.

A shirt's value was determined, to a large degree, by how the team did that day at the Sprints. Even though Yale hadn't won, it maintained its high asking price of a racing shirt, and maybe even a windshirt if the shirt was from a lesser rowing school like Columbia, for a single betting shirt. Yale oarsmen don't trade racing shirts. Even though I didn't have any currency of my own, since I had lost my shirt, I wouldn't have traded for another school's shirt. I wanted to earn my shirts on the water.

Around the docks where the Yale boats shoved off, family and alums fluttered about. A group of older men wore blue blazers with white trim. The pockets of these jackets were embroidered with a Y and crossed oars. These were Henley blazers, and the only way to get one was to row at the Royal Henley Regatta in England. Undefeated boats went to Henley to test their skills against some of Europe's fastest crews.

It was hard for me to believe that some of these men in their fifties and sixties, some sporting pretty serious beer guts, had been rowing gods at Yale. Would Hard and Morley end up looking like these guys? Hell, would I?

One man's blazer featured the Y and five linked circles, each a different color. I had seen him before. He was one of the men in the photo at the boathouse. He had won a gold medal in the 1956 Olympics. This man, unlike the others, looked as if he could step into any boat right now and make it go faster. His shoulders were huge beneath his blazer, and his legs carried him swiftly from admirer to admirer. This man still dwelt on Mount Olympus and I was awed by his presence.

FOURTEEN

After the bus ride back to New Haven, we all went back to our rooms, showered, and changed into coat and tie for the annual year-end crew banquet, held in the President's Room of Woolsey Hall. The food was plentiful and delicious. And pitchers of beer magically materialized at our tables the moment the previous ones had been drained. Since all of us were still light from sucking weight to make our pre-race weigh-in weights, the beers went down easily. The atmosphere got festive quickly.

Dave was the master of ceremonies, and managed to behave himself, except when he referred to the alums he hoped to get to donate to the program as "geriatrics." But he did also say that with so many underclassmen returning, and because the JV could have romped on almost any other school's varsity boat around, the future was promising. He thought, in spite of the Sprints, the year had been a great success.

The seniors sat on the dais with Dave and he thanked each one individually for being a part of Yale Crew for four years. I hadn't gotten to know many of the seniors very well, so I wasn't that nostalgic as Dave bade them farewell. In three years, I'd be sitting up there. I wondered what Vogel would have to say about my years rowing for the lightweights.

Then Rick got up and reviewed the freshman campaign. Although we hadn't won all our races, Rick judged his season a success because all the oarsmen planned to come back and row for the varsity next year. He had overlooked the six from his second boat that would never touch an oar, run the stairs, or pull and erg again. They were quitting, which seemed to neither surprise, nor even concern, Rick.

There were three awards given to freshmen. The MVP went to Jigger and Matt Burlage. Everyone figured that Jigger would get it, but no one thought Burlage would share in the honor. Matt deserved it, though. After the MIT race, when Rick put him at stroke, his toughness and leadership accounted for much of the boat's ensuing success and improvement.

Lincoln got the award for most improved. The last award was a sort of joke called the Commodore's Award. It was a makeshift trophy made up of a wooden rowing seat with a blue and white Styrofoam head on it, a boater's hat on top of the head. On the "trophy" was written, "To be awarded each year to the Freshman Commodore."

Unlike any other award, this one had no stated criteria. "This year's winner," Rick announced, "...is Mike Danziger."

I walked up to receive the award. I wasn't sure why I had gotten it. But I knew that Steve Gavin and Jim Faust, the seven man in the varsity, had won it when they were freshmen. I was on my way to becoming Captain Danziger, Fine Rower.

The rest of the evening became a bacchanalian blur. I remember walking into a Wa Wa convenience store and bobbing for pickles in a large barrel. Boy, did that sting my eyes! And I had to buy the entire barrel as the store owner wasn't too happy with my little stunt.

I think I remember going to Dunkin' Donuts. And I still have no idea how I woke up in the Davenport Courtyard with dried blood all over my arms, legs and chest. Some reports had me diving headlong off the Wright Hall gate. Luckily, I had the pavement to break my fall. My last conscious recollection was watching Steve Gavin howling in laughter as he threw up in the bushes. Very Gavinish.

When I awoke — I guess "coming to" better describes it — from my stupor-induced slumber, I found that my trophy was missing. I briefly attempted to mentally retrace my movements from the evening before, but quickly abandoned that fruitless pursuit. That summer, I swiped a seat from the Fordham boathouse, and Mom bought a head and a boater's hat and fashioned a brand new Commodore's trophy. She sure came through for me.

Though the Sprints marked the end of the rowing season for the lightweights, the heavies used the races in Worcester as a springboard for the beginning of training for perhaps their biggest test of the year: The Race. The four-mile race pitting Harvard against Yale, held each year on the Thames River in New London, Connecticut. In 1852, boats from Harvard and Yale squared off on Lake Winnipesaukee in the first-ever intercollegiate athletic competition. The pomp and ceremony that surround the race exemplify the sense of tradition and ties with the past upon which both schools pride themselves. It is a very big deal.

Harvard had won eighteen straight races since 1963. In

1981, Yale broke the Crimson's streak. In 1982, Yale won the Sprints, and were odds-on favorites to begin a streak of their own. I didn't want to miss it.

Much of what I knew about rowing at Yale, and especially the Yale-Harvard Race, I gathered from Stephen Kiesling's 1982 book *The Shell Game*, which was an account of his rowing experience at Yale as a member of the class of '80. He was in the first freshman boat, and then spent three years in the varsity, winning the Sprints a couple of times along the way. However, a victory in the duel with Harvard evaded Kiesling's grasp every time.

I read Kiesling's book while I was in Tampa. Like me, Kiesling had come to Yale with almost no knowledge about crew. He became "addicted" to the sport, and through hard work, made the top boats, and eventually the U.S. National Team. I admired Kiesling's dedication and was envious of his success. I had no doubt that if I focused on crew the way he had, I would reap the same results.

Though I respected all the wonderful things Kiesling achieved, I doubted very much that he would like me, and as a consequence, I'm quite certain that I wouldn't have cared for him. For starters, the only people that seemed to matter at all to Kiesling were the guys in the top boat with him. He never even mentioned the ones who worked really hard but just didn't have the skill that he had. In fact, he stayed away from the guys who weren't in the "major" boats, for fear that their lack of prowess might rub off on him. He stressed effort only as it related to success. Someone who worked hard but made the JV might just as well have not worked at all. After all, as Kiesling said, "friendship, even identity, had to be proven on the water." I wondered what he would have thought of a loud mouth lightweight in the second freshman boat.

Even though I thought Kiesling was probably an intolerable asshole, his book did a great deal to pique my interest in crew, and The Race. So in mid-June, Lincoln, Tim Cotton, and I journeyed up to New London to watch the Harvard – Yale race.

We finagled our way on to a large party boat which was anchored at the finish line, and immediately hit the bar. Many beers later, we cheered deliriously as the Yale varsity cruised by our vessel well ahead of Harvard. I watched the two boats pull together after they had stopped paddling. The guys from Harvard slowly stripped their crimson shirts from their bodies, and handed them over to the counterparts from Yale. Then the two shells separated themselves from one another, and the Harvard crew rowed bareback down the river, while the Yale guys rowed with their new prizes draped over their shoulders. I was proud, excited, and jealous, all at the same time.

As I turned to walk off the boat, a man with a pen and pad of paper in his hands approached me. "Excuse me," he said hesitantly, "aren't you Stephen Kiesling?"

Dressed as I was, in my crew jacket, and standing six foot four, as Kiesling did, I could, perhaps, be mistaken for the well-known author by someone who had maybe never seen Kiesling before.

"Yes I am," I replied. History, as Napoleon asserted, is lies agreed upon. So if both of us concurred that I was Stephen Kiesling, then in fact I must be.

"I'm from the *New Haven Courier*. Do you have any comments about The Race?" the reporter asked me, staring intently, pen poised and at the ready.

"Well," I said, as he began to scribble, "Harvard's streak is a distant memory." He was actually taking this down. This was fun, so I continued to lay it on. "A new day has dawned on Yale rowing. With the program Tony has in place, and the talent that Yale has, it could very well be quite some time before Harvard sees another victory." I stopped and looked at the reporter. Was I good copy? He didn't seem fully satisfied

"Is that all?" the reporter asked.

"There is one other thing," I said quietly. The reporter peered up at me. "I just wish I had what it takes to win The Race."

The reporter couldn't believe that I had exposed myself like that. I had just alerted the media to the fact that when it came time for a gut check at the three mile mark, Stephen Kiesling found he was wanting. This was a scoop. The reporter thanked me and I walked over to join Tim and Lincoln.

"Zig," Tim asked "who was that?"

I was nonchalant. "Oh, some reporter. He wanted to know what I thought of the race."

"How come he interviewed you?"

"Tim," I explained "when it comes to crew, nobody tells it like the Commodore."

"Right you are."

The three of us split up for the summer, with visions of being in the varsity boat that would avenge this year's loss at the Sprints.

FIFTEEN

Coming back to Yale sophomore year was a little like starting over. Instead of the cozy confines of Old Campus which had become home by the end of freshman year, I was now a new member of Branford College. I barely recognized anyone and the upper-classmen certainly didn't know who I was. Stephen, J.D. and I were still rooming together, and John Rowley joined our now quadrumvirate to make up Room 889.

One of the great things about living on campus at Yale is that there is very little sense of class. Nearly everyone sleeps in roughly the same accommodations, eats the same food and dresses in similar fashion. Of course, every now and then you get some douchebag who has a great off campus apartment, wears designer clothes and eschews the dining hall for restaurants. But these posers are seen for whom they are and the exception to the rule.

I was completely unaware of who may have been rich or poor, because quite frankly, that wasn't really relevant to how I lived my life. There was no networking going on, beyond sharing lecture notes and maybe befriending a girl so you could hit on her roommate.

This isn't to say there weren't cliques; there most certainly were—jocks, the artsy crowd, the super intellectuals—but economic lines didn't seem to matter much at all. Not only was I unaware of what other people may, or may not, have been worth, I didn't even really have a sense of my own wealth.

The only time I was aware that I was more fortunate than others was on Saturdays, when I would meet with Jaymie. His circumstance was so distinct from my own that I couldn't help but be so grateful for everything I had been given, solely because my parents were wealthy and his were poor. My clothes, my car, the fact that I was at Yale, my certainty that all my essential needs would be met without question. My sense of oblivious entitlement would have only grown had I not become part of Jaymie's life.

I was given $1,250 a semester in spending money from my parents. It was put into a checking account, and if I wanted cash, my dad introduced me to a salesman at J Press who worked there when my dad was a law student 25 years earlier. I was told to make a check out to J Press, and he would give me cash. Not quite as handy as the ATMs that were five years down the road, but it worked well for me. Every now and then, I'd feel badly that I only came into the store to get cash, so I'd buy some socks, maybe a belt.

I sucked with money. Whatever I had, I spent. If I went to Rudy's with ten dollars, I'd have a great time and leave with my pockets empty. If I happened to walk in with thirty dollars, I'd have the same great time, buy a few extra rounds, and leave in the same condition. Half way through each semester, I'd go to

J Press, only to be told that my checking account was empty.

So I did what many of my friends did: I got jobs to supplement what I'd been allotted. What I didn't realize is that some of my friends were working upwards of 20 hours a week so that they could help pay their tuition, and even send some money home to chip in for expenses. I worked odd jobs where I could find them so that I'd have some spending money.

I delivered pizza for Naples, which kind of sucked because I was only paid a few dollars an hour and was supposed to make it up on tips. But since there was a delivery charge on top of what the pizza cost, there weren't many students in the mood to tip the guy on the bike. But I did it anyway because I believed in the product, it was fun to bike around campus, and I got to see a bunch of really stoned students with the munchies nearly tear the pizza boxes off my bike before the kick stand was down. I liked that.

I also opened and closed the penalty box gates at hockey games. This was kind of cool because I was near the action, right on top of it, actually. The games were always packed, the crowds were really into it, and I sort of got to know the players. But, like delivering pizza, it wasn't all it was cracked up to be. Every hockey player I got to "meet" was in a shitty mood. He was in the penalty box after all, and he was pissed off. So my small talk wasn't welcome. Dan Poliziani didn't want to talk to me about Joannie Dea, the sensational Canadian girl in my class who he was dating. Bob Brooke, who would play for the Rangers the next year, wasn't interested that I thought I had seen him at the keg the night before at Feb Club. No, they really only wanted to tell me whether I should open the gate when their two or five minutes was up, or if they'd rather jump over boards. After a while, I got to know the players' preferences, and I'd say, "hop over, right?" and they'd nod, without smiling.

The job I hated most, and sucked at the worst, was working security at football games. I had two jobs, and couldn't do either of them at all. The first was going into the stands after a field goal or extra point and getting the ball back. I had an orange vest on, which made me look official, but totally lame, and I'd be positioned in the end zone, about 10 rows up. The end zone wasn't the student section. It was for folks from New Haven, mostly. And I guess people from New Haven love souvenir footballs, because there was no way I was getting a ball away from any of them.

When a kick ended up near me, I'd go to the person with the ball and ask to have it back. They'd laugh at me, usually, or tell me to fuck off. Then I'd reach for the ball, at which point, the guy would toss it to a friend a few rows away. I'd then hustle up to that seat, and sure enough the ball would get thrown to yet another person. Since I was being paid eight dollars an hour, I did feel as though a certain amount of effort, and attendant humiliation was due from me. But after a while the game of keep away, in front of 40,000 people, just wasn't worth the 30 dollars a game I was getting.

Luckily, there was another part of the security detail that I could fail at. This one had higher stakes than getting the ball, and I had no chance of fulfilling my mission. If a game was really close, or if we were going to upset a heavily favored team, or at the Harvard or Princeton game, I, along with a few other guys in orange vests, were in charge, get this, of stopping students from pouring onto the field when it ended, and, more importantly, making sure the goal post didn't get torn down in the ensuing celebration.

Please. The orange vest bestowed no authority and certainly wasn't a deterrent. In fact, as the minutes ticked down, and we positioned ourselves at the perimeter of the end zone, facing the stands, we'd hold our hands up, letting the fans know that they were not allowed to run on the field. This didn't do the trick. In fact, the sight of us was like a red cape in front of a bunch of drunken bulls, some of whom had footballs that I had failed to wrest away from them. And they'd chant, "Goal post! Goal post!" taunting us while making their intentions plain.

When the final whistle sounded, the first several rows would empty onto the field. I'd make a pathetic attempt to stop the first couple of people, especially if they were my size or smaller and I thought I had even a chance. After that, it was a free for all. Great job, if you can get it.

I almost had another job, but it fell through at the last moment. Sometime sophomore year, I came across a posting at Yale Station, the post office, from a fertility clinic. It seems they were looking for sperm donors. Not only that, they paid $80 a "specimen"! Talk about getting paid for doing what you love. I had to learn more.

A couple of days later, I drove down to the clinic. I shaved, and put on a nice button shirt and pair of khakis, so I might look like the sort of a guy who has sperm that a woman would want.

I filled out some forms—background, education, height, weight, age of parents and grandparents, that sort of stuff-- and gave some blood so they could make sure that I was relatively healthy. This was going to be easy money. I never, for even a second, thought about how it might be to have lots of little Ziglets running around, who didn't know me, and whom I didn't know. For me it was all about the 8/10 of a Benjamin!

I noticed that there were some men who had already been cleared. They walked up to the counter, got a little cup, and headed off into little private rooms. I wondered what those rooms were like? Did they have magazines, show movies, or were you left to your own? If you can't figure out how to make that happen without some sort of outside assistance, then I don't think you'd be the sort of fellow whose sperm would be much in demand anyway.

I did determine that there must be some magazines in those rooms, because one guy, who may have been in his late 30's, walked in and came out moments later. He sheepishly looked at the receptionist and told her that he had forgotten his glasses.

After a week or so, I got a call from the clinic saying that I had passed the screening and could I come in to discuss the procedure and sign some documents that probably meant that I would never know my child (this would be my child!) and he or she might have the right to hunt me down—imagine the disappointment!—depending on the state.

"Sounds good," I said. "Why don't I come in today, sign the papers and give you my first specimen?"

"When was the last time you ejaculated?" she asked me, as if she was asking what my cholesterol was.

"Let me see," I said, pretending to search my memory. "Last ejaculation, you say. That would be, if memory serves me, this morning."

"I see, " she said, now that she knew when I ejaculated last. "Then the earliest you could come in would be three days from now, which is Friday."

"Why's that?" I asked.

"Well, you can't give a specimen within three days of your last ejaculation. We want to make sure there is plenty of volume."

"So," I said, seeing my career as a sperm donor go up in

smoke, "I have to wait three days between ejaculations before going into a room with magazines and cup?"

She laughed. "That's right."

"No deal," I said firmly.

"You must have quite a girlfriend," she said.

"Actually, I don't. Not now." I found that once the word ejaculation gets used for the fourth or fifth time, you can get quite candid. "Between girlfriends, huh?" she asked.

"I guess so," I replied. Ok, so I wasn't that candid. It wasn't really between girlfriends at all. I had yet to have a girlfriend. So I guess I was more like before girlfriends than between them. "Anyways, I don't think I'd be able to stick to your rule. Plus, do you really think the world needs a bunch of kids running around who are this selfish about their ejaculations? I think I'm doing everyone a favor by pulling out—so to speak—now "

"Really?" she asked, a bit surprised. "It's not like you have to wait three days all the time, just before you come here. It could be once a month."

My mind was made up. "No dice," I said. "Can't do it."

I could tell that she thought about trying to convince me to think it over, but decided not to, because maybe my seed wasn't so great after all.

"Ok," she said. "If you change your mind, let us know."

"I won't, " I said.

She laughed and hung up.

John and I shared a room, and he quickly let me know that he wasn't about to tolerate my utter disregard for normal human hygiene. Our room, he informed me, would be neat. If I couldn't stand being tidy and needed to make a mess, John had accounted for just such an inevitability. There was a large cardboard box in the corner called the Messy Box. If I felt the urge to be a slob,

I could throw clothes, garbage, food, anything I pleased in this box. What an entire suite couldn't contain last year was now condensed into a box. What had I gotten myself into?

———————

Three days into the year, I found myself in the more familiar confines of the Cooke Boathouse for the first day of fall practice. Dave addressed about 30 guys who hoped to make the top boats in the spring.

"It's good to see you all back," he began. "For you sophomores, welcome to the varsity. The fall is a fun time. We work hard, but I think you'll see there's a lightness that isn't there in the spring. We've got a lot of new people on the team, so it will take some time getting used to rowing together. The Head of the Charles is a big party, but I take boats up there to win, not to fiddle fart around. So by the end of October I hope that in addition to having a good time, we'll have put some quick eights together."

Then Dave stopped his speech to take roll. Hard, Morley, Bradley, all the big names were there. I couldn't believe that I numbered myself among this group. Dave read off the names of many of the guys in my boat last year. Moore. No answer. Gramaglia. Again, silence. Ritten. Absent for good. When Dave finished reading the roll he asked if there was anybody present whose name had not been read. I raised my hand.

"Oh, Zig," he said, surprised. "Good. I'm glad you're here. Welcome."

I was hurt. Dave Vogel, the man who would choose the boats in the spring, didn't even consider me among the top thirty. I wasn't in a position of resting on the laurels that I had earned last year. I had a long way to go to prove myself.

Vogel split us up into four eights, and moments later I was in a shell for my first varsity practice. Aside from being in a boat with eight guys with whom I had never rowed, I was in a new boat, a carbocraft. Freshman year, I rowed in the Newbury, an old wooden shell. The pretty boys rowed in the Butler, a gleaming white, brand-new carbon fiber boat called a carbo. A good measure of the envy we second boaters had for the guys in the first boat was derived not so much from the fact that they were in the first boat, but that they got to row in a carbo, while we were still in a wooden boat like the ones we learned on in the lagoon.

As I adjusted my foot stretchers on this first day of practice, I found that my jealousy was well founded. In fact the carbo was far different from the Newbury. For starters, the foot stretchers in the carbo were actually sneakers—Pumas — whereas in the Newbury we put our feet on boards with metal heel cups and fastened them with hard leather straps. The carbo was also a lot quieter that its wooden ancestor. There were no odd squeaks and rattles that typically punctuated every stroke in the Newbury. In the carbo, I imagined, you could really focus on rowing together and pulling hard without any distractions. I really liked my new environment.

After rowing up river by fours, and doing a few half-power tens to warm up, Dave instructed the coxswains to get the boats even. The first drill we did was called the pick drill. We started rowing arms only, and then slowly added backs, quarter slide, half slide, until we were rowing full strokes. This drill harkened back to the first day in the tanks with Rick Ricci. The purpose of the drill was to get us thinking of the stroke as a series of connected movements, as well as to work on timing.

"In together, out together," Dave would yell into his blue megaphone. "Let's see some snap at the catch, a little action. I know we're only rowing quarter slide, but I want to see some pop at the catch. Make it happen right from the start. Get on it."

Clearly catches were a priority for Dave. I made a note of that. Last year I worried about my finishes so I wouldn't crab; this year I would focus on catches. Mark Block, a senior, and stroke of last year's undefeated Sprint-winning JV was sitting in the four seat just in front of me. I tried to copy his movements precisely. I was mirroring him, or so I thought, until a voice from my left shattered my concentration.

"Danziger!" It was Vogel. I tensed up and almost stopped rowing. "Work with the boat, not against it. I want to see your oar going in with the rest of them. Don't think you can row to your own beat this year. Get with it."

I was devastated. I hadn't even gotten a chance to pull full power, to show off my enormous puddles, and Dave had shot me down. I didn't exactly savor the idea of enduring his brand of instruction for three years.

While we were turning around at the four mile point, Mark turned around and said, "Don't worry about Dave, Mike. He's just that way. He shits on everyone, and I'll tell you something, it doesn't mean a thing."

I thanked Mark sincerely for his comforting council, and we rowed back to the boathouse doing drills with a few tens sprinkled amongst them. Mark was right, Dave did yell at a bunch of people, regardless of their position in the hierarchy.

David Holt Vogel. His name was synonymous with Yale

lightweight crew because he was involved with the program, as both an oarsman and the coach for over fifteen years. Dave rowed for four years while at Yale and was captain of a solid, if unspectacular, squad in 1971. After Yale, Dave rowed for the U.S. National team, and was a world championships medalist. Then Dave returned to New Haven and was named lightweight coach. He was married briefly, but I hear his wife got tired of playing a lesser role in Dave's life than crew did. She gave him an ultimatum, and Dave promptly grabbed his megaphone and stroke watch, and left.

Since then, Dave's life has been lightweight crew. The Yale administration only considered Dave's coaching duties as a part-time job, so Dave worked "full-time" as an alumni co-ordinator. Anyone who has ever met Dave Vogel will tell you that coaching lightweight crew at Yale was not a part-time job for him. It was his life, how he defined himself. Jim Bouton ends his book *Ball Four* by saying, "You spend a good piece of your life gripping a baseball and in the end it turns out that it was the other way around all along." Dave had the same unhealthy relationship with the oar handle.

A symptom of Dave's obsession with crew was his treatment of oarsmen. During my freshman year, I saw him time and again scream mercilessly and unremittingly at oarsmen who were clearly trying as hard as they could. Some could shrug it off as Vogel's problem, not their own. Others, however, were really hurt by his remarks. I wondered how I would react to his relentless volley of verbal abuse.

I'm used to loud voices directed at me. My father has a prodigious temper, and will often bellow at me for anything ranging from neglect to proper table etiquette to not dressing properly. People who have seen Dad unload on me often wonder how I can tolerate such lambasting. The response is simple and self-evident: I love my father and admire him as much as I look up to anyone else I've ever known. He has a tremendous temper, but I know that he loves me — even though he doesn't say it —and would never do anything to harm me. Dad's tantrums were sometimes scary (and were often mere parodies of themselves), but they are part of him and I have learned to accept them, and see them for what they are: his idiosyncratic way of showing me that he cares.

———————

I didn't know how I would respond to Dave, on the other hand, because I wasn't sure that I trusted him. If he was going spend three years calling me a worthless bag of shit, that was fine, as long as there was a purpose behind it other than abuse. Some people thought that Dave was an asshole so that the team could have someone in common to hate. The theory held that if everyone could focus their animosity on Dave, we would pull together as a team. Rick Elser, who coxed under Dave for three years before becoming a coach threw those fancy postulates away. "Vogel is an asshole," Rick once explained, "because he's an asshole." I was suspending judgment, but thought that my opinion would probably end up aligning with Rick's.

My ruminations on the cause of Dave's behavior were interrupted by Lincoln, who had one of his frequent fine ideas.

"Zig, I'm thinking of going up to Smith this weekend.Why don't you join me?"

"Do you know someone up there?" I asked.

"Nope, but there's bound to be a party, and I'm sure we'll be able to find some girls who would be delighted to have us stick around for a sleepover."

It was set. Lincoln and I would journey to Northampton for a time honored right-of-passage for Elihu Yale's horny sons.

Thursday evening, my parents called to find out how their little boy was faring in his first week at school as a sophomore. I told them that I was still shopping for classes, which really meant that I hadn't been going to all that many but it didn't matter because I didn't have to hand in my schedule for a week. Crew, I informed them, was going well.

"What are you up to for the weekend?" Dad asked.

"Lincoln and I are heading up to some obscure girls' school in Northampton."

"Michael," Mom whined. She had gone to Smith.

"Sounds like fun," Dad said. "I can remember some pretty good times I had up there."

"Richard." Mom again.

Dad then shifted into his advice mode. "There's a spot up there called Paradise Pond. I think you'll find a swing near the pond that might be of some use."

"Gotcha, Dad."

"Now really, Richard," Mom protested, "don't you think our son can find his own place to make out."

"Just thought I'd steer him toward a place I liked."

"Appreciate the tip, Dad."

"Anytime."

SIXTEEN

Lincoln and I arrived in Northampton around seven o'clock Friday evening. We drove around until we found what seemed to be a happening quad. After parking, we asked a few of the women if there was a party going on that night. One of them told us that Ziskind House was having a four-kegger. Would we like to come? You bet. We wouldn't miss one of Ziskind's legendary four-kegger extravaganzas for anything.

The party wasn't a whole lot different than most of the college parties at Yale. There was music, lots of beer, and many more guys than girls. I guessed Lincoln and I weren't the only two guys who thought there would be easy pickings at an all-women's college. Guys from Harvard, UMass., and Amherst were all there, too. There weren't too many women at the Ziskind bash because Smith is a pretty small school.

There didn't need to be many, just one, and I had spotted her. She was a vision, as she changed the tap on one of the kegs. A gentle zephyr moved her shoulder length blond hair across her gorgeous face. Her legs were long and fit. She was perfect.

I imagined the scenario. I would ask her to dance, and the entire floor would clear to watch us rekindle memories of Fred and Ginger. Then, I would sweep her off her feet, and carry her to Paradise Pond. The swing would be waiting for us, and we would kiss gently for hours. Later, in her room, we would wrap each other in the majesty of our embrace, and make love until the angels wept. A tearful farewell would be followed by vows to keep in touch. We'd call everyday and see each other on the weekend. Three days after graduation, we would marry and begin a storied life together.

I took a tug at my beer and headed over to her. How could I miss? We were meant for each other. Without each other, we were like the sound of one hand clapping. Plus, I was wearing my crew jacket. One of the guys on the varsity said that this jacket worked like fly-paper at Smith parties. I couldn't wait to find out.

Within seconds, I found myself standing next to the most wonderful girl I had ever seen near a keg. No courage was necessary, as our enchanted fate was already sealed.

"Would you like to dance?" It was almost a rhetorical question.

She gazed soulfully into my eyes, and opened her mouth to utter forth the mellifluous syllable meant for me alone. "No."

This couldn't be happening. She was defying destiny. "How about sometime later?" Now I was bargaining.

"No, really," she insisted, "I'm with somebody."

"Blow him off," I protested. "He's not right for you."

"How do you know?"

"Because he's not me."

Without a word, she turned and left, leaving me alone with one of Ziskind's four kegs. I heard a sermon once on television early one Sunday, just after Davey and Goliath, and just before NFL Today. The preacher said that when the Lord closes a door, He always leaves open a window. As I turned away from the slamming door, I bumped right into my window. She was tall, about five ten, with short brown hair and a lovely smile.

"My name's Sophia, let's dance."

After a couple of songs, we stepped off the dance floor and tried to carry on a conversation above the din.

Sophia was a junior at Smith from Rochester, New York. I tried to find out what house she was in, but couldn't quite make out what she said. But I understood every word when she asked me if I'd like to go outside where it was quieter.

"It's better out here," Sophia said.

"Sophia," I said, retrieving information I had learned in Mr. Mitchell's fifth grade social science course, in which we had to memorize the capitals of every country in the world. Until this moment I hadn't seen the purpose of that tedious drill. "Isn't that the capital of Bulgaria?"

"Yes, I think it is."

"You're lucky your parents didn't name you after the capital of Upper Volta," I informed Sophia.

"Why is that?"

"Because then you'd have to go through life being called Ouagadougou." Sophia laughed. I was feeling very clever now.

"Is that a lacrosse jacket you're wearing?" she asked. It was kind of dark out, and easy to see how she could have mistaken my oars for lacrosse sticks. "No. Those are oars. I row crew."

Then I did something I didn't need to do, and certainly shouldn't have done. I fibbed. Well alright, I downright lied to Sophia. "This is the jacket they give to the Most Valuable Oarsman at the end of every year."

Sophia was no idiot. I could tell that even before I started bullshitting her. She looked at me incredulously. "I thought you said you were a sophomore. You got that when you were a freshman?"

I decided to stick to my story, no matter what. "It's rare, but yes, I did." Change the subject, Zig. "Hey, let's go for a walk. I hear there's a wonderful place called Paradise Pond somewhere around here."

Sophia peered at me skeptically. "That's what you hear, is it? Why don't we go back inside instead."

"Come on," I said, grabbing her hand. It was smooth and small and fragile. "Let's go to the pond."

"You just won't take no for an answer will you?" Sophia said with a smile.

"You wouldn't like me as much if I did," I said with a swagger in my voice. My response was lifted directly from Burt Reynolds in Semi-Tough. I just prayed she hadn't seen the movie.

Sophia hadn't seen it. Or, if she had, she too knew it was too good to pass up. Some guys use lines from Shakespeare like, "A rose by any other name…" I quote Dan Jenkins.

"Come on," she finally said. "Let's go to the lake."

As advertised, the swing is a super spot. Dad had done me right with this tip. Sophia and I spent some time there before heading back to her room, where we groped for a while before she finally shut me down.

I was sorry to leave the next morning, but I hadn't seen Jaymie all summer, and we had planned to spend the afternoon together. I told Sophia that there was a big party at Morse College in two weeks, and it'd be great if she came down for it. She said she'd try.

It took me a while to find Lincoln, but I finally spotted him outside of Wilson House, where he had found friendly refuge.

———————●

Two weeks later, Martha Reeves and the Vandellas were belting out *Dancing in the Street* over a huge sound system at Morse College's annual Motown party. I was there with Killenberg, Sloan, and a bunch of the other guys on the team, when I saw Sophia wading through the crowd in my direction. I was super glad she had come, and I pushed through to meet her. We kissed, then I took her over to meet my friends.

After hanging around the same group of people for awhile, it's easy to overlook certain characteristics. In this case, I had forgotten the crew's sartorial practice of only — and always — wearing the crew jacket. Sophia noticed this right away.

"Mike," she asked, in a voice that all the others guys heard, "I thought you said that your jacket was an MVP jacket. What's the deal? Everyone's got one."

Nailed. Grilled on the skillet. She certainly had me. The guys could barely conceal their laughter.

"MVP convention?" I offered weakly.

Sophia launched into me with Vogelesque furor. She was pissed. Not so much that I wasn't the great oarsman I had previously advertised myself as being. But I had made sport of her, and she certainly wasn't about to suffer that kind of shit.

I don't remember how she phrased it, but from her tone and gestures, I gathered that Sophia was suggesting that perhaps our relationship had reached the stage where it might be best that we start dating other people.

As Vogel had promised, rowing in the fall was fun. Each day, the boatings were different, and I invariably found myself in the same shell as one of the stars from last year's varsity. Rowing in a boat filled with talented oarsmen made it easier for me to improve my technique. The boats were almost always set, so I didn't have to worry about fingers getting jammed against the gunwales. Instead, I concentrated on applying pressure on the blade right from the Catch.

We typically rowed nine miles a day on the Housatonic. Naturally, there would be moments during practice when I wasn't rowing so well, but overall I felt as though I was getting better each day. My name was broadcast with less and less frequency over the speaker system, which meant that I wasn't fouling things up as often.

I began to keep a diary of my progress in crew. Each day, I'd write down how many miles we had rowed, what the workout was, and any part of my rowing which I thought might require special attention. At the end of an entry for a practice in mid-October, I wrote the following:

> After practice today, I was putting my oar back in its rack when Dave came up to me. He said, "Zig, you are one of the sloppiest oarsmen I've ever seen out there. Your body is all over the place when you row. You've got a long way to go before I can see you in a top boat, but I really like the way you're working." Coming from Dave, that's a real attaboy.

Any words from Dave had a profound affect on me. If he

yelled at me, I was certain I had been relegated to the rowing wilderness forever. If he said something encouraging, like he had that day in October, I read it as a sign that he was grooming me for a seat in the varsity.

———————

Jaymie became interested in my progress on the team only because he enjoyed going out to Derby. One Saturday, J.D. and I drove over to the Turpin's to pick up Andre and Jaymie for the afternoon. In the car ride back to Yale, the two boys revealed their careers plans to us.

"Know what I want to be?" Andre asked.

"What?" said JD

"A cop."

"Why do you want to be a police officer?" J.D. asked. He hoped that Andre would talk about the great satisfaction he hoped to derive from keeping the streets safe for children, in making sure that right triumphed over wrong.

"So I can have a piece," Andre explained.

"A piece?"

"Yeah, a piece. You know, a gun? Bang Bang?"

"I know what a piece is, Andre," J.D. said. "What's so great about having a gun?"

"No one can push you around."

Jaymie jumped into the conversation. "Know what I'm going to be?"

"What's that?" I asked.

"A dentist," said Jaymie with a wide grin.

I was really surprised and pleased that Jaymie would

choose a field like dentistry to pursue. "Why do you want to be a dentist?"

"Because then I can clean people's teeth, and maybe they won't lose them when they get old."

I was gratified. "Terrific. I know you'll make a super dentist, Jaymie."

"There's one other reason it's good to be a dentist," Jaymie said.

"What's that?"

"I get a drill, and if some one makes me mad, then I can drill his head till he's dead."

Ah, there's the rub. Jaymie didn't want his D.D.S. for purely humanitarian reasons. That would be too much to ask. "I'll make sure to avoid you if I ever need anything more complicated than a cleaning."

The four of us split up when we got to Yale. J.D. and Andre went to the Peabody Museum, and I took Jaymie out to Derby to watch a practice.

After I introduced Jaymie to Dave, I went to the locker room to change. When I came out, Jaymie was running along the docks with a bright orange life-jacket on over his winter coat. He couldn't wait for practice to begin.

Having Jaymie at practice was terrific. I got a kick out of looking out of the boat to see Jaymie smiling as the launch swept him over the river. He was loving it. The other reason I liked having Jaymie along was that his presence mitigated Dave's temper. Vogel rarely yelled, and never directed his comments at me while Jaymie was sitting by his side. Jaymie was having a blast, and I was getting something in the deal, too.

Being Jaymie's big brother was perhaps the most rewarding thing I did at Yale. I loved hanging out with Jaymie because just being with him put all my petty troubles in their proper perspective. I also derived pleasure from seeing Jaymie so happy. The final reason I relished my moments with Jaymie was that it seemed people who saw me with him thought more of me. "Oh, Zig," they'd say, "I didn't know you were a big brother. I think that's fantastic." I'd beam in response. But this was troubling. Would I have made the commitment involved with being a big brother if I didn't get the strokes from everyone who saw me and Jaymie together? What portion of my enjoyment did I get from my relationship with Jaymie, and how much came from everyone telling me what a hero I was? Would I do it if no one knew? These questions bothered me because I honestly didn't know the answers.

After practice, Dave thanked Jaymie for helping him coach, and Jaymie thanked Dave for letting him ride in the launch. I showered quickly, changed, and met Jaymie at the car.

"What do you feel like having for lunch, Jaymie," I asked. "How 'bout Wendy's?"

"A Big Classic would taste great right now."

"Yeah," Jaymie added. "They got those soft Kaiser rolls on 'em now." That ad campaign had certainly worked on this hungry six-year-old.

As we pulled towards the drive-thru, Jaymie asked if he could steer. I said sure and pulled him onto my lap. We narrowly missed colliding with the speaker stand, but managed to place our orders. As Jaymie maneuvered us out of the lot, I thought how happy I was to be with him. And it didn't matter at all if anyone knew that we were pals or not.

SEVENTEEN

For reasons known only to a son who so desperately wanted to please an unpleasable father, I majored in art history. Luckily for me, art history was a major your could bullshit your way through, unlike, say, mechanical engineering, so I had a fighting chance.

So it was that I found myself sitting in Vincent Scully's Renaissance Art History class. Images of art from the 15th and 16th centuries flashed on the screen as he described the themes the artist may have been dealing with, the influences, and on and on. All of a sudden, a slide of a sculpture that riveted me appeared on the screen. It looked to be unfinished, but perhaps that was part of the artist's intent. The sculpture was of a nude man with enormous and well-defined muscles. He was bent over and seemed to be struggling to lift the weight of the marble off himself. Even more, it was as if this man was emerging from the marble itself.

I put aside whatever utterly unrelated notes I was doodling and stared at the screen.

"The *Awakening Slave*," Professor Scully explained, "reflects three themes that Michelangelo was exploring. Let me begin with the most abstract. While Michelangelo was in the court of the Medicis, he not only honed his craft as a sculptor, but, as a member of the court, was privy to the scholarly discourse of the day. One school of thought that was in vogue then was Neo- Classicism. Neo-Classism has many facets to it, but as this is a survey course that I bet many of you are taking credit/fail…" Here a bunch of students laughed, but I did not as I was, for the first time, genuinely interested. "I will focus on the aspects of Neo-Classicism as it relates specifically to Michelangelo, and more particularly to the *Awakening Slave*, which you can now observe in the Academia in Florence or in the Boboli gardens, just across the Arno. Those of the school of Neo-Classicism believed the soul was trapped in a bodily prison and was in constant struggle to free itself and rise to heaven. Through faith and good works, the soul could achieve its end. We can see this theme very clearly in Michelangelo's slaves." Scully tapped his long wooden pointer at the screen, at the big slab that the slave seemed to try to heave from his shoulders. His voice rose with passion and, what seemed to me, love and admiration for this artist, dead for four centuries. "Can you see how the slave, like the soul itself, struggles to free itself from this prison? Every muscle straining, veins bulging, in this the most important task of all. In fact, eternity depends on it. The stakes couldn't be higher and we are lucky to witness the supreme quest."

Scully seems nearly exhausted, but also exhilarated, describing the *Awakening Slave's* challenge, and I am right with them: Scully and the slave.

"On another level," he continues, regaining his breath, "we have the slave himself struggling for freedom from his physical, not spiritual this time, bonds. This is the most literal meaning ascribed to the work. Michelangelo is depicting, as no one had ever dared do before, the human body almost from the inside out. And Michelangelo literally risked his life to learn to sculpt this way. In order to show the musculature we see here, Michelangelo snuck into morgues and secretly performed dissections so he could see how the human body worked, from the inside out. Only then was he able to carve a man such as this. This deltoid," Scully jabbed the pointer at the massive muscle connecting the neck to the shoulder, "is rendered only because Michelangelo saw for himself the inner workings of the tissues, muscles, and tendons. He was a man fully committed to his craft."

"Finally," Scully intoned, "we can see here what made Michelangelo such a genius and why his sculptures seem," here Scully corrected himself, "not seem, they are, imbued with the soul of what he intended to create. Michelangelo believed that the first, toughest, and most critical job a sculptor had was to determine what form the marble held inside of it. He believed with all that he was that each piece of white marble had within it a form that yearned, like the soul referred to by Neo-Classicists, to be free. Michelangelo had to ascertain the form within, and then, with skills he alone had, free it.

"In other words," Scully explained to me, and anyone else who was lucky enough to be listening, "no matter how wonderfully rendered a sculpture might be, if it didn't depict the form held within the stone, it would only be beautiful, but would have no soul. For instance, if a piece of marble held the *Pieta*, but the sculptor created from that stone Moses, it may look exactly as Moses should have looked, but it wouldn't be imbued with the man's being. "Just look at the *Awakening Slave*. On the base and sides of the sculpture, Michelangelo leaves the marble as he found it when it arrived from the quarry. Rough hewn, and greyish. Here, as more marble is removed and the slave starts to emerge from the marble, the color and texture change. And finally, in the legs and of course in the agony-etched face, we see an almost alabaster color, smooth as can be. In this work of art, of towering genius, we see the process of the shape emerging from the stone itself. The only thing that could have come from this rock was this man, and Michelangelo knew.

"On three levels: the soul, the slave, and the form itself, were trying to free themselves from a sort of prison. Michelangelo expressed this theme with honesty, passion, courage, and without flinching. That, class, is why Michelangelo was the greatest artist the world had ever known, or may ever know. Next slide please."

I loved the passion Scully had for his subject, the passion Michelangelo had for his, and the beauty of process, so brutally portrayed in the *Awakening Slave*.

As I left the lecture hall, I couldn't get that slide off my mind, nor Scully's beautifully worded explanation, and I was determined to see the *Awakening Slave* for myself. I also tried to imagine how the theory of a fixed form yearning to be freed might relate to my own life. Perhaps, before I decided what I would do with this one and only life of mine, I ought to look inside my own "marble" and determine who I really was. Only then, when I had determined who I was, could I think about what might be the best expression of the real me. If Michelangelo were to look inside of me, what would he discover?

Was I, against all my determined intentions, having a scholarly thought? Was I connecting on a deeper, more personal, more intellectual level with something I'd learned? More than likely, this was a really interesting fluke, since what lay inside my marble was most certainly not a Scholar. But this fundamental truth didn't need to stop me from being moved from time to time and savoring the moments when my courses struck a nerve.

———

As the fall wore on, I got used to Dave's eccentricities and he to mine. One thing I liked to do was wear a pair of silk Everlast boxing trunks to practice for the weekly Friday choose-up races. I would prance around the dock, shadow boxing, and calling myself "Kid Nasty" or "The Master of Disaster", or whatever ring name I had just given myself.

I was less spectacular in the boats during choose-up races than I was on the dock. I was never in a boat that won a three-mile race. As a matter of fact, all of the boats I was in finished DFL. Not once did I ever cross the line before another boat.

One Friday, after slogging in to yet another last place showing. I joined my team mates at the keg on the dock. Most of the guys had already had a couple of beers before we even got out of the water, so they toasted our return with zeal.

"Do you get a prize or something for finishing last every race?" I asked.

"Yes," Ben Norris, a perennial third boat oarsman, replied, "you get to be in the 4v."

"There isn't a 4v," I pointed out.

"Exactly." Even though I wasn't exactly setting the crew world afire with my performances in the choose-up races, I was undaunted. The fall didn't count much when it came time for picking boats in the spring anyhow.

Besides, I was getting better with each practice. The main thing I had to work on was shooting my slide. That happens when an oarsman is at the Catch and moves back up the slide without his blade moving. The movement of the seat ought to be transferred to the blade in the water. Shooting your slide was an inefficient way to row because you are rowing with your back more than your legs. Dave kept after me to "connect the drive," which meant that I should be concentrating on hooking into the stroke with my legs, instead of shooting my slide and wrenching through the stroke with my back. This was easier for Dave to say than for me to do (and to explain), but each day I tried to feel more connection between my seat and my blade.

When it came time for Dave to pick boats for the Head of The Charles, he took three. He chose two boats from amongst the juniors and seniors, and a sophomore shell. The week before he made his selection, Dave announced that there would be a little ergonometric exercise: a ten-minute piece at four and a half pounds.

The erg workout was the only day we were indoors during the fall. The piece was just as menacing as I had remembered. The first couple of minutes were easy. Then there was a moment of dread at about three-and-a-half minutes, when I realized that I was fading, hurting, and not even close to being done. The middle minutes vanished in a whirl of lactic acid and oxygen debt. And the final two minutes were a desperate effort to gain precious revolutions before the clock mercifully signaled an end to it all.

My score was just shy of 5,500. A lot better than I had ever done last year. Among starboards I placed ninth. But within my class, only Jigger and Potter had better scores, and Potter just barely nosed me out. I had beaten Burlage, Sloan, and Rowley (Hard and Morley both broke 6,000, as did Tim Bradley, who was the strongest starboard oarsman). By my reckoning, I should be sitting in the four seat of the sophomore boat at the Head of the Charles, rowing in front of over 300,000 delirious rowing fans.

Dave's reckoning, as it would on many occasions, diverged from mine. He took last year's first freshman boat to Boston. I was disappointed, of course, but not discouraged. They had rowed together for a full year, and were probably the best combination of sophomores. I looked forward to rowing in the Head as a junior.

Aside from the disappointments of not winning many (okay, any), choose-up races, and not being chosen for the Head of the Charles, I was thrilled to be on the team. The guys on the squad were terrific, and we hung out a lot together even during the few hours that we weren't practicing. Each Tuesday, a different guy would have a small keg in his room, and a bunch of us would go over and drain it. Every few weeks, the whole team would do something like go bowling together. Some of us brought really shitty old shoes with us to the bowling alley, and left them as a deposit for a pair of bowling shoes. That way we could keep the bowling shoes. I thought our new shoes would start a fashion craze like the ripped sweatshirt look that Jennifer Beales had launched with her role in Flashdance. I was wrong, but got a kick out of wearing the new shoes around.

One night, Niccola, a woman in Jonathan Edwards College, told me that her college was having a party called "Jonathan Edwards Strips It's Image." Jonathan Edwards College had the reputation of being a sissy, artsy college. Niccola wanted to change that image. So she had the idea to have a huge bash. To get women to come to the party, Niccola dreamed up the concept of having male strippers perform in front of a women-only audience at the beginning of the party. Then they'd let the men in.

The only catch was that Niccola had to find some guys willing to strip down to G-strings in front of a couple hundred women.

"Zig," Niccola said, "Pergande, Burlage, Grant, and Potter said they'd do it. We need another stripper. You willing?"

Willing? I'd be delighted. But I decided to try to negotiate a deal anyhow.

"What do we get? How about a keg of beer?"

"Done."

I told Anne Wilson, a woman in my class, what I was planning on doing. She was predictably flabbergasted.

"Zig! Aren't you going to be embarrassed, mortified?"

My explanation was simple. "I don't get embarrassed. It ought to be a blast."

Many people ask me why it is I never seem to get embarrassed. How can I drop a tray full of food in the middle of Commons, to the amusement of hundreds, and not miss a step on my way up for seconds? How, they wonder, can I accidentally spit in a girl's face when asking her to dance, and not worry that the fact that my saliva on her cheek might make her think that I'm an asshole? Let me explain....

When I was a junior in high school, I went to St. Maarten with my family on spring vacation. Upon arrival, I found that Lawrence, a classmate of mine was also spending the break on this delightful Caribbean isle. Lawrence and I were far from best friends, but we greeted each other with enthusiastic high fives, and promised to spend the entire week together (It's interesting how people who normally couldn't care less about one another magically become blood brothers if their vacation plans happen to coincide.). Lawrence told me that he had a motor boat, and would like me to join him for an afternoon of water skiing. Though I had never tried the sport before, wild horses couldn't keep me from spending time with my buddy.

Lawrence was quite an expert water skier. He skied on bare feet and did tricks that seemed to impress even the driver of the boat who didn't seem to thrilled to be spending the afternoon dragging us across the water in the scorching heat.

After climbing into the boat, Lawrence gave me some quick pointers, and I jumped into the water. Let me just tell you that water skiing has got to be the easiest, and stupidest sport of all. If you can hold on to a bar and have any degree of balance at all, then you can water ski.

I got up without a problem, and was cutting across the wake on one ski in no time (You should know, however, that even though this sport is ridiculously easy, I have been told that it is a rare feat for some one to drop a ski on the first try. Keep this in mind, since the end of the story is somewhat humiliating, and I want to be thought of not only as a buffoon, but as a marvelously gifted athlete as well). I was gliding along effortlessly, when all of a sudden, I wiped out. I fell right on my posterior, and felt a warm jet of Caribbean water shoot up my ass. I didn't think too much about it, although it did occur to me that this was a strange aspect of the sport.

After I was finished, Lawrence and I congratulated each other, and he told me that he had a house on the island. Would I like to come over for dinner? I told him that I would love to, and that I'd be right over as soon as I changed. No need, Lawrence told me, come as you are.

The house was a charming cottage overlooking the bay. I met Lawrence's parents who were in their late fifties, so I guessed it made sense that they weren't the hippest folks in the world. They were, in fact, a bit stand-offish. In the middle of dinner, I had to take a leak, so I excused myself and headed for the bathroom.

I never made it to the bathroom. I got about three steps from the table, when, all of a sudden, I blew a huge diarrhea shit all over the white shag dining room rug. Needless to say, I was quite shocked, so I panicked and began to sop up the shit with their linen monogrammed napkins. I was totally ambushed by this shit, taken utterly unaware.

Though they couldn't have expected me to shit on their

floor, Lawrence's parents were very uncool. They wanted to know what the hell was going on, and how I could have done something like that. I had no explanations, only lame apologies as I finished wiping my shit off their carpet.

I don't remember much of the rest of the evening, though I am quite certain that I didn't stick around for port and cigars after dinner.

When I got home, I spoke to Dad about my day with Lawrence.

"Hey, that's great," Dad said. "You got up on one ski? It took me several tries just to get up on two. How was dinner?"

"Oh it was fine. They've got this really cool house. It's right on the water. We had fish and some mousse for dessert. It was good. But one thing was kind of strange."

Dad leaned forward. "What's that?"

"In the middle of the meal, I got up to go to the bathroom and accidentally crapped all over their rug. It was quite awkward."

Dad was amazed. "I'll say. I'll bet when you wiped out, the sea water softened your bowels. You had some sort of time release enema."

I was happy to get an explanation, but that didn't change the fact that I had just been through the most humiliating moment ever. I knew right then that nothing that I would ever do, no matter how mortifying, would ever embarrass me. Shitting on that rug had freed me forever from perhaps the most inhibiting emotion.

———————

Even though I was sure that I wouldn't be embarrassed as a stripper, an hour or so before we were to take the stage,

Potter, Grant, Burlage, John Pergande (a heavyweight in our class), and I tapped the keg and began consuming as much liquid courage as we could. We choreographed a little routine to a Pretenders song, and put on preppy ties and jackets over our matching red G-strings.

With the bright lights in our eyes, it was hard to see the audience. That made gyrating and stripping down a lot easier. When we were through, we accepted what I took to be a huge ovation, and hurried back to polish off what was left of our keg. It was a good night.

The next Monday, our picture was on the front page of Yale Daily News. That publication would never again print my likeness. My legacy would be that of a stripper.

EIGHTEEN

By mid-term of sophomore year, I really felt as though I had both feet on the ground and was going at a pretty good clip. I wasn't breaking new ground with any of my scholarly research, but I was doing adequate work in my classes. The only course that concerned me was biology. I had never been a math or science wizard, but had a distribution requirement to fill. Bio seemed like a good choice. Plus, in case it was too hard, I had opted for the credit/fail option. All I needed was a D and I'd get credit for taking the course. The first test was easy. The question was about monkeys, and why they had such great eyesight and the ability to swing from branch to branch. I wrote that they developed these skills so they could see their enemies in the nighttime and escape. I got an A for this insight, and immediately changed from credit/fail to a grade. After all, I'd be stupid to pass up an easy A.

The next test was about RNA and how the body produces some sort of genetic something or other. I didn't do so hot on this test; I got a 17%. Med school applications and studying for the MCATs were no longer on my to-do list.

I sidled into the final exam with a solid C-/D+ and just wanted to pass the course even if it meant getting a D instead of the "Credit" that would have showed up on my transcript. The exam had almost no questions on it that I could even bullshit my way through. I tossed a couple of terms like meiosis and mitosis around, mentioned Gregor Mendel's experiment (I had learned about this in tenth grade and knew it would come in handy someday) and hoped for the best. Actually, I did more than hope; I begged. At the end of the exam, I wrote a pathetic, ass-kissy note to whatever grad student drew the straw that meant looking at my exam. In the note, I asked for mercy and a passing grade. In return, I promised never to take a science class again, set foot in the science building, or even joke a about a career in science or medicine. I even signed it, "Pretty please!" Anyway, I got a D, which actually worked out well, because my grades that semester were an A, a B, a C, and a D. An accomplishment of sorts, I guess.

Aside from academics, other parts of my life at Yale were prospering. I was getting along really well with Jaymie, and seemed to be learning as much from him as I hoped he was from me.

The only part of my life that I felt was lagging was crew. By December, we had moved indoors and I didn't get a feeling that I was getting any better. Each day, Dave screamed at me about my technique in the tanks.

"Come on Danziger," he'd yell. "If you're going to row like a pussy, why don't you get out and let someone take your place who wants to do it right?"

He was relentless. The constant verbal pounding was demeaning and discouraging, even though I knew that there were lots of other guys eating his shit, too. I began to believe what he was saying. Maybe I did suck. Maybe I was a worthless oarsman. I certainly didn't have the erg scores to contradict Vogel's words. I wanted to do better, but I seemed to have stagnated at a low plateau.

One day, I bumped into a guy outside the gym who I vaguely recognized. He was tall and thin, with thinning blond hair and glasses. Where had I seen him? He seemed to recognize me as well, only even more faintly than was my recollection of him. Finally, I introduced myself.

"I'm Mark Groshek," he said. Of course! How could I not have known? Mark Groshek was in the varsity boat last year. He had graduated and was at Penn Med School, or something like that.

"Are you still rowing crew?" He asked.

"Yup."

"How's it going this year? Is Vogel on your case?"

"Isn't he on everyone's?"

"Listen," Mark said, "can I give you some advice on how to get ahead with Vogel?"

I couldn't believe that Shek, as he was known, was even talking to me, let alone letting me in on some of the rowing secrets that propelled him to the top. I was all ears.

"Practice in the morning," Shek began. "I know it's tough to discipline yourself, but try to get in the gym a few times a week in the morning in addition to rowing in the afternoon. Do some tank pieces. There'll usually be someone there to let you in around 7:30 or 8:00. There's no way I would have ended up in the V if I hadn't gotten some extra work in. Plus, Dave will see that you're there, and it'll let him know that you care enough to improve. Face time can't hurt."

Shek and I talked a while longer, and then cordially parted ways. I went back to my room and called Lincoln.

"Hey Linc, listen, I just bumped into Mark Groshek. You know, from last year's varsity? Anyway, he said that if I practice in the morning a few times a week, I'll make a better boat. Want to join me?"

Lincoln Benet was already shouldering a course load of seven courses, three more than I had. And none of his were nickname guts, either. I don't know how he managed to take, and ace, all those courses and row crew. And go out drinking several nights a week. I figured a few morning practices would be spit in the ocean compared to the rest of his schedule.

"I'm psyched," he said. "Why don't we shoot for Monday, Wednesday, and Friday, right after Christmas break?"

"All right with me." I was excited to try out Shek's success formula.

———————

Just before Christmas, Rowley and Sloan announced separately, but on the same day, that they were quitting. I wasn't surprised about Sloan's decision. He had rowed at Groton for a few years and had just burned out on the sport.

But Rowley had worked harder than anyone in our class to improve in crew. He never missed a practice and went to the gym on weekends to lift weights. By the end of November, his body was rippling with muscles and his erg scores were way up. His style in the tanks must have been pretty good, because I never heard Vogel making any untoward remarks about Rowley's mother while John was rowing. Still, John had had enough. John was so into rowing that I thought he'd have a hard time giving it up. But as soon as he decided that he was going to quit, he left crew behind completely. He didn't ask about how practice was, or what Dave was up to; he separated himself completely from crew. He would row intramurals for Branford, but Yale crew held nothing for him.

I was genuinely disappointed to see John and Sloan leave the team. I had rowed with both of them in the second boat the year before, and looked forward to rowing with them some more as varsity oarsmen. More importantly, I really liked being around both guys. Sloan had a distinctive WASP voice that belied his goofy sense of humor. John's intensity and sincerity as a teammate was something to be around. I didn't miss John so much because I still roomed with him and the messy box.

The only bright side to their departure was that both Sloan and John were starboards. Both were better than I was, so now there were two less people I had to beat out in order to make a top boat.

Although there were eight seats in each boat, there were really only four that I cared about: the starboard four. It didn't matter if there were ten ports better than I was; I just had to be in the top eight starboards to make it into the JV boat.

I had a list of starboards, ranked from best to worst. At the top of the list were Bradley, Faust, and Bain. They had been in the varsity the year before, and even with my inflated view of my rowing abilities, I couldn't fathom stealing their seats. Aside from those three, there were eight others who I conservatively ranked above me on the starboard side. That put me at number twelve, which would be the last guy in the fourth boat. And since there was no fourth boat, it wasn't such an ideal situation at all. When

John and Sloan called it quits, I moved into the number ten spot on my own list, just two seats away from a berth in the third boat.

That was my worst-possible-scenario list. My optimistic list had me, after John and Sloan's departure, rowing in the JV. I just prayed that Dave's list would end up looking more like my second list than my first.

Winter training with Dave was so much more intense than it had been with Rick, mainly because Dave was way more intense than Rick. There was no goofing around in practice. We were there to work, not socialize. Any slack behavior was met with some of Dave's unique brand of public verbal flagellation. I tried, therefore, not to slack off, at least not where Dave might catch me.

The workouts themselves were also much tougher under Dave. More was expected from varsity oarsmen. As freshman, so much time was put into teaching us how to row and getting us used to the program, that we could only be asked to work so hard. As members of the varsity squad, the emphasis was on work, and plenty of it.

Though ergs were still the most dreaded item on the agenda, stairs were not far behind. Most days, we would run the 187 steps and nine flights to the solarium, five or six times. This was not easy. Running a set of six stairs was roughly equivalent to climbing to the top of the Duomo in Florence and down, three times. Only the view from the top of Payne Whitney isn't nearly as breathtaking.

This was hard enough when we ran the stairs at our own pace. Every couple of weeks, Dave timed us. He stood at the top of the stairs with a watch, and had a contraption down the stairwell on the fifth floor. Different color lights would flash, telling us when to start running. We would do six sets. These were called "stair relays" although there were no teams, just individual times.

Stair relays didn't sound so difficult to me, and I waited casually for the elevator to take me from the basement to the fifth floor (no reason to walk up any extra flights of stairs) and my first stair relay. My mood quickly shifted from nonchalant to worried when the doors to the elevator opened. There was Eric Brende, a junior. He didn't look well. His face was blanched and he leaned against one of the elevator walls for support. As the doors opened, he took a shaky step forward, and pitched on to his face.

I got in the elevator and pressed five. In a moment, the doors opened. I walked towards the stairwell, pausing briefly to sneak a look in at the aerobics room where dozens of leotard-clad women worked through a sensual hip movement class disguised as exercise.

"Let's go, Zig." It was John Biek, one of the coxswains. "Your group is up next."

I walked into the stairwell on the fifth floor. There was dried spit all over the base of the wall. Guys had been retching their cotton-mouths out all over the wall. The other guys in my group were stretching their legs and opening and closing their fists to relieve nervous energy. Jim Faust was up first. After him, we'd leave in fifteen second intervals.

"Go!" Biek shouted. And I was off. I leapt up the stairs two at a time, and grabbed on to the banister to help swing myself around as I neared the top of each flight of stairs. With two flights to go, I was huffing pretty hard. I saw Faust hustling down the stairs, so he'd have as much time as possible to rest at the bottom before his next set.

"That's the way, Zig," Jim yelled. "You're almost there. Push it hard for another flight." Jim was one of my favorite people on the team. He had been in the varsity as a sophomore, and was everyone's pick to stroke the boat this year, because Vogel thought that Jim Faust was the toughest competitor on the team. His fierce drive forced everyone around him to examine his own effort and then raise it a notch to try to match his.

Aside from being such a great oarsman, Jim was the kindest person I knew at Yale. If someone was down, he took time to find out what the matter was; and if there was any way he could help. He was, unlike Hard and Morley, utterly human and approachable. It was impossible not to like and admire Jim Faust.

So Jim's words of encouragement fueled me the rest of the way up to the top. As I rounded the corner, I heard Vogel chanting my time. "53...54...55 seconds, Zig." Not bad for the first set. I tried to catch my breath before heading down.

By the fourth set, my time was up over a minute and five seconds. I no longer slung myself around each corner with the banister; I used it to drag me up the stairs, like a mountain climber uses a rope to get himself up a steep section of rock at high altitude.

My lungs were burning and my legs were stiff and weak. Faust would now pass me with his cheerful words of encouragement as I still had five flights to go. It seemed as though Jim had taken the elevator to the top and was walking down. He was hardly out of breath. He ran all six of his sets within three seconds of one another. His average time was 49 seconds. Mine was well over a minute.

At last, I finished. My last set took just under 70 seconds. I stood at the solarium, bent over at the waist, my hands on my knees, gasping for breath. I tried to spit some of the vile saliva out of my mouth, but it was so thick that it landed on my shoulder.

"Ok, Zig," it was Vogel, "let's get moving. Hit the tanks." I didn't move.

"Come on," he said derisively, "get going. You don't see anybody else standing around waiting for sympathy. And everyone else didn't walk up the last flight either."

I straightened up and started on my way down the stairs, as the third group of runners began their ordeal. I thought about Dave's comments. What he neglected to mention was that everyone wasn't in the gym working out at eight o'clock that morning. I was.

Lincoln and I had started on our Shek two-a-day program. I had gotten a set of keys to the tanks and the erg from Rick. Three times a week, Lincoln and I would row some pieces in the morning.

I am not a morning person. My earliest class, aside from the freshman English fiasco, was scheduled for ten o'clock. And I even managed to snooze through that from time to time. Getting out of bed at seven thirty on a cold winter morning to row in the tanks took a huge amount of effort. The alarm would go off, and I'd instinctively smack the snooze bar for a precious eight extra minutes. After a couple of these, Rowley would get annoyed and tell me to get my ass out of bed so he could get some sleep.

Bryant Gumbel, in talking about his job at *The Today Show*, mentioned that he had to get up at four in the morning every day. He said that there are two things about waking up early that hold true for everybody: "Nobody likes it, and five minutes after you're up, it's okay."

It's okay if you're Bryant Gumbel and five minutes after waking up you're being spirited to work in the back of a nice long limousine. It's not so okay if you're Mike Danziger and you're bundled in sweats, high-stepping through snow drifts on your way to a morning workout.

Against every desire I had to stay warm and comfortable and asleep, I'd be at the front door of Payne Whitney three mornings a week a couple of minutes before eight.

Lincoln and I would stretch for a few minutes and then hit the tanks or the ergs. There were a few other people who were there most days. Dave was there a lot, as were Alex and Ruth, two women on the women's varsity crew. They were terrific rowers; controlled and very quick at the catch. I learned a lot just by watching them practice.

When Lincoln and I had the tanks to ourselves, we mostly did three minute pieces. Three minutes was a good length because it was short enough that we could concentrate fully throughout the body of the piece, but long enough to be a good workout. Also, seat races in Tampa, which were the most determinative method Dave had of choosing boats, were three minutes long. We'd typically do five or six of these pieces. Sometimes we'd join Dave and the others in the tanks, and do whatever workout they had planned. Dave did a lot of long pieces, ten or fifteen minute ones. Those were tiring both physically and mentally, but rowing behind Dave, and trying to stay with him was good for me.

Lincoln and I did ergs less frequently. But we kept at it with the hopes that when we were tested we would improve. We soon learned that any erg practicing goes out the window when the cox puts the weight in the basket for real.

The workouts in the morning were helpful. I sensed, though I couldn't tell for sure, that I was rowing better. I was worried at first that I'd not be as sharp in the afternoons because of the morning routine, but the opposite turned out to be the case. By spending extra time in the morning, I felt as though I had more invested in the sport. I worked even harder than I might have in the afternoons. Pretty soon many of the other guys on the team knew what Lincoln and I were up to. They knew we were serious. We were gaining on them. We were going to kick their asses in Tampa.

A couple of weeks into the second semester, Roy Kiesling, Stephen's younger brother, was pulling an erg. He was in the undefeated JV boat as a sophomore the year before, but got mono right before the Sprints and had to be pulled from the boat. Nonetheless, he was still a really good oarsman, and way ahead of me on the starboard side pecking order.

Halfway through, his splits were nothing special, but he was doing fine. Then, for no apparent reason, Roy stopped rowing and got off the erg. He let go of the oar and said, "I just don't feel right," to no one in particular. With that, he walked out of the room.

Roy was back at practice the next day, and stayed with crew for another week or so, but I don't think anyone was surprised when he finally quit. One of, if not the cardinal, rule of the ergometer is "never quit." Quitting can not be an option on the erg, no matter how bad it got. If you were injured and didn't think you could finish, then you better not get on. Once you strapped your feet into the foot stretchers, you're there for the duration. If I were to get off the erg midway through a piece, then every other time I was hurting I'd know that quitting was a recourse I could choose. If that were the case, there's no way I'd ever finish another erg. I'd get off every time.

By quitting the erg, Roy had also lost the trust of the rest of the team. What would happen in a tight race, maybe the Sprints, when everyone was in agony and the cox decided to call the rating up? Would Roy be there? Perhaps he would. But no one could be sure. And as I learned in the Sprints the year before, if, and only if, all eight oarsman are sure that each of the others is pulling his balls off, only then can the boat be competitive. If there was so much as a hint that one man wasn't there one hundred percent, then the boat would disintegrate. Without that mutual trust, a boat is worthless.

Roy Kiesling was one less starboard I had to beat out, and one more oarsman in my rear view mirror. With Roy out of the picture, my optimistic list had me seventh among starboards. However, my more realistic roster put me somewhere around eleventh or twelfth on my side. I was on the bubble, and had less than two months to prove myself to Vogel before he picked the guys he'd be taking down to Tampa in March. A lot can happen in two months of winter training.

To say that winter training lasts three and a half months does not accurately describe its duration. Being in the tanks doesn't lend itself to measurements of time at all.

Every day is the same. The temperature stays the same. The sights, sounds of the ergs, weights, and oar, and the dank smell of chlorine mixed with perspiration are constants. The human population in the tanks is not a variable; the same people are there every day. On occasion, a stranger would watch practice from a balcony above the tanks, but the intruder would quickly tire of the monotony and leave.

Since there are no seasons in the tanks, there really was

no sense of time, and therefore no awareness of its passage. I would find myself standing next to a barbell thinking that today was just like yesterday, and tomorrow will be another duplicate. There really was no feeling of "today," since that is a term relative to "yesterday" and "tomorrow," which couldn't be clearly delineated.

It is hard to carry on, much less with enthusiasm, in a timeless, static environment. What about this sport compelled me to show up each day in an attempt, as Dr. Benjamin Spock, an Olympic gold medalist himself, described it: to turn a series of unnatural movements into an instinct, an almost involuntary reaction?

The answer was simple: I loved being on the team. Crew itself held a certain amount of fascination for me. But I must confess that if I had been contacted by the fencing coach rather than Rick Elser, I probably would have found myself on the eighth floor of Payne Whitney everyday, foil in hand, instead of in the tanks. Being on a team, sharing a common goal, is something I have always cherished. I have always striven for excellence, mastery of a skill. But being on the team itself gave me the most pleasure.

In seventh grade, I tried out for the baseball team because all my good friends were planning to join the squad. Additionally, Mr. Cook, one of my favorite faculty members, was the coach. I convinced my parents that I needed a pair of cleats. Without cleats, I insisted, my place in Cooperstown would be in great jeopardy. Not wanting to be the ones to keep me out of the Hall of Fame, Mom and Dad presented me with a pair of black cleats the day before tryouts began.

Naturally, I left my treasured cleats on the crosstown bus on my way to school. I couldn't bear to tell my parents, so I played the entire season in my penny loafers. Actually, that isn't quite true. I didn't really play at all. I wasn't good enough to be one of the starting nine, but I did have my place on the team. Mr. Cook would hit balls to the infield and outfield everyday during practice. The players would field the ball and throw it back to Mr. Cook. Coach Cook was a rather rotund man, and had trouble bending over to pick up the baseballs at his feet. So each day I would stand next to my coach, pick up the balls, and hand them to Mr. Cook. I only played in one game (I drew a walk, bounced out to the pitcher, and caught a fly ball in right field), but I had a great time because I was on the team. I had a uniform, and got to hang out with Solly, Wags, Sav, and the rest of my buddies.

I was one of the smallest boys in my class. In eighth grade, Greg Knapp and Courtney Ward would stuff me into a trash can during homeroom each day. This was enjoyable for Greg and Courtney, but I found that the novelty wore off surprisingly fast.

I wasn't supposed to be small. My Mom is tall, 5'10", and everyone always told me that I took after her, and that I'd be tall, too. By sophomore year in high school, I stood just over 5'4" and I started thinking, "What gives? Where's all this height people have been promising me I'd get?"

Luckily, Mom's genes were not recessive. By the end of eleventh grade I was 6'2"; I had grown almost ten inches in one year. This was great. I would finally be the athlete I always dreamed I could be. There was a catch, however, to growing so fast all at once. Sprouting up at such a rapid rate soaked me of most of my energy, and all of my limited coordination. Tennis was my best sport, and I struggled to keep from stumbling around the court.

Unfortunately, my newly-acquired height was not accompanied by a commensurate gain in weight. At 6'2", I weighed in at a paltry 120 pounds. I was quite a sight, actually. Greg and Courtney no longer crammed me into trash cans, not because they couldn't; I just didn't fit so well anymore. One of my favorite stunts was slipping my entire body through the frame of any unstrung tennis racket (and this was in the days before the oversized rackets). A friend of mine, who deemed himself to be as emaciated as I was, tried to fit himself through a racket and got it stuck around his chest. We almost had to butter him up to free him.

Needless to say, I wasn't an imposing sight on the tennis court. Nevertheless, since Collegiate's best athletes migrated towards baseball and track, the tennis team was thin on talent. Thus, I was the number one player on the team — a sacrificial lamb of sorts.

Even though my victories junior year were two and far between, I had a terrific time being on the team. Trips in the van to Queens, watching my teammates play, and announcing our results in the school assemblies on Thursdays were all part of the team experience, which I thrived on and required.

Perhaps the photograph which most fittingly summed my tennis career at Collegiate was the image of me leaping over the net after an intra-squad match. My face reflected the boundless joy that I got from competing. I was smiling broadly, my arms thrust in the air. I wasn't holding a racket; I had already hurled it into the stratosphere as the moment of victory became mine. A closer look at the picture reveals that my front foot is about to catch the top of the net. In an instant, I would be splattered on the cement. No matter, I was thrilled for a moment. The pain and embarrassment of my landing would pass. The feeling of jubilation is still a vivid memory.

The feelings that I had as I soared over the net and plummeted to the ground were duplicated during the Penn-Columbia race freshman year. Milan's comforting words immediately following the outcome had lingered without fading. Catching a boat-stopping, race-losing crab was a downside risk I was willing to take in order to feel part of the team.

NINETEEN

While sometimes it was fun to go on excursions with Jaymie — to the tanks, to a football game, or to a museum — some of the best times we had were just hanging out in my suite, or playing in the Branford College courtyard, pushing him on the swing, or maybe working on his blazing fastball. We were sitting on my couch one Saturday and Jaymie issued me a challenge.

"I bet I could whip you in basketball, Zig."

"Oh yeah?" I countered, "I think I could destroy you in basketball."

"I've been practicing with Andre, and he tells me I'm getting pretty good."

"That's fine," I reminded him, with a mock seriousness that Jaymie totally got, "but Andre's 10 and small. I am 19 and tall."

"Well you row, and don't practice basketball like I do."

"My record against six-year-olds is quite good," I told my

dear Jaymie Turpin. "I think I'm 16 and 5 this year."

"You've been playing against other six-year-olds? Who?" he asked.

"None of your business. But I'm ready for you."

We didn't have time to go the gym, and it was too cold anyway. So I fashioned a hoop out of a wire coat hanger (our coats ended up slung over chairs or on the floor, so there were plenty of hangars to choose from) and I bent the part that hangs on the rod over the doorway. A rolled-up sock served as our ball.

To even things out a bit, I agreed to play on my knees. We wouldn't have to dribble the sock, but we had to make the dribbling motion with the sock in our hand. We could pass off the walls.

The game was spirited and close most of the way. Lots of trash talking both ways.

"Zig, is that all you've got? I don't how you beat any of those other six-year-olds."

"Hey, JT, how's that smelly sock taste when I swat your weak shot back in your face?"

With five seconds left in our game, we were tied and Jaymie had the ball. I counted down slowly, and he drove past me as I gave chase on my knees.

"Two… one…" I said, and he lofted a two footer towards the hangar. "BUZZZZZZZZZZZZZ" I said as the sock hung in the air. It fell through the wire.

"And there was pandemonium in Branford Arena! The fans are charging the court. Oh the humanity!!" Jaymie danced around the room, and I crumpled to the floor in utter despair.

I reached out my hand in a gesture of sportsmanship and Jaymie lunged at me with the enthusiasm and energy of a six-year-old who had just schooled a 19-year-old on the hardwood.

He went to give me a high five but sort of stumbled and ended up slapping me in the face. There was zero malice; he was just trying to join the celebration.

Nonetheless, he nailed me in the face with the palm and heel of his hand and it stunned me.

For an instant, I was enraged and found myself ready to grab him, and maybe even strike him back. That reflex lasted a fraction of a second, and I soon realized what had happened. Instead of lashing out, I grabbed him in an embrace, wrestled him to the ground, and pretended to be on his team in a celebratory pig pile. It was wonderful, but could have been the opposite. At that moment, I understood how a parent could fly off the handle and maybe even do the unthinkable, which is exactly what hitting Jaymie would have been — an act without any thought at all. What would my relationship with Jaymie have been like if I reacted in anger, even without violence? It would have changed everything forever, and that's how long I would have regretted it.

———

I had a only a few weeks left to prove to Vogel that I was deserving of a spot on the Tampa squad. During February, Lincoln and I increased the intensity of our morning workouts. We would typically do a couple of ten minute pieces followed by a few threes. That way we were tired by the time we got into the intense, shorter pieces that we both knew would determine the boatings once we got down to Florida.

A week before the bus was scheduled to leave for Florida, we still hadn't heard from Dave about whom he was planning to take south. I was anxious to find out if I had made the cut. It was all I talked about in my room. Finally, Stephen looked at me with exasperation.

"Listen, Mike," he said in his deep, slow Southern drawl, "why don't you just go on over to Dave's office and tell him that you want to know whether or not he's taking you to Florida. You've got a right to know."

That made such simple sense, as did a lot of the advice that Stephen gave during the four years that we would room together. With his resolve ringing in my ears, and reflected in my stride, I marched across the street to the Alumni House where Dave worked.

"Is Dave busy?" I asked the secretary at the top of the stairs. I was almost hoping that he was, so that I could say that I had gone to talk to him, but that he didn't have time to speak to me. She shook her head, smiled, and pointed down the stairs.

My shirt was soaked with sweat even though the heat inside didn't nearly compensate for the near freezing temperatures outside. I was more nervous about walking into Dave's office than I had been at the start of the Sprints.

Vogel's office was to my left as I got to the bottom of the large spiral staircase. His door was open, so I peered in. He was on the phone. Now was not a good time. I'd see him later. I turned to leave. Dave covered the mouthpiece and said, "Come on in, Zig. I won't be long."

Now I had to stay. So I stepped into the office and looked around anxiously as Dave talked to someone about the upcoming season. He was saying that he thought we'd be really fast, had a terrific crop of juniors, and some seniors left from last year's HYP boat. Things were looking bright for Yale Lightweight Crew, Dave boasted to the listener.

Dave was an Alumni coordinator, but it was clear from glancing around the room that he was a crew coach first and last. There must have been twenty crew pictures on the wall. He was in some of them, but most were of the boats that he coached. The one that caught my attention was a picture of the 1979 varsity. They were the last varsity to win the lightweight Sprints. There they stood, each wearing a different shirt from their vanquished opponents. In front of them lay a pile of some 200 racing and betting shirts, their booty from that year's successes. I didn't recognize any of the faces, but I knew their names. There was Eliasberg, Kannapan, Reichenbach, and the rest of the gods of '79. Their deeds were part of the past, but Dave invoked their names enough to keep the memories of these oarsmen alive. They would remain immortal as long as Dave spoke of them. I was sure that in years to come Hard and Morley's names would be added to that pantheon. WWhether or not I would ever breathe the rarefied air of Mount Olympus was still not clear. Nor did I care. What mattered most to me was getting a seat on the bus down to Florida.

Dave finally hung up, swung his feet onto his desk, clasped his hands behind his head, and smiled. "What can I do for you, Zig?" He asked.

Well, Dave, you could take me down to Tampa and stick me in the varsity.

I didn't say that.

"Dave, there's only a week left before spring break, and I'd be lying if I didn't tell you that I was curious about whether I was going down to Florida. I was just wondering if you'd made up your mind."

"I have," Vogel said, still not revealing my fate. "You have come a long way this year, Zig. Last year you weren't worth a whole lot in the boat, but you have worked hard and have really improved." Dave paused. This was sounding good so far.

But this intermission after some praise I figured would be followed by a qualifying conjunction. Here it came. "But... as of now, I just can't justify taking you down to Florida. We've got a really deep team this year. I think a lot of boats are going to win a lot of races. I'd love to take you, and I know the guys on the team would love to have you and your spirit down there, but that would mean leaving someone behind who I think could help us more."

I was stunned. I was through. In less than a minute Vogel had nullified everything that I had struggled to obtain. "Does this mean I'm cut?"

"We don't make cuts," Dave was almost mocking me by repeating Tony's words when he was asked about cuts during the introductory meeting last year. Of course I had been cut. I couldn't make a boat if I didn't go to Florida. I had been offed.

But since Dave left me an opening, I decided to take it. "Well, if you want me off this team," I informed Vogel, who was still smiling in his reclined position, "you're going to have to kick me off, because if you don't I'm going to be at practice every day."

"Suit yourself."

"See you in the tanks, Dave," I said. I turned and left. The '79 crew was still smiling on Dave's shelf. He would always remember them as gods, undefeated, winners. The image that Vogel would carry of me, if indeed he ever paused to consider me, was of a guy walking out of his office who had just been shut down for good. I was through, history, a loser.

For some reason, I was now more determined than ever to make the squad. Elizabeth Kubler-Ross, the foremost expert on dying, described five stages in the process of coming to terms with any sort of mortality. The first is denial. I was going through that stage as I faced the end of my life as an oarsman. I couldn't accept Dave's words. He, the ultimate authority, had just sentenced my rowing future to death. This was beyond my capacity for acceptance.

The secretary smiled sweetly at the top of the stairs. I smiled back and walked out into the chill March air. My eyes began to water as the wind slapped against my face.

Stephen took the news of my departure from the rowing world nearly as hard as I did. "It isn't right," he said, "that you could work so hard and never be given a chance to prove yourself better or worse than the others." Then a smile appeared on Stephen's face. "Fuck Vogel. Fuck crew. You and I are going to Fort Lauderdale for Spring Break. We're going to have some real fun."

We sealed the plans with a high five and a week later loaded up my car for the 24 hour ride on I-95 to the mecca for drunken college hedonists.

We took turns at the wheel and sped our way through nine states, and finally reached Lauderdale. It had taken a little over a day, and Stephen and I were exhausted and sick of the three tapes that we had brought along for the trip. No matter. We were in Lauderdale and we were going to have fun.

Fort Lauderdale is a bizarre phenomenon during March and early April. Tens of thousands of college students converge on this seaside resort which is little more than a string of bars and bathing suit shops. The idea, as I understood it, was to get as drunk as possible and try to get laid.

"Zig," I was told before I left Yale. "If you can't get fucked in Fort Lauderdale during Spring Break, you don't have a dick. Everyone gets laid."

After a few days, I was forced to take a peek down my

trousers. I did indeed still have the brilliant refulgence of my male principle. Was I the only person in the entire town who had managed to avoid, albeit involuntarily, to find a willing woman?

I was intimidated by the scene. Huge frat boys crushed beer cans against their heads and chewed glass in an attempt to impress the sorority girls. There were a lot of girls, though. However, it didn't matter. None of them was really my type. Okay, the converse was actually more to the point: I was not their type.

I discovered an important rule: the number of girls present in one place is totally unrelated to my chances of meeting one. What is crucial is the number who would be interested in meeting me. In Fort Lauderdale, the aggregate number of the thousands of women in the scores of bars that I had been to who might want to spend some time with me was zero. Not a one.

I was relieved to find that I wasn't the only guy not to get laid on spring break. In fact, I didn't know anybody who scored down there. For starters, there weren't that many hotels in town, so it was about 12 to a room. I didn't even have enough privacy to take a dump, let alone get laid. And I assumed no one else did either. The truth is this: anytime someone tells you that "everyone gets laid there," that really means that no one has ever gotten laid there. But such a pervasive myth has been perpetuated that people are afraid to admit that they were the only ones not to get laid. Let me end the ruse forever: Nobody gets laid in Fort Lauderdale during Spring Break. This has never, in the history of recorded humanity, taken place. And as far as anyone can tell, no one will ever get laid there.

People did get drunk in Lauderdale. That part of the equation was true enough. Bars stayed open late, and there were drinking games all day long. My favorite spot was a place called The Button. This wasn't such a huge bar, but it did so much business during Spring Break that it was Miller Beer's biggest account.

But it wasn't the drinks alone that drew so many to The Button. The main attraction was the daily wet t-shirt contest. Representing their schools, girls would take to the stage in a Button t-shirt and strip down to nothing in order to win glory for their alma maters. The packed bar would go berserk as these girls competed.

I must admit that I cheered as lustily as anyone, chanting "Show us your tits!" with the rest of the barbarians. All the while, however, I was filled with a vague sense of discontent. I didn't belong in The Button. I was supposed to be somewhere else.

One afternoon, after a couple of beach-side margaritas, I told Stephen that I didn't feel right being in Lauderdale. Tampa was where I wanted to be, with the crew.

Stephen looked around at all the gorgeous women, took a slug of his tropical concoction, and said resolutely, "Then let's get in the car and go to Tampa." He gladly and immediately forfeited a week of his vacation to satisfy my desperate desire to drive across the state in order to see my teammates on the crew. I never knew a better friend in college.

Five hours and several hundred miles later, we pulled into Tampa Bay. I knew that the team was staying at the Hyatt (quite a step up from the barracks), so we drove straight to the hotel. I saw a few of the heavyweights wandering around, but the lightweights weren't anywhere to be found. It turns out that this was their one night out on the town, and Vogel had organized a field trip to Mons Venus, a strip joint.

Armed with that information, Stephen and I drove off in search of the Mons Venus. We found the sleaze district and ducked into a few bars on the strip to ask where this particular establishment was. The management of these places seemed reluctant to steer us towards the competition, but our persistence paid off and at last we found our place.

The Mons Venus was Dave's kind of place. The lights were low, there was smoke in the air, and the clientele was plumbed from society's depths. As I looked around, I expected to see Dave, wallowing in his element, with naked women in his lap swinging their tasseled nipples 'round and 'round. But he wasn't there. I asked the owner if he remembered a group of guys lead by an older man with a moustache. Sure he had. Good lads, they were. But they had left not five minutes earlier.

"Sit down and have a drink," the manager said, motioning towards two stools at the end of the runway where a young woman, my age, was dancing somber-faced to the strains of Peter Gabriel.

"Thanks, but we've got to go," I replied. Turning to the door, I glanced back at the girl on the stage. She smiled sadly at me. I felt sorry for her, and the image of her grinding herself into Vogel's lap while he laughed and stuffed a five-dollar bill into her hand made me angry.

Back at the hotel, we finally ran into the guys on the team. They were surprised to see us, but it was great to see them.

"Zig!" yelled Eddie Schmults from down a hallway. Eddie was Hard's roommate. The two of them were also in the varsity boat together. Like Hard, Eddie was a terrific oarsman, and strikingly handsome. Between them, they had stolen virtually every girl's heart at Yale. If his erg scores had been a bit higher, Eddie might have joined Hard atop Olympus. As it was, he was just a notch below.

"It's great to see you," Eddie said, his palm extended for a high five. I knew enough to touch it gently, as I was sure his hands were covered with blood blisters. My hands, by contrast, were getting soft.

———————

That day, the Yale boats had competed in the President's Cup, an annual race in Tampa Bay that Yale always wins. This year was no different, and I peeked in one of the hotel rooms, and saw some of the heavies drinking out of the victor's cup. Everyone seemed thrilled to see me. They wanted to know how often I got laid, what the girls were like, and lots of other predictable stuff concerning my sojourn to Fort Lauderdale. Of course, I lied, thus perpetuating the myth that draws people to Spring Break.

A lot of the guys seemed jealous of me. I didn't have get up at five thirty every morning. The grueling two-a-days weren't part of my schedule. I could chase girls and drink all I wanted, whereas they had to concentrate on timing and keeping the set right.

Naturally, I smiled while I regaled them with the licentious, and fictitious, tales of my adventures during the past week.

Finally, it was time for the guys on the team to hit the sack. After all, they did have get up early to row the next morning. Lucky me, I got to sleep in. Stephen crashed on the floor of one of the rooms. I went downstairs to go to the bathroom. As the door of the bathroom closed behind me I crumpled to the floor, with my face in my hands, sobbing. It had been years since I had shed a tear, and I hadn't cried this hard since I was maybe five or six years old. I was crying so hard that I could hardly catch my breath.

The guys on the team were happy to see me but I was just a visitor whom they really liked. I was, for the first time since seventh grade, not on a team. The Tampa experience defined the squad, and I wasn't a part of it. The team would come together without me. All I could do was cry my hardest, because I had never been so devastated in my entire life.

And like I did when I was six years old, I cried and cried until I could cry no more. Then I fell asleep on the floor of the bathroom.

The next morning, Stephen and I joined the team for breakfast at the University of Tampa cafeteria. No heavyweight was going to cut in front of me this time. I wasn't a lightweight anymore. I was a visitor. Plus, Stephen was standing by my side and no one dared push me around with him near by.

After the meal, I said good-bye to the guys on the team, wished them luck in their seat races, and got in the car for the drive back to New Haven.

I told Stephen how I felt. He was very sympathetic. "You looked like you were just smiling through the tears," he said. "What are you going to do now?"

"I don't know."

We sat in silence for most of the way through Florida and Georgia. Stephen realized that I needed to sink into my self pity in order to step out of it, and he graciously granted me this luxury.

Our silence, and my depression, was interrupted in Beaufort County, South Carolina, when we plowed into a stop sign. Luckily, no one was seriously hurt. But I felt a certain amount of discomfort when the sheriff arrived and saw that a Jew with vanity plates from New York had just taken out his road sign.

Stephen, who lived in South Carolina, did the talking for us. He eventually convinced the officer that we were in the wrong, we would gladly pay for any and all damages, that our fender bender did not constitute a crime against humanity, and it would be best if he didn't take us downtown (I personally thought the sheriff was bluffing when he suggested we "go downtown" because as far as I could tell, Beaufort County, South Carolina had no downtown).

TWENTY

When the rest of the team returned from Tampa, I joined them at the boathouse for practice. The boats had been set, and needless to say, I did not make one of the top three boats. But neither did seven other guys. Rob Wilen, who coxed a few of my races freshman year, was aced out of the third boat by John Biek, a junior. The nine of us waited in the boathouse as the others went out to row.

As the rest of the squad showered, Dave called the nine of us together. "Listen," he said, "you all have a decision to make. Either you can quit, or you can row together in a fourth boat." This sounded fine with me. Dave's next words didn't make rowing in the 4v sound quite as appealing. "I've never carried four boats at the varsity level, and I won't be able to pay much attention to you out on the river. There aren't many other schools with four boats, so your schedule will be different from the rest of the team's. I can't even guarantee that you'll get that many chances to race. But if you want to stick around, you can row in the Newbury. What will it be?"

Nobody looked at anybody else. If one person wasn't up for it, then we'd all have to abandon our hopes of being on the team. I looked around. No one looked too psyched. Dave was getting impatient.

Then Ivor Benjamin, a senior and two-year veteran of the 3v, spoke up. "We'll do it, Dave. Just give us a boat and try to get us as many races as possible. We want to row." Ivor's words and eager tone had galvanized us all. We were ready to be the 4v.

For the next two weeks, we practiced not knowing whether, when, or against whom we were going to race. Those seemed to be almost trivial considerations. The important thing was that we were on the water with the team and getting better.

The Newbury was the boat I had rowed in the year before, so I was used to its idiosyncrasies. The other guys weren't so happy with the old wooden shell. Though we couldn't expect Dave to give us a carbo, there was some hope that we might row in a Schoenbrod, a shell which was in-between what the varsity rowed and what we found ourselves in.

Crew is one of the few sports in which the less-skilled members of the team were saddled with inferior equipment. The low guys on the tennis ladder didn't have to play with old wooden rackets, while the top guys dueled it out with oversized graphite weapons.

The reason coxswains tried so hard to be light was that for

every extra pound, the shell slowed one foot per six-minute race. If that was the case, then the Newbury (300 pounds), compared with the carbos (250 pounds), cost us almost a length before we even got in the boat. Not only were we slower by virtue of the fact that we were poor oarsmen, we were handicapped with extra weight as well.

What made it even more infuriating to row in such inferior equipment was that there was a long waiting list of alums who were just dying to fork over 25 grand to have a boat named after them. The only condition, however, was that it must be used by the first boat. The Jv and 3v got to use carbos once the varsity had rowed in it for a few seasons. The 4v got no hand-me-downs.

"Someday," said Ivor after practice, "I'm going to make a bunch of money and give Yale a state-of-the-art boat, better than any they'd ever had. It'll have a tremendous speaker system, the works. And I'll stipulate that no one can set foot in that shell unless he's in the lowest boat."

Ben Norris had another idea. "I'm going to give the same type of shell to Harvard. And my only proviso will be that they have to name the boat the David H. Vogel. I'd love to see Dave's face when a Harvard boat with his name all over the bow shlongs one of his crews." We all smiled at Ivor and Ben's methods of reprisal.

Just as Hard and Morley occupied a unique and exalted place in the crew hierarchy and were inextricably tied to one another, Ben and Ivor represented another aspect of Yale crew. Both guys were seniors and had rowed together as freshman in the second boat, as sophomores and juniors in the 3v, and now found themselves in the 4v. Aside from being in the same boat every year, these two guys had one other thing in common: an uncamouflaged loathing for one another.

Ivor was the stroke of our boat and Ben sat in the six seat, though Ben believed all along that he should be stroking the 4v instead of Ivor. After each practice he would tell Ivor that the rating was either too high, too low, or too rushed. There was always something the matter with Ivor's rowing.

Ivor had the same measured, calm response each time Ben pestered him. "Shut up, Norris," he would say in his nasal voice. "I'm the stroke, not you." This went on every single day, and reached a point of self-parody quickly.

The most celebrated set-to between Ivor and Ben came in their sophomore year. Ivor was stroking the 3v, and once again, Ben found himself in the six seat. Before the HYP's that year, Ben was busily scouring the boat, trying to rid it of any dirt that might cause drag in the water.

Meanwhile Ivor was relaxing and quietly getting ready for the race. Ben took exception to what he took to be Ivor's apathetic attitude and threatened to "wring his fucking neck" if he didn't pull his nuts off.

Sure enough, when the race was over, their boat came in third. As tradition stipulated, the 3v pulled next to the victorious Princeton boat and gave up their shirts. It was a cold day and Ivor had a t-shirt on underneath his racing shirt. The rest of the boat was bareback. Ben was livid.

"Ivor," he screamed, "why the hell did you wear a t-shirt?"

Ivor answer was calm. "Because I didn't want to freeze on the way back to the dock."

With that, Ben leapt over the seven man and grabbed Ivor's neck with both of his hands. He was actually trying to strangle Ivor. The rest of the boat, not to mention the crowd on the banks of the river, looked on in shocked disbelief. Finally, the seven man pried them apart. The two never cared much for each other after that.

Another person who wasn't one of Norris' biggest fans was Vogel. This wasn't so much because Norris was a lousy oarsman, although I can't think of many shitty rowers that Dave has allowed himself to admire, but more because of a storied altercation that Norris had with Dave in the tanks.

When Norris was a junior, he had signed up for a tank session and was sitting in his assigned seat, warming up for the workout. The tank was filled. Just then, Hard, a sophomore at the time, wandered into the tanks.

"Hey, Mike," Dave yelled towards Hard, "why don't you hop in the tanks now?"

Hard saw that the tanks were full. "That's ok, I'll do some weight circuits instead."

"Nonsense," said Dave. "I'll make room for you." He scanned the tank for an available seat. His eyes came to rest on Ben. Norris sat in his seat with his yellow skin, matching hair, and omnipresent scowl. "Norris, you're out," Dave bellowed. "Get out of the tanks. Mike, get in."

Ben didn't budge.

"Get out Norris," Dave repeated.

"I'm signed up for this session," Ben protested. "I'm not leaving."

"Get out right now." Dave was getting pissed. Norris was unfazed.

"Why don't you try to make me." Norris dropped the gauntlet.

Dave picked it up. "Fine with me." He made his way towards Ben's seat. Still, Ben wouldn't move. He wasn't bluffing. The rest of the guys in the tank, along with whoever was nearby, watched the drama unfold.

When Dave finally got to Norris, he reached down in an attempt to pull Ben's oar up on the gunwale. Norris would have none of this. He grabbed Dave and started wrestling with him. What a ludicrous scene this must have been. Here was the varsity coach grappling with one of his least talented oarsmen over a seat in the tank which Hard wasn't even dying to use. After a brief struggle, Ben flipped Dave over and wrenched Vogel's knee. For the next several weeks, Dave needed crutches to get around. Norris' rowing fate was set in stone. Whatever the lowest boat was, he would be in it.

Whereas many people were put off by Norris, everyone liked Ivor. He was cheerful, properly cynical, and fun to be around. Ivor graduated with both a B.A. and an M.A. from Yale. In addition, he had a thriving on campus hi-fi dealership. Crew mattered to Ivor, but he wasn't about to fight Vogel over a spot in the tanks.

Ivor and Ben couldn't have been more different. But they were alike in two fundamental aspects. Aside from their common distaste for one another, they shared one other thing: an unquestioned dedication to crew. I was proud to be in their boat.

The 4v was comprised of three seniors, three juniors, and me and McManus from the sophomore class. Rob Wilen coxed us. Though Rob was without argument the worst coxswain on the team, just as we were certainly the poorest oarsmen, his job was tougher than what the other coxes had to handle. He was essentially our coach.

Dave paid, as he warned us, very little attention to the 4v. We often rowed in the wake of his launch as he zipped ahead to watch the other three boats, all way ahead of us. Sometimes, he would send us off on our own. Rob Wilen would have to come up with a workout and implement it while we were on the water. With no one to compare ourselves to, we could only sense that we were improving from day to day. In the first couple of weeks, our set became more solid and consistent, and that allowed us to pull harder and go faster. One thing we never achieved was swing.

"Swing." That elusive feeling that all boats aim to achieve. Supposedly swing occurs when all eight oarsmen are in perfect synchronization. Not only are their oars entering and exiting the water at the same time, but they are applying the pressure to the blade as one. The feeling was supposed to be almost transcendental. I had never come close to being in a boat that swung.

One day, on the way out to practice, I was sitting next to Alex and Ruth, the two stars of the women's program. I heard them talking about swing. I had to interrupt.

"What is swing?" I asked.

Alex looked at me. She was strong and very feminine. A tattoo of a butterfly on her shoulder made her seem exotic, risky. I found her really attractive but hadn't ever screwed up the courage to talk to her.

"It's hard to explain."

"Try."

"Well," she began, "it's when the boat is going really well, when everything's clicking just right."

This didn't help me at all. I had heard all of this before. "What does it feel like when the boat is swinging? How do you know if you're swinging?"

"You just know," Alex said. "That's all, you just know. It's almost like an orgasm. You can't describe it, but you know when you're having it. And it feels so good."

This was the best description of swing that I had ever

heard. Also, just hearing Alex say "orgasm" to me was a thrill.

"Well," I asked, trying to be witty, "Can you fake swing?"

Alex and Ruth laughed. "Nope," Alex said.

After this discussion, I was more disappointed than ever that I had never swung in a boat. I was missing out on more than just a good row, so it seemed.

After a couple of weeks of practice, the top three boats prepared for their opening race with Coast Guard. Since they didn't have a fourth boat, we didn't have a race. But on the Wednesday before that Saturday's race, Vogel told us that the University of Rhode Island's JV had agreed to race us that day, at the same place that our other boats would be racing.

This was great news! We would be racing after all. The only troubling aspect was that I weighed one hundred sixty six pounds. Our boat average had to be one fifty five, with no one weighing more than one sixty. The seniors determined who would weigh what, and it was decided that I should tip the scales at no more than one fifty five. I had two and a half days to lose eleven pounds before Friday's weigh in.

———————

Drip. Drip. Drip. I sat on the top bench of the boathouse sauna, with my elbows on my knees, and my head in my hands, and watched two circles of sweat darken the wooden floor beneath me. One circle was formed from sweat dripping from my nose, the other from my balls. I counted the drips, seeing which would reach one hundred first. This wasn't so much a scientific experiment, the results of which I would publish in *The New*

England Journal of Medicine, rather it was a way of keeping my mind off of the excruciating heat and boredom of the sauna. For the record, my nose dripped one hundred times to my balls' eighty two. The sauna was cranked up as hot as it could go, and the thermometer indicated that I was in an oven. The temperature was over two hundred and twenty degrees. Every five minutes or so, I'd have to leave this inferno, take a shower, and then return.

Sitting in a sauna, trying to sweat off one last pound from a body already dehydrated by over a day of no food or water, and more than two days of no food at all, was torture. None of the present translations of Dante's *Inferno* refer to the sauna, but I'm quite sure that Dante himself reserved this level of Hell for those poor souls who were too stupid to have figured out a way to make weight by Friday's practice. I had lost ten pounds in less than three days, and had to lose one more before the four o'clock weigh-in.

There were two other guys in the sauna with me. Tim Bradley, a senior who had become callous to the discomfort of the hot box. He sat quietly, reading the *New York Post*. This had become a Friday ritual for Tim. Sitting in the sauna was almost part of his preparation for the race.

Josh Chernoff, a sophomore, sat on the lower bench. From there he could pour water on to the scalding rocks. This would raise the humidity and increase our sweating. The air was so hot that it hurt to inhale through my nose. Also, we were warned to leave any jewelry outside the sauna, as any metals became branding irons in that small room.

All of a sudden, Josh's face lit up He rose and announced, "I've got to take a shit!" This was indeed big news. A shit, even a small one, had to weigh at least several ounces. And that was equivalent to plenty of time that Josh would not have to spend sweating. Tim and I looked at each other ruefully. We were jealous of Josh's turd.

It had been more than a day since I had so much as urinated. And even then, my body was so depleted of water, that all I could produce was a couple of drops of thick yellow liquid.

The weigh-in was scheduled for four pm, with Dave presiding. At three thirty, I got out of the sauna and stepped on the scale. I couldn't believe it. I was 153 ½!

"Lincoln," I hollered, "get over here with my cookies." In a moment, Lincoln showed up at my side with a box of Entenmann's chocolate chip cookies in his hand. "Load me up," I said, with my arms outstretched, hands cupped together.

With that, Lincoln began to pile the cookies into my hands. I watched the scale. It hit 154, and I asked him to bring me my sixteen ounce bottle of Coke. I learned in ninth grade that, "A pint's a pound, the world around," so I knew that the cookies I had in my hand and my Coke would get me exactly to my target weight.

I gobbled the cookies. Sure enough, they weighed the same half-pound in my stomach as they had in my hands. I drank the Coke as slowly as I could, keeping one eye on the needle. As I drained the bottle, the scale announced that I weighed precisely 155 pounds. I had made weight.

After all the boats made weight, Dave called us together. He had three or four cardboard boxes at his feet. "Time to get your shirts," he announced, reaching into a box. This scene harkened back to the fall day my freshman year when Rick Ricci tossed us each our first Yale rowing shirts. Only it was different with Dave. Instead of giving everyone a team shirt, he called the boats up one by one. The varsity and JV got blue shirts with the white sash, white trim around the arms and neck. The only difference between what the two boats got was that the second boat shirts had a JV next to the Y. The 3v shirts had no sashes, and ours were like theirs, except without the trim.

I was bothered by the fact that my shirt wasn't the same, let alone as fine as the varsity shirts. I had worked just as hard as anyone else. I had earned my spot on the team. This was a team, after all, wasn't it? Or was it four separate teams rowing under the Yale name?

When I looked at the yearbook after freshman year, I turned to the page that had the picture of the lightweight crew. There were only nine guys in the picture, all from the first varsity boat. The other two-thirds of the squad were not accounted for. The message was clear: The first boat was the Yale lightweight crew team. The rest of us merely rowed under the Yale name. I could think of no other sport in which only the starters appeared in the team picture.

The lower boats rowed in inferior shells and were clothed in less spectacular uniforms than the top boats. It was easy to see how a sense of class consciousness could arise.

Not only were there levels of society that were equated with one's ability to row well, but the levels were pretty well fixed. There was very little mobility within the caste system Dave had set up and deliberately perpetuated. Ivor and Ben were at the bottom of the heap when they started, and it was no surprise to anyone that they would be there when they left. By the same token, Hard, Morley, Faust and Bain had unconditional residence at the upper echelon of society. There was a bit of movement between the top two boats, but a guy in the third boat was deep in slumber if he thought he would one day be in the varsity.

It hadn't always been this way. In fact, the famous Dr.

Spock, the "Baby Doctor", started out in the thirteenth freshman eight. Four years later he won a gold medal in the 1924 Olympics.

When I was a freshman, I was eleven boats ahead of Spock's pace. But the two boats between me and the first boat would be harder to get through than the thirteen that Spock traversed sixty years earlier. Ed Leader, his coach, did not have the rigid hierarchy that Dave had.

The next day, the other guys in the 4v and I stood around the dock of the Coast Guard boathouse, preparing to launch our boat for the race against Rhode Island. To our surprise, as we got ready to get into our shell, several of the oarsmen from URI came over to us. When they found out that they were racing against Yale's 4v, and not the JV, as they expected, they saw it as a great opportunity to win some Yale racing shirts. They wanted to make sure we were racing for shirts.

There had been no question in any of our minds that this was a race for shirts, but since they brought up the issue, we took it up with Vogel, just to make sure.

"Listen," he explained, "these guys are good oarsmen. They made the finals of the Dad Vails last year." (Dad Vails are the small school equivalent of the Sprints.) Dave continued. "You can bet your shirts if you want, but I'll be damned if I'm going to pay for a new set of shirts every time you lose. Bet them, fine. But if you lose, you're either going to be rowing bareback for the rest of the year or you can buy your own shirts."

Ivor looked at us. "That sounds like a 'yes' to me," he said. With that, we went over to our competition and informed them that of course we'd be racing for shirts.

With 500 meters to go in the race, it looked as if we were either going to be rowing topless for the rest of the year or we'd have to come up with some money in order to put new shirts on our backs. The Rams of URI took almost a length lead after the first 40 strokes, and it seemed as though they weren't about to relinquish it. Neither did we seem capable of gaining on them. Our tens were worthless, just words that Rob barked out. We weren't moving a bit.

As we passed the 1,500 meter mark, a pleasure cruiser pulled along our starboard side. It slowed up along side us to get a look at the race. After a few seconds of inspection, the people must have decided that crew is not the greatest spectator sport, even when viewed up close. The driver pushed the throttle down and the boat sped away.

Moments later, I heard Rob Wilen say, "Surf's up, boys. Let's wax up the boards and prepare to hang ten and ride it out with a twenty on this one!"

Just as Rob started counting out the power strokes, a wave broke over my left shoulder. We were hit by a couple more breakers, and the Newbury quickly had almost half a foot of water sloshing around the hull. Whatever set our boat had was gone, and it was difficult to get our oars in the water the way we were being tossed about. But since Rob had warned us of the wake and had gotten us focused by calling a power twenty, we managed to avoid falling apart completely.

That is exactly what happened to URI's boat. The wake hit them by surprise, and when the waves started hitting them they didn't know how to respond. While we slugged it out the best we could, they all but stopped rowing in an attempt to ride out the turbulence.

We more than weathered the storm. By the time we finished with our power strokes, the water had become calm again. More important, we had moved through URI. Rob announced that we had half a length on them. In typical 4v fashion, we all looked out of the boat so that our eyes could be witness to the incredible news that our ears had just received. Sure enough, Rob was right. The Rams were behind us and fading. We continued to pull away until we reached the finish line a full two lengths ahead of URI.

What an unbelievable feeling! To come from behind, row through a wake that would have caused any other race to be re-rowed, and beat a talented crew. No matter that we were the fourth boat and that our opponents were a team that Yale had never rowed against, and would likely never race again. The feeling of unbridled satisfaction that accompanies an extraordinary effort was not diminished because we weren't top oarsmen. Talent was irrelevant. The amount of joy one feels is never bounded by skill; rather it is a response to dedicated work.

The first time Jaymie was able to throw a basketball through a regulation hoop, after countless afternoons of trying, he pumped his arms in the air and ran around the gym, as if he had just sunk a buzzer-beater to win the seventh game of the NBA Finals. And to him, he did. His smile came not in spite of his relative lack of skill; it came from the feeling of accomplishment which Jaymie could lay no less claim to than could Magic Johnson.

After catching our breath, we paddled into the dock. Dave was there to help pull our boat in, and congratulate us on our win. The URI boat docked right next to us, and after they got their boat out of the water, we waited for them to come over and surrender their shirts to us. Their shirts were cool, too. They were long sleeve with a patch in the middle of the chest.

The guys from URI didn't come over to hand us our spoils right away. We all were excited to get our shirts, my first as a varsity oarsman, and the third of my career, but we weren't about to ask for them. Protocol requires that the losers come over and give up their shirts, not that the winners demand them. Maybe after they finished derigging their shell they'd pay off their cottony debt to us. Nope. That wasn't going to happen. They loaded their boat onto a trailer and began to head over to their team van.

"Looks like they forgot about the bet," said Pete Calabresi, our seven man.

"I guess we're not getting shirts from them," said Eric Brende. This was awkward. We had won. Those shirts were ours. But no one was going to ask for them.

"The hell we're not." I had forgotten about Norris. He had no qualms about demanding the shirts. The situation wasn't in the least bit uncomfortable to him. They were welching on a bet, and he wasn't about stand for it.

He marched over to one of the guys on their team and said, "We agreed that this race was for shirts. Now pay up." Diplomatic Norris. I wished I could be that up front with people.

The URI oarsman shuffled around before saying, "Our shirts are back at school. We'll be sure to send them to you." That's right. The check's in the mail.

"How about what you're wearing?" Norris asked. "Those are racing shirts. That's what we bet, racing shirts. You owe us those shirts."

"We can't bet these shirts. These are racing shirts. We bet betting shirts. Like I said, we'll get them to you."

"Terrific," said Norris. And he turned to return to us.

"Well done," said Ivor, sarcastically. "I'll be checking my mailbox tomorrow. I'm sure they'll FedEx them."

"Those guys are assholes," Ben groaned. "They didn't

bring shirts cause they figured they'd get shlonged by our JV. They could say it was a scrimmage. Then, they find out they're racing us so they bet, counting on us sucking. What dicks. They're probably too classless to feel embarrassed about this."

"That's right, Norris. A class guy like you would have been all broken up over it," Ivor pitched in.

"Shut up Ivor."

We loaded our boat and returned to New Haven.

TWENTY-ONE

The next few weeks, which was practically the entire season, were pretty dull. We didn't get a chance to race much, except as a third entrant in some of the 3v races. Invariably, we would get creamed by both our 3v and the other team's boat. It was frustrating to come in third in duel races all the time. Wilen insisted that we were getting faster, but none of the rest of us saw it at all. We were trying hard. But with little coaching from Dave, and no races of our own, it was increasingly difficult to maintain enthusiasm.

One day after practice, I was showering when Norris walked in and turned on his shower. He was in an unusually sour mood, even for Norris, because the computer he was working on had freaked out or shorted or something and swallowed up his entire senior essay. He had two weeks to do it over. This troubled an already troubled man.

"Zig," Ben said to me, "are you going to quit at the end of this year?"

"No."

"Why not?"

"Because I like rowing."

"How can you?" Norris asked. "You suck. I mean you are one terrible oarsman. We all are. We are so inept that Dave had to create a whole new level for us to sink to."

Norris was a brooding guy by nature, but this tone was downright grim, even for him. I hadn't seen him this down about rowing since Dave took the weight off of Norris' erg in the middle of a piece and told him that he was worthless. Norris was disconsolate then, and he was now.

"Rowing has been a gigantic waste of time for me," he continued. "If I knew that I was going to end up rowing in the six seat of the 4v, I would have been gone long ago." I doubted this very much. Even though Ben Norris was upset to be in the bottom boat, and to be rowing behind his nemesis, Ivor, he liked crew and was proud of his accomplishments. He had to be. I just knew it.

"Norris," I said, "I'm not going to end up in the 4v. This is a weigh station for me. I'm going places in this sport. Next year, I swear to God, I'll be sitting pretty in the stern four of the 3v, knocking on the door of the JV."

"Wake up, Zig." Norris said, as he squinted and tried to get some soap out of his eyes. "Let's look at the situation for what it is. You are in the three seat of the 4v. The three seat. Who rows in the three seat? The stern pair sets the cadence. The six, five, and four men are the engine room, the power of the boat. And the bow pair keep the set. What's left? That's right, the three man. You, Zig. The worst man in the worst boat. The three seat of the 4v is the black hole of rowing. Nothing happens there. And wait, it gets worse. Whoever gets sucked into that black hole will never get out. You're stuck, and fucked. No rowing future." Ben finished his speech, shrugged his shoulders, and turned his palms up. Those are the facts, Zig, he was trying to tell me, just thought you ought to know them.

I stopped shampooing my hair (I still used the palms-up method even though I didn't have any raw blisters on my hands, it had become habit). and looked at Norris gravely. "Jesus, Ben," I said, "I didn't know it was that dire."

"You bet it is," he said, completely missing my mocking tone. "Get out while you can."

I thanked Norris for his pep talk, rinsed off, and got out of the shower before I started to believe him.

Since there was no 4v category in the Sprints, the HYP's would be our final and most important test. It was that race on Lake Carnegie that we were aiming for. During some power pieces in practice, Rob would tell us that we were neck and neck with Princeton or Harvard, or both, with twenty strokes to go. In those pieces we would always eek out a victory by a bow ball on the last stroke. Even though it was make believe, Rob made it real, and it got us psyched for the race.

A week and a half before the big race, Dave called us together after practice. The crew budget, he explained, was pretty tight. He hadn't counted on taking four boats to Princeton, and he didn't think he could justify spending the extra money to bring us down and put us up in a hotel. We were, he concluded, not going down to Princeton for the HYP's. There was no emotion in his voice. No concern. No regret. He was just delivering the news.

We regarded Dave in stunned silence for an awkward moment. Then Ivor stepped forward, and looked Dave Vogel right in the eye.

"You listen to me, Dave," Ivor began, in a slow stern voice. "Whether you choose to recognize it or not, this boat is as much a part of the team as any other boat. And I know I am speaking for everyone in the 4v when I say that we are willing to pay money to prove this point to you. We will be at Princeton to race in the HYP's, budget or no budget. That I guarantee you. Make arrangements for our transportation and lodging, Dave. Tell me what it costs, and we will find a way to pay our way."

Not once did Ivor divert his eyes from Vogel. Vogel looked back at him with a look of surprise and admiration (though Dave himself probably didn't recognize the admiration part). Finally, Dave said, with a hint of contrition in his voice, "I'll make the reservations."

Then Ivor nodded, and we all headed up to the locker room. I had never seen anyone shut Vogel up. But Ivor's message was irrefutable, and even Dave knew it.

Dave's agreement to take us to the HYP's did not, however, signify a fundamental change in his attitude towards his lowest boat. Three days after Ivor's oratory, we raced Trinity's JV. Dave didn't join us for this race, nor did he provide us with any mode of transportation. We would have to drive ourselves to and from Hartford. But our coach did see through to lending us a trailer to bring our shell to Trinity.

"Let me know how you do," Dave told Ivor the day before the race. He said it with a tone that betrayed passing interest at best. "Give me a call or something."

It had been three and a half weeks since our victory over URI. Since then, we hadn't won a race, or so much as a piece in practice. We had no idea how fast or slow we were. We knew that we were a lot slower than any 3v around. Our confidence was pretty low, and we really needed a win against Trinity to set us up for the HYP's. It wasn't so much that beating Trinity would be any sort of gauge as to how fast we were, relative to Harvard and Princeton. What really mattered was that our boat get reacquainted with winning a race. If we went into the HYP's with the feeling that winning was an alien experience, we would surely lose — a self-fulfilling prophesy. This was a must-win situation.

Trinity's JV was just the tonic we needed. We annihilated them. Wasted them by 23 seconds. We pulled away right away, and continued to widen our margin until we crossed the finish line a full four lengths ahead of our opponents. Guys in the varsity referred to the distance between our boat and Trinity's as "the curvature of the earth," or, more simply, a "horizon."

Could it be that more than three weeks of getting wailed on by our 3v had actually made us faster? We thought all along that we stunk, because we kept getting beaten in three minute pieces by horizons, but maybe we were actually getting better, even though the improvement was indiscernible.

We were excited about our showing and everyone had a quiet confidence about our chances at the HYP's. Everyone except Norris, naturally. He threw a wet blanket on our hopes by saying that he refused to view any part of the season as a success until, and unless, we won the HYP's. If we didn't win the race, he continued, the season would be one gigantic waste of time for all of us.

For the entire week before the HYP's, we focused on getting length on every stroke. Rob sensed that our puddles weren't adequately spaced, even at low ratings. "Reach out, hook on to some water," he'd say over and over in his familiar nasal twang, "and really send those puddles down the river."

We also sharpened up our starts, working on getting the rating up in the water, rather than just flying up and down the slides at break-neck speed. "Let the boat run out from under you," Rob instructed. "Really feel it glide."

———————•

The day before the race, after Dave put the other three boats through their final paces, he brought his launch over to us and said, "Let's see what you guys can do over two minutes."

We took the boat out at a paddle, and when it seemed to Dave that our set was fine, he told us to take it up to full. All at once our blades hooked into the water as one. The catches were strong, and we kept the water on the blade straight through to the finish. Stroke after stroke we put our blades in at precisely the same instant, applied the pressure together, and came out clean and as a group.

All of a sudden, the Newbury became light. It felt as if it had been transformed into a carbocraft right there on the water. Even lighter than a carbo. Our old wooden shell was like a flat stone skipping across the water.

———————•

Also, the water seemed different. Before, our blades moved through the water sluggishly, like the Housatonic was made of mud. Now, the water yielded immediately to our blades as if we were rowing on champagne, light and bubbly.

I couldn't hear Rob's voice. Perhaps he wasn't speaking at all, like a jockey whose horse is running perfectly eschews the whip and just enjoys the ride.

Dave told us to paddle, and that was the only time in my years of rowing that I wasn't glad to hear those words. I wanted to keep going. It wasn't even hard, we were rowing so well.

We had experienced swing. Elusive swing. So that's what it was all about. I felt as if I had finally been let in on a terrific secret that many of my friends had been keeping from me.

We had swung, and it was wonderful.

As advertised, swing was truly transcendental. We went far beyond what all of our talents combined could possibly have produced. Alex was right. Swing is hard to describe (witness my attempt), but you know it when it happens.

Like an orgasm? That far I don't think I'd be willing to go, although for Alex it might have been an appropriate analogy.

I couldn't believe that the varsity guys experience the feeling of swing almost every day in practice. If not on every piece, at least during a few of them.

"We were swinging there during that second eight, right in the middle of it," one would say to another in the bus on the way back to Yale, "but we lost it towards the end." How frustrating it must be to be swinging, and then, all of a sudden, not to be swinging. The difference is a quantum leap.

On the other hand, how amazing it must be to expect to swing during practice. If that were the case with our boat, we would be dying to go out to Derby every day. For us, practice was a chore we endured in order to improve. Ben wouldn't have thought his efforts were a waste of time if our boat swung every day. That would be a joy. Even for Norris.

Dave pulled his launch alongside our boat and said, "Nice piece. Take it in." Though his words didn't betray it, we could tell he was shocked with what he saw.

On the dock, I overheard him tell Rick, in a very matter-of-fact voice, that we would win. There wasn't even a trace of doubt in his voice. Vogel had been around boats for almost two decades and he knew a winner when he saw one. He was looking at a winner.

When we arrived at Princeton late that afternoon, we found that Vogel had indeed been true to the letter of his word, if not the spirit, when he told Ivor that he would handle the accommodations for our boat at Princeton. He had provided lodging for us in the same hotel as the rest of the team. That was uncharacteristically thoughtful of Dave, considering his attitude (or lack thereof) towards us the rest of the season.

Lest you think he had turned a corner about us, he arranged a single room. For all of us. Nine guys. That was more like the Vogel we had come to know and loathe.

After making weight (I had learned my lesson after the URI weigh-in, and only had to go on a hunger strike for a day to get down to weight this time), our boat had dinner together and then headed back to the room. Dave was making the rounds, talking to each boat about race tactics. It wasn't so much a strategic talk as it was a pep talk. From what I heard, Dave was great at getting boats psyched for the race. Real fire-and-brimstone type stuff. Knute Rockne addressing his squad before the Homecoming Game. That type of talk.

So of course we waited with baited breath for Dave to arrive at our cramped quarters. At nine o'clock, there was a knock on the door. Dave walked in, looking deadly serious. Our double room was already set up for the night, with box springs off the beds, and blankets spread for guys who didn't even get to snooze on box springs. There was little room for Dave to stand.

"Tomorrow," Dave said, his voice calm, preparing us for the dramatic juxtaposition of his passionate, voice-cracking tone that was to follow, "you race Harvard and Princeton." He paused so that the enormity of the moment would settle on each of us.

I immediately recognized that Dave's introduction was clearly an allusion to the famous speech Tad Jones gave to his football team before they took the field against Harvard. "Gentlemen," Coach Jones told his players many decades ago, "You are about to play Harvard. Never again in your lives will you do something so important."

Would Dave echo Jones' words, or had he come up with a variation on the theme? Dave glanced around the room, making meaningful eye contact with each of us. We leaned forward, awaiting his next utterance.

"The bus leaves at eight o'clock sharp. Be on it or you will not race." With that, he turned and left the room. An interesting departure from Tad Jones' speech to be sure.

"What a dick," McManus said.

"Don't worry about Dave," Ivor assured the rest of us. "As long as we row like we did yesterday, we'll be fine. No one will stay with us."

Norris chimed in, "That is if you can get the rating above a 33, Ivor."

As one, we all spoke Ivor's refrain. "Shut up Norris."

Within a few minutes, all of us had managed to fall asleep, dreaming of fulfilling Dave's vision for us. We would make that bus.

Sure enough, the bus left at eight sharp, and we were on it. The day was bright and sunny. A not insignificant crosswind would make setting the boat harder, but the conditions were nothing compared with what we were used to on the Housatonic. Andrew Carnegie had seen to it that his lake would be well-protected from the winds.

After the customary race day warm-up of a bunch of power tens and twenties and a few practice starts, we backed into the stake boats at the starting line. We had drawn the outside lane. Harvard was in the middle, off to our port side, and Princeton was on the inside. I looked over at the Harvard boat. They were all wearing tennis hats with H's on the front. Typical Harvard dorks. Then the coxswain started passing bananas down the boat. Everyone had a banana and was eating it. I had never seen this before a race. What was it, some kind of snack, like juice and cookies?

Wait a second, hadn't I read somewhere that bananas were an excellent source of potassium? Yes I had. That's it. The Harvard dorks were loading up on potassium before the race.

The sight of those guys eating bananas in the shell made me happier than ever that I went to Yale and not Harvard. Not that I even applied to Harvard; not that I could have gotten in. I hate bananas. I hate them so much that I won't even try them. Never have, never will. They just seem gross. So mealy, and with all those tiny seeds. Not for me. Plus, I'm not too crazy about the flavor of bananas.

And I know the flavor because Katie once had a banana-flavored chapstick, and I used it. Tasted atrocious. That's as close as I'll ever come to eating a banana.

At any rate, as I was giving thanks that I was in the Yale boat, and not in the Harvard boat eating bananas, the race official was getting the boats set for the race.

"Touch it up, Princeton bow."

"Okay," Rob said quietly into the microphone, "this is it. just like yesterday and we'll leave 'em all in our wake. Good luck."

Jim McManus put his hand on my shoulder. I turned around and he smiled and winked. I patted Eric Brende's shoulder and he kind of shrugged in acknowledgement.

"All eyes in the boat," Rob reminded us. "Focus."

I glued my sight to the back of Eric's neck. His blonde, straw-like hair was darker at the ends, which hung just above the top of his shirt. His collar was turned slightly backwards, the white tag crawling straight up his neck. In blue, upside-down writing, I could see the brand name of the shirt: ImPrint. There were also some washing instructions. Warm water, tumble dry. My eyes would not waver from this tag. If, at the end of the race, I still had my shirt, I vowed to treat it properly. I would wash it only in warm water, after which it would be treated to a tumble dry. The next voice I heard was that of the race official. "Êtes-vous prêt? Partez!"

We were off. Like in the Sprints the year before, it all came down to this one race, and as soon as the official started us, the nervousness was gone, replaced by puddles in the water.

We were rough off the start. There was no rhythm, certainly no swing. Where was the swing from yesterday? Would it be back, or was it like a one night stand?

Even though we weren't rowing well at all, Rob informed us that we were neck and neck with both Harvard and Princeton. If we could row badly and still hang in there, when we got straightened out we'd blow those boats away, potassium-loaded oarsmen or not.

For 1,000 meters, the three boats traded power tens, but

no boat could gain so much as three seats on the other two. This race was turning out to be, as Yogi Berra liked to say, "a real cliff-dweller."

———————

Close races were rare among lower boats for two reasons. First, there is usually a greater spread in talent at the bottom than among the top rowers, and secondly, lower boats tended to give up if they fall behind more readily than do their JV and varsity counterparts. Today, these three boats seemed to be evenly matched, and it was obvious no one was going to concede.

Close races are so much more difficult than blowouts. In blowouts, even though both boats are rowing at full power the entire way, the outcome has been determined early on, taking the mental pressure off of each stroke.

In a tight race like the one we were having, every stroke was critical. Ease up for a second, and the opposing coxswains would sense it, take a ten, and be long gone before you knew it. The first thousand meters were a battle, and no one was giving a quarter.

"All right!" Rob yelled. "1,000 down, and we're dead even with Harvard and Princeton. This is the third 500 of the race. We own the third 500! It's ours. Let's prove it with a 20. On this one!"

If we owned the third 500, we had just leased it out to Princeton. They raised their rating four beats for 20 strokes and were gone. At the end of their flutter, they had three quarters of a length on us, and a half a length on Harvard, who was subletting some of our real estate in the third 500 as well.

We sagged when we should have surged, and the race was over. As they had last year, Princeton and Harvard battled it out for first, while we headed for home in third place.

With 20 strokes to go, Rob used a call he had been dying to try all season. The other boats were about to cross the finish line (Princeton ahead of Harvard by almost a length) when Rob yelled, "Let's see it guys! Our season's not complete until we eat some Tiger meat!"

Had we even been in contention, or better, in the lead, that might have been an inspirational call. As it was, it seemed unnecessary, almost mocking. We paddled back down the racecourse towards the dock, in silence. As we passed the 1,000 meter buoys, I wondered where we had gone wrong, how we had fallen apart so quickly.

Once at the dock, the Princeton 4v was there waiting for us, all smiles, ostensibly there to help pull us in. Their real purpose was clear: They were vultures, and they wanted our skins. We complied, stripping off our race shirts, me for the second time, Ivor, Norris, and Dave for the fourth, and handed them over. We stood on the dock, naked to the waist, as the Princeton team disappeared laughing, a sea of blue cotton.

A few of us stood in the shade of some trees near the boathouse. I looked around. This was Princeton? How could Fitzgerald possibly have described this setting as if it were the Elysian Fields in *This Side of Paradise*? He had it all wrong. The setting was gloomy, forbidding, ugly. At least it seemed that way to me.

Ivor, commiserating with his girlfriend, Brende, walked around dazed from the effort, not fully realizing yet that we had lost the only race that really mattered all year. And Norris was going on about how this just proved that his entire rowing career, and all of ours for that matter, had been one huge, flaming waste of time.

I had the same thought that the Gauls probably had 20 centuries earlier after taking on Caesar and his troops: we came, we saw, we lost.

Even though we hadn't won, the day was not a wash by any means. The first freshmen kept their hopes of an undefeated season alive by trouncing both Harvard and Princeton. Lincoln and his third boat mates cruised to victory. And the JV won after one of the guys on the Princeton squad fell off his seat and couldn't get back on. Princeton alums on the banks of the Carnegie were complaining about it being a cheap win. But it was a win.

Unfortunately, the varsity ran up against a superior Tiger crew and had to settle for second. I saw our previously unbeaten first boat as they were de-rigging. They weren't so much sad as they were shocked. I don't think it occurred to them that there was any boat that could even stay with them over 2000 meters. A bewildered look masked what sorrow and frustration they must have felt.

Only Jim Faust had a different appearance. He took his seat off the rollers with a determined scowl on his face. He was already looking towards revenge in two weeks on Lake Quinsigamond for the Spirits.

At least the varsity had a chance for paybacks. Our season was through. And once again, I would go home without a Yale Crew shirt.

My visit at Princeton, however, was not a total loss. After the race, I spent the night going to houseparties with a good friend, Billy Ullman. It was at parties like these that Fitzgerald must have gotten his inspiration. We were transported back half a century, to a time when men dressed in dinner jackets and women wore shimmering ball gowns. Many eating clubs threw lavish parties, and each that did had a band and plenty of beverages.

There was no way to be glum at a houseparty. It was so festive and grand. As I listened to the Marvelettes sing, and asked a lovely young lady to dance, memories of the morning's loss became faint, replaced with thoughts of trying to figure out a way to get Melissa to join me at the Cap and Gown party down the street.

TWENTY-TWO

A few weeks later, I found myself leaning against a railing on the Ponte Vecchio at 6:30 in the morning. The famous gold shops wouldn't open for another couple of hours. Soon there would be wall-to-wall tourists, buying jewelry from goldsmiths who ran little shops that had been on the old bridge for more than a century. Little had changed in these small family operations, except now they took American Express and Visa.

I wasn't down this early to beat the rush. Even when the shops opened, I probably wouldn't have gone in them. All that glitters was confusing to me.

I was homesick and jetlagged. So I took a walk from my *pensione* down to the river. I had liked Florence right away. The streets were narrow and twisty. I imagined that they were the same as they had been when the Medicis ruled back in the 14th and 15th centuries. Now cars and Vespas and pedestrians fought for position on the little thoroughfares.

Old ladies hung their white linen out to dry and waved as I yelled, "Ciao!" to them.

I liked the streets and the old ladies more than my *pensione*. My first night, I lay in bed, looking up at the ceiling. It struck me as odd that walls of my room were white, and yet the ceiling was black. Two-tone was kind of fancy for my cheap little hotel. Then I noticed something even more disconcerting: The ceiling seemed to be moving. Not the ceiling, really, just the black paint. It kind of swayed. Upon closer inspection, I came to the dreadful realization that the black "paint" was actually a sea of cockroaches blanketing my ceiling.

I had lived in New York for eighteen years and wasn't too squeamish about roaches, but this was too much. I went downstairs and explained to the night watchman that I was sharing my room with some half a million black creepy crawlies. He nodded and handed me some bug spray. I gave him my most gracious "grazie" and went upstairs for some serious cockroach genocide.

After emptying the entire contents of the family-size aerosol can in my tiny room, I left to air out my body and clothes.

I returned ten minutes later and looked at the ceiling. Sure enough, the roaches were gone. The stuff that guy gave me must have been pretty heavy duty. Unfortunately, they had fallen on my bed and all over the floor.

I slept in the lobby that night. At six, I got up and walked through the charming narrow streets, past the old ladies hanging their sheets out, to the Ponte Vecchio. There I stood, farther away from home than I had ever been by myself. There was nothing even mildly familiar about my new environs.

I was in Florence for six weeks with the University of Pennsylvania Summer Program. I would be studying Italian Renaissance Art on location. A few weeks earlier, I decided that I would major in art history at Yale. I had been frightened away from English by my first teacher, and I really liked the courses I had taken in art history. The art was almost always interesting, and sometimes beautiful.

And I found that once I learned the art historian vocabulary, I could cruise through any course in the field. For instance, in every paper and exam that I wrote, I was sure to mention a certain piece of art as being "the artistic manifestation of the joyous celebration of the boundless potential of human endeavor." That is art history-speak, and every time I used that phrase, I would get a check in the margin, or maybe even a "yes, indeed!"

The thirty or so other people in my summer course seemed more like shoppers than scholars. The main topic of conversation during my first supper at the *pensione* was how not to get ripped off in the open markets, and why you should wait and buy leather in Rome.

I heard one pundit talking frantically to her mother. "Mom," she said with genuine concern, "you said I was going to Florence. What am I doing here in Firenze?"

As I worried about my predicament, my eyes followed the Arno as it flowed under three other bridges. A familiar sight caught my eye. It was a pair, rowing on the river. I waited for the shell to get nearer the bridge on which I was standing, and as it passed under, I ran off the bridge and followed the boat from a road about fifty feet above the river bank. The shell pulled up to a dock right under the Uffizi, and about sixty yards (meters, I was in Europe) from the Ponte Vecchio.

I climbed over a three-foot wall and scampered down a slope to the dock. The men and their boat had disappeared into the boathouse, so I cased the outside of the place in hopes of finding someone I could talk to about possibly joining this club.

A short man with a shock of black greased-back hair came out of the archway that led into the boathouse and regarded me with dark skeptical eyes. I stepped forward, offering him my hand. "Hi. My name's Mike Danziger. I'm here for the summer."

The man took my hand cautiously. "Cosa vuole? What do you want?" he demanded.

"That's right," I said cheerfully. "I'm with the Penn Program? Out by the Central Market. I'll be here for six weeks."

"E uno cannotiero?" (Are you an oarsman?)

"I sure am happy there's a boathouse in Florence," I said, completely oblivious to his question. "This looks like a great club you've got here. Any chance of my joining up for the summer?"

The man turned to walk away. He seemed more frustrated with our dialogue than I was.

I didn't speak much Italian. In fact I spoke next to no Italian. I had already used all the words I knew in talking to the night watchman (grazie) and the old ladies doing their laundry (ciao). But I had noticed a few things about the language: first of all, it seemed to me that were a preponderance of vowels, mostly o's, at the ends of words.

Also, talking with your hands was part of the grammatical structure of the language, as far as I could tell. Armed with those two bits of "knowledge," I began speaking "Italian" to this man.

"Momento, please," I said. The man turned around. I must have been doing something right. "My name is Michaelo Danzigero. Americano." I was waiving my hands and arms furiously through the air, like a blackjack dealer gone berserk.

The man watched me with stunned amusement. But he wasn't leaving. So I continued.

"I row at Yalo Universitato."

This he understood. For he said, "Si?"

"Si," I repeated. Now we were talking the same language.

I took out my wallet and produced my Yale identification card.

He looked at it, and then said, "Vuole rogare qui?" (Would you like to row here?")

I hadn't the foggiest idea what he had just said, but he was smiling, so I took it as an invitation to join the club. "Si," I said, extending my hand which he now grabbed readily. "Grazie."

With that, I became a member of the Società Cannotiere Firenze.

The man, whose name was Piero, was the club's boatman. He made sure that all the boats were in proper working condition, and he was the guy you went to when you wanted to take a boat out on the river. I was glad we were *paisanos*.

The next day, after class, I wandered through town, past the Duomo, into the Piazza Vecchio, and through the Uffizi gallery, where statues of Cosimo de' Medici, Michelangelo, and Alberti watched me as I went by. The sense of history and romance of this Tuscan city was inescapable, and as I got more and more acquainted with it, I felt somehow linked to those heroes of the Renaissance under whose gaze I passed on my way to row.

The boat club was directly beneath the Uffizi, and it was a great place. There were pictures hanging on the walls of members who had gone on to glory in the Olympics and World Championships. There was also a bar (a bar out at Derby? Never!) and a large changing room. There was a weight room, a still-water tank, and lots of great old wooden shells.

On my second day at the club, a man approached me. At 6'3", he was taller than most of the other Italians I had seen, and looked as though he was carved from some of the leftover Carrara marble that Michelangelo didn't use for the *David*.

He introduced himself, "Mi chiamo Roberto."

"Mi chiamo Michael." I was catching on.

"Michele," he said, obviously mistaking my mimicry as a knowledge of his language, "Vuole rogare insieme con mi?" (Would you like to row together with me?")

I had no idea what he was saying, but he motioned that I follow him out to the boat racks. He spoke to my old friend Piero for a bit, and asked me to help him get the pair out in the water.

After we got our oars on the dock, Roberto said "A uno adestro," and he held out his right hand, "O uno sinestro?" he held out his left.

I understood. He wanted to know whether I was port or starboard. "Adestro," I said.

"Va bene. Andiamo." That's good. Let's go.

With that, we got in the shell and shoved off. Roberto stroked, and I sat in the bow seat. He rowed very smoothly, and at a low rating. We were just paddling, but I could feel the boat jump with his catches. I was concentrating on rowing with him, keeping my timing sharp. After making a trip up the 1,500 meter strip of rowable water, Roberto turned around and said, "Per dieci." (For Ten)

I nodded. After a few more strokes on the paddle, I heard him say, "Prosima." (Next) And then, "Quest'uno." (This one). Our oars locked into the Arno, and we were off. Roberto was much stronger than I was, and the boat pulled starboard. I sensed him letting up a bit, to keep the boat going in a straight line. We did a few more tens, a couple of twenties, and then went full power for a minute.

It was exhilarating. Rowing in a pair, I could feel everything that was happening in the boat. The Catch, how the boat ran out from under us. I had heard Dave talking about these things, but I had never really experienced them. Rowing this way clarified everything he said.

It was also a charge rowing under the Ponte Vecchio and having the tourists whip out their cameras and take pictures of us. No longer was I a Yale oarsman laboring under obscurity for thirty minutes of unattended racing in the spring. I was a tourist attraction.

When we finished rowing, Roberto and I thanked each other, and he headed for the weight room. A man approached me. He spoke English quite well.

"How did you like rowing with Roberto?" he asked.

"It was great. A real pleasure."

"Roberto, he is one of our best rowers. Last year he finished third in the Italian Championships and rowed in the finals of the World Championships," the man informed me.

"Well it was great to row with him. I hope I get a chance to do it again."

The man smiled. "I am sure he will row with you again. He is that way. Roberto is a very nice man." With that he turned and walked away.

I was stunned. Roberto was a better — far better — oarsman than anyone on the Yale team, and yet he rowed with me. That never would have happened at Yale. I was lucky to catch a meal with guys in the varsity. They'd never row with me. At the Società Cannotiere Firenze, there was no class consciousness derived from one's rowing ability. Rowing was enough of a bond; there didn't need to be delineation based on puddle size.

After a few weeks, Piero called me over to his shop. I followed him into a little room behind the boat racks. The room was filled with the tools of a boatsman's trade: rigger wrenches, old seats, slides that needed fixing, and oars that had broken collars.

Piero reached into a box and pulled out a shirt. It was a white tank top with broad red horizontal stripes across it. In the middle of the chest was a patch that had the club's name and seal on it. Piero held the shirt out to me.

"Porta la" (Wear this), he said. "Ch'e la tua manicha" (This is your shirt). It was a rowing shirt, just like the one Roberto and everybody else at the club wore. This was no stripped-down, lesser version like the ones I wore for Yale... the shirts Vogel passed out to those not in the top boats. The fact that I was clearly an inferior oarsman, and not even a Florentine, didn't matter to Piero. He saw that I liked rowing and had become friendly with several members of the club. That was enough for him. I was honored to wear my shirt.

I took the shirt and tried my best to thank him with what humble Italian I had learned. "Mille grazie. Molto contento portare questa manica. La portero con spirito." (Thank you so much. I am very happy to wear this shirt. I will wear it with pride). I must have gotten at least a few words right, because Piero put his hand out and looked me in the eye and smiled when I took it.

Roberto and I rowed together a couple of times a week for the six weeks that I was in Florence. My rowing improved and so did my Italian. The other Yale lightweights were probably pushing papers at some desk job on Wall Street or chasing girls in Newport or Martha's Vineyard. I was becoming a better oarsman.

TWENTY-THREE

Fall training for me would merely be an extension of what I had been doing in Florence. I wouldn't be rusty the first couple of weeks like the others. Surely Dave would notice this. How could he not? He was, after all, a terrific coach who knew good rowing when he saw it, and could draw the best out of an oarsman if he thought there was anything to be drawn. So far he had not seen that I had any real potential aside from the fact that I was taller than any other lightweight in the country (I was now just over 6'4") and therefore in theory, I should have been able to move more water if I learned how to row properly. The part about learning to row properly is where Dave had his doubts about me.

A couple of days after returning to Yale my junior year, I wandered by Beinecke courtyard. Sure enough, there were the shells, and there were Dave and Tony talking to prospective oarsmen about the program.

My mind was cast back two years to when I had first seen the strange vessels, and Dave had asked me to be at the introductory meeting. I was thrilled. And the following two years had been wonderful, my every expectation was fulfilled and more. Crew had been, so far and without qualification, a joyous part of my college experience.

Vogel's voice snapped me out of my revisionist history. "Hey, Zig," he said, "are you going to be out there spinning your wheels for another year?"

"You bet, Dave. I'll see you out at Derby tomorrow."

He shook his head and smiled. "Suit yourself." Then he turned his attention to another promising freshman.

I turned and walked away. Even though Dave's words were cloaked in laughter, that couldn't disguise the way he thought about me as an oarsman, or rather the way he didn't think of me as an oarsman. Unless he overcame the idea that there was no way in the world that I could make it, he would most certainly be right.

Two weeks after the Princeton weekend, while the other boats were practicing for the Sprints, my phone rang. "Hello?" I said.

"Mikey." It was Coach Byrnes from Collegiate. He added an "ie" or a "y" to everyone's name. No one else called me Mikey, except sometimes my Mom, and her voice sounded different than Coach Byrnes'. I played in a poker game at Coach Byrnes' house once, and the other players were Richie, Patty, Birdy, Andy, and Ray (Ray's a tough one to add Coach's favorite suffix to, so he was just Ray, or Rayzer).

"Hi Coach!" I said. "It's great to hear from you. How are things at school?"

"Just fine. Trying to stay out of Barter and Boss' way. Hey listen, I know you're busy, so I won't keep you long." (This was his way of saying that he was busy and didn't have long. Without crew practice, I had all afternoon to chew the fat with Coach Byrnes). "We've got the athletic banquet coming up in three weeks, and we've decided to do something a little different. We used to get guys like McGuire, Gondrazec, you know, celebrities, to come and speak. We think it'd mean more to the kids if one of our own gave the speech."

"That sounds like a terrific idea. Do you want Solly's number? I think I've got it here somewhere." John Solomon had been the most celebrated, even though he was certainly not the most talented, athlete in my class. He had no grace, very little coordination, and a lousy shot in basketball. The only thing he could do was win. If there was a way to win, Solly would find it. He was an inspiration to me, and a legend to the kids to whom he'd be speaking.

"Actually," Coach said, "I was hoping you would lead things off for us. Solly would be great, but we'll ask him some other year. This year we would like you to speak."

I was really flattered and, even more, shocked. After all, my accomplishments paled next to those of many other kids in my class, and they were invisible next to John's. "What should I speak about?"

"I don't know. About sports. What they meant to you at Collegiate, and maybe what it's like to be on a team in college. You'll be great. The banquet's on May 16. I'll send your folks an invite. Can't wait to see you, Mikey."

I wasn't sure that I was the right guy to be giving this kind of talk. But if Coach Byrnes wanted me to do it, then I wasn't going to say no. "See you then, Coach."

I grabbed a pen and one of my previously unmarked spiral notebooks, and headed over to Richter's, a bar that Rick Elser opened earlier that year. It was a quiet place during the afternoon. Plus, if I got stuck for words, a beer might be just the thing to free up the block.

I had been sitting in the back room at a large wooden circular table for a couple of hours, jotting down ideas, themes, possible opening lines that weren't that creative, basically trying to get a feel for what I might try to say to a bunch of kids who were expecting a celebrity and got a nineteen year old athletic ne'er do well.

Just then Vogel walked in, and without asking sat down at my table, at once robbing me of my privacy without affording me any companionship in return.

"Hey, Zig," he said as the corners of his moustache turned up, "what are you writing?"

"Actually, I was just asked to give a speech at my old high school."

"About what?"

"It's a sports banquet, and I've got to come up with something to say about my involvement with sports in high school and in college."

"They better have other speakers," Dave said.

"Why's that?" I asked, genuinely curious, forgetting to whom I was speaking.

"Because if you're the only one they have talking about college sports," he said with a laugh, "it's going to be an awfully short speech."

Did he really think the crew experience was available to only the guys in the top boat? Did it ever occur to him that the speed of the boat was completely separate from what crew was really about: the training, the common goals, the perseverance? In all his years of rowing and coaching, had that essential truth escaped him? I wasn't about to try to explain it to him.

"No, Dave," I explained, "the reason they asked me was that the rest of the banquet, the awards and stuff, take so long that they needed a thirty second speech at the end. So I guess I'm their man."

"Guess so," he said with his moustache straight across his upper lip.

As Dave left I turned my attention to my speech, but I couldn't help thinking about what Dave had said and what he might actually think of my rowing experience. Sometimes Vogel could be so dismissive of me and the others who rowed in lower (face it, lowEST) boats. On the other hand, my experience was so different from Dave's and from those in the top boats. At the level that defined his career as a rower and his expectation for his boats, fitness and skill were a given. It was all about fine tuning the nine men in the boat, developing chemistry, and working to become recognized as the best in the country. They operate at the highest level. It's a different mind set.

The guys in my boat were still learning the elusive simplicity of the stroke, much less doing it as one. We raced whomever Vogel could cajole into taking us on. The Sprints didn't include us. All the goals that motivated the varsity were alien to us.In that way, Dave didn't understand why anyone would want to hear what I had to say about crew. It was in many ways unrecognizable to Dave. He didn't get. How could he?

But still. The reason Vogel even bothered to pull up chair and and discuss crew at all with me, spoke to the part of crew that was common to both of us. The unrelenting work, the repetition, the reliance on every one else in the boat, the focus. The crew experience is unto itself and can't be fully explained (this book is testament to that) to the uninitiated. Those who share the common experience that so few understand, care about, let alone dedicate themselves, are a rare lot. And even though the team is split into boats, each getting different uniforms and rowing in different types of shells, whatever it is that gets each of us to the tanks all winter, or out to Derby and back the rest of the year matters too. And that's why even though it seems like Vogel either doesn't care about what happens to me as a rower, and sometimes even ridicules me, I can't help but knowing that he cares and is intrigued by whatever it is that motivates me. And that I have more in common with vaunted crew of 1979 than either of us could really define. A rower is a rower. Even, and maybe especially, the crappy ones.

Two weeks later, I went to New York and delivered my speech to Collegiate's athletes. I talked fondly about my days as an athlete at Collegiate. My victories in dodge ball and red rover got particular attention.

Then I talked about rowing. I never hinted that I was anything other than a mediocre oarsmen, and even that was stretching it since I was in fact one of the worst. Instead, what I emphasized were the rewards of being on a team, and how that made me feel more a part of the school.

The speech was fairly well received, considering it came at the end of a three-hour banquet. My message, the pill which I wanted the students to swallow, was mushed up in hilarious anecdote after hilarious anecdote. They laughed, but I doubted that they'd all rush out to be oarsmen.

———————

The Sprints yielded the same results as the HYP's, except this time the Princeton guy who fell off his seat managed to keep his ass in position, allowing his boat to beat our JV. The varsity lost by four tenths of a second to Princeton, and our 3v rowed away from the field to capture the championship, as well as conclude an undefeated season. By far the most exciting race was the first freshman final. The only boat that stayed close to Rick's crew was Dartmouth, and we had beaten them by less than half a second at Derby.

Dartmouth had revenge on its mind. With 500 meters to go, they held a length lead on our boat. Unless one of their oarsmen could duplicate my crab at Columbia, it seemed certain that The Big Green would win.

But Jamie Fosburgh, the stroke of our boat, was not willing to let that happen. Instead, he did something even more incredible. He picked up the rating. The boat had been rowing at a 35, quite a high rating for a freshman crew. Jamie cranked it to a 37, and the boat followed. Then the rating went up to a 40. Coaches on the bank of the river were looking at their stroke watches in disbelief.

With 20 strokes left in their season, Jamie asked his boat to follow him up to 40 strokes per minute, a higher rating than they had started the race at. The boat complied, and they seemed to pull even with two strokes to go.

As the two boats crossed the finish line as one, all sixteen oarsmen collapsed. Only the two coxswains were able to listen as the official motioned that Yale had won — by a tenth of a second! The total difference in time between these two boats in both races was under half a second.

It was astonishing. These guys had given everything they had. There was nothing left as the 2,000th meter of water went under their bow ball. That is how a race is supposed to be rowed.

At the trailer, the Dartmouth oarsmen came over and surrendered their shirts. Some of them were crying. The Yale freshmen didn't look much happier. They were drained and would appreciate what they had accomplished later. Two Dartmouth oarsmen were unable to bring their shirts to the Yale trailer;

they were in ambulances on the way to the hospital, suffering from acute exhaustion.

At the banquet following the Sprints, the mood was somber. Even though the fresh and the 3v had won, the top two boats hadn't come away with a victory, and that was unsettling.

Still, there were lots of alums in their Henley blazers saying, "Well done… Nice going…" Mostly they gathered around the varsity oarsmen, who, even in defeat, were the stars of the show.

———————

The eight oarsmen and coxswain who made up the varsity boat carried themselves differently than everyone else. At least it seemed that way to me. I saw them as being at the top of the ziggurat that Tom Wolfe details in *The Right Stuff*. They had climbed to the highest perch of crew mountain (venerable Mount Olympus) and from there we all looked up at them, in reverence.

Physically they looked no different than the other oarsmen. They were no taller, for I was the tallest on the team. They were no stronger, as Kem Edwards could lift far more weight than any of them. Yet they possessed something, a quality that was exclusive to their group. Whatever they had that made them varsity oarsmen affected other parts of their lives as well.

Things came easily to these men, both in and out of the water. They excelled in classes (five of the eight oarsmen in the '82 varsity had Phi Beta Kappa keys), they were popular with women, and men admired them. Hard and Morley were selected, along with 13 other men in their class, to join Scroll and Key, one of Yale's oldest and most prestigious secret societies. Gavin had been in that mausoleum on College Street his senior year, too. What went on in that windowless edifice, no one knew for sure.

But being tapped was about as Gavinish as you could get. Like the Apollo astronauts, I believed the guys in the varsity had "the right stuff." I did not. What was this unquantifiable stuff? In what area was I wanting? What did they have that I did not? Again I looked to Wolfe's book for the answer. The one attribute which the astronauts and the varsity oarsmen had, and I, a member of the 4v (the three man, for God's sake!), lacked in sufficient amounts was, quite simply, manhood. I was convinced of this fact. I felt jealous, envious, and inadequate, all at the same time.

At the banquet, Faust was elected, more like anointed, captain for the following year. Dave gave out the awards, and then turned his attention to the seniors, seated with him on the dais.

Dave had words dripping with praise and admiration for Bradley, Schmidt, McGlashan, and a few of the others who had rowed in the top boats. Then he came to Ivor, Ben, and Dave Kaminsky, each of whom had never rowed in anything but the lowest boat all three years.

Ivor, proud Ivor, who had stood up to Dave so many times, squirmed as Dave looked at him and tried to think up a sugar coated way to say, "He sucked, but for some reason that completely escapes me, he stuck with it for some reason, and I guess that's worth something." What Vogel came up with instead was something on the order of, "Ivor has earned his varsity letter by rowing for four years. He can be proud of this achievement."

Completely insincere. Ivor tried to smile, but he didn't really manage to summon much more than a twitch of his lips. He didn't need Dave to be throwing him a bone. Ivor knew what he had accomplished. He certainly didn't require Vogel's hollow approval. And I could tell that Dave was just as uncomfortable giving it. If Dave had anything to do with it, guys who rowed for four years but never made a top boat wouldn't get a letter just for their efforts. Why, Vogel wouldn't have given Norris the steam off his shit, yet he forced himself to give Norris a varsity letter. You could tell Vogel hated doing it.

The most moving moment, in an otherwise artificial atmosphere, was an unscheduled one. The freshmen had just given Rick Elser a gift: a watch. Engraved on the back were the words, "To Rick. From your undefeated EARC Champion Crew of 1983." It was a great present, and a ballsy one as well, if you consider that they had to get the watch engraved before the Sprints. The same cocky spirit that got them to get the bold engraving in advance is what made them great.

At any rate, after they gave this present to Rick, Vogel was supposed to thank all the alums and ask them to give freely and often to the Crew Association. Before he had a chance to begin, Jon Leone, a member of Rick's boat, stood up unexpectedly. "I have something to say," he began.

"Sit down and shut up Leone," Rick said, not wanting his crew to steal too much of Dave's time.

Leone persisted. "It'll just take a second." Rick glanced down in resignation. Dave glowered from the podium.

"We have had a great time rowing this year," Leone began. "And not just because we had a successful year on the water. This year has been a terrific year for all of us because you upperclassmen have made us feel such a part of the team. Especially the seniors." The room was dead silent.

"Chuck," he said to McGlashan, "thank you for all you've done to welcome us on to the team. There's not much more I can say," and here his voice began to crack, taking everyone by surprise. "But I would like you to have this," Leone said, his voice now really strained with emotion, as he lifted a blue shirt up. "It was my shirt that I wore as the captain of my high school crew. I'd be pleased if you'd take it as a token of our appreciation for the job you've done."

No one knew what to do. This was certainly as impromptu as it was moving. We all clapped as Chuck walked, dumbfounded, towards Jon. As Jon handed Chuck the shirt, all Chuck could say was, "Thanks, dude."

As it had the year before, the banquet eventually degenerated into a drunken celebration of a long year's effort, and spilled out into the bars and convenience stores 'til dawn broke the next day. As with the last post-banquet partying, I don't recall much, except that my hair smelled like pickle juice in the morning.

TWENTY-FOUR

I got back to the room and found Stephen Anderer sprawled across a couch with a beer in one hand and Aristotle's *Nichomachean Ethics* in the other. Stephen had just returned from his second football practice of the day. He was exhausted and I didn't want to bother him. I slumped down in one of the chairs and rummaged around the pile of magazines on our coffee table until I found a fairly recent *New York Times* sports section.

Stephen looked up from his book. "How's it going, Michael?" He was practically the only person at Yale who called me Michael.

"Not bad. How was practice?"

"Brutal. They had us in pads for both sessions. Coach Storey ran us ragged all day."

"How does the depth chart look?"

"Pretty good for me. They've got me at the top for left guards. I'm in decent shape, which is a whole lot more than some of the other Toads can say." Toads was what the offensive linemen called themselves. "You ought to see Otto. He's enormous. 'Roids, I reckon."

"Well," I said, "with Andre back, at least you'll have someone to block for." Paul Andre was a returning tailback. I followed Yale football pretty carefully, mostly because of Stephen, and through him I knew a lot of guys on the team.

Stephen sat up from his couch and looked at me. "You looked pissed off, Michael. What is it?"

"Nothing."

"It's got to be something," he said in a concerned tone. Then with a touch of humor, "What'd Vogel do, cut you already?"

"Not in so many words."

"You've got to be kidding me. What did he say to you?"

"Well," I explained, "he said that I would be spinning my wheels if I went out for crew again this year."

"Fuck him," Stephen said. "Fuck that asshole. He hasn't even seen you row this year. Does he know you rowed all summer? Of course not. He wouldn't ask. He's a dick. And you're going to show him, Michael. He's going to be sorry he even thought of writing you off."

Stephen was more upset about the way Dave had been treating me than I was. I guess I had learned to accept Vogel's attitude as a given.

"What do you mean?" I asked.

"Listen to me," Stephen began, "you worked hard last year, and you're going to work even harder this year. You are going to get so strong, and be so technically superior, that there's no way he will be able to overlook you. Remove that option from his repertoire. He will be forced to give you a shot when you show him how good you really are."

I was told that when I went to Yale I would meet people that would humble me. Stephen Anderer was one of those people. When I walked into my suite freshman year and saw Stephen, he struck me as a big dumb jock who I'd probably have a great time hanging out with. He was six foot two, weighed 225 pounds, had a pitted complexion and a nose that looked like it had been broken many times. His voice was deep, and hailing from South Carolina, he had a slow Southern drawl.

A literary theme I gleaned in the two weeks that I took freshman English was that of appearance versus reality. In no person was that borne out more convincingly than in Stephen Anderer. Though he was big and strong with a lumbering carriage, and played football, he was anything but stupid. In fact, he may have been the brightest of my roommates, two of whom ended up Phi Beta Kappa and Summa Cum Laude.

Stephen led an examined life at Yale. He loved questions, issues, and the debates they led to. Because he was a natural lawyer, few people stood a chance against Stephen in a verbal dispute. Another advantage Stephen had was that at first glance, no one took him seriously as an intellect. His lazy southern drawl lured them into his trap. He was his own mark. A typical discussion might have gone something like this:

Unsuspecting debater (in a very condescending tone): "Well Stephen, maybe you don't understand Plato's ideas on Truth. They are difficult to understand. I took a course on them and I think you'll find that my point of view is correct."

Stephen (shifting into an intellectual gear far beyond anything his outmanned adversary has ever dreamed of possessing): "I audited that class for a while. Didn't you do the suggested reading on the *Poetics*? Once you've read that, even though the translation is a bit foggy, your premise sinks under the weight of its own implausibility."

Unsuspecting debater: "I think I will read that if I get a chance."

Stephen: "Good. Then come back and maybe we can talk seriously about Plato. After all, he would want us to seek the Truth, don't you think?"

I didn't admire Stephen for his intellect alone; there were plenty of people around who blew me away with their smarts. I looked up to Stephen for his sense of honor and his loyalty as a friend.

He moved from Philadelphia to South Carolina when he was 13. Because of this, Stephen had a mixture of urban street smarts and Southern charm. Women found that combination irresistible.

Soon after moving to South Carolina, Stephen's father moved to Saudi Arabia to be on a construction project, leaving his wife to raise three sons and a daughter. Whereas I grew up in a house where no one ever wanted for anything for even an instant, the Anderer's were not so well off. Stephen had to work to put himself through college, help with his younger brother's tuition, and send some money home to his mother, who was not in good health. One summer, Stephen worked the 9 pm -5am shift at a loading dock, and then worked out for football during the day. I couldn't conceive of the work ethic he had and the hardships he endured, but I respected him immeasurably for those qualities.

His burdens increased countlessly when tragedy struck in the fall of our sophomore year when his father died suddenly of a heart attack. These awesome burdens must have matured Stephen awfully fast, for he handled each hardship like a man, and never complained about the yoke he had to carry. In fact, I didn't know of half of the hardships until years after we graduated. Stephen didn't want to burden anyone else with his affairs. He was tempered by the troubling realities which he faced. The way he dealt with them, and how that process matured him, was a lesson I would never forget. Stephen Anderer was the most impressive person I ever knew at Yale.

Another characteristic that set Stephen apart was that he did not like to be challenged or trifled with, and as a consequence he seldom was. He was toughened up by his older brother, who would knock Stephen to the ground, sit on his chest and punch Stephen in the face until he cried. And then he told Stephen that he would stop punching him when the crying stopped.

One day, on the football field during practice, he and another lineman got into a skirmish on the field. It was no big deal, and after a couple of minutes, they were separated and practice continued. Later, in the showers, Stephen went up to the other guy and said he was sorry about the fight. It was hot and he just lost his temper. They were both on the same team, Stephen reasoned, so it was certainly best that they just forget about the whole incident. Then Stephen put out his hand.

The other guy, who was about Stephen's size, just looked at Stephen's hand, letting it hang in the air for an awkward moment.

"If that's the way you want it," Stephen said, deadly serious, "that's fine with me. But I'm going to kick your ass every day until you shake it."

The other player grabbed Stephen's hand immediately, and the issue was settled.

There are many people who do not like to be insulted, and will fight to defend their honor. In this way, Stephen was not exceptional. However, Stephen took equal offense if one of his friends was confronted in a way he didn't think was right.

A few weeks into our freshman year, Stephen and I went to

the gym to lift weights. I was doing some bench presses, when a guy with a Yale Wrestling shirt came up to me and said, "Hey pal, why don't you get out of here and come back when you've got some meat on your bones."

I couldn't believe this guy was for real, so I assumed he was kidding around. "Speaking of meat," I said, jabbing him in the stomach, "you could probably stand to lose some yourself. I'd be glad to take some of your extra weight."

He didn't smile. And standing next to him, I noticed plainly that he was a big boy. He could probably throw me clear across the gym if he wanted to. "You want to take it outside?" He scowled.

What was this, a Western? I decided to play along. "Oh yeah?" I said making a fist. "I wouldn't if I were you, because when this lands, no one gets up."

"Let's see," he said, and he started pounding me in the face with my own fist, which I had stupidly kept clenched, even after he started wailing on me with it. This was getting kind of humiliating.

———————

All of a sudden he stopped, and he let go of my wrist. He was looking over my shoulder. There was Stephen, who was boring a hole in that other guy's forehead with his eyes.

"You don't need any help with this clown, do you Michael?" Stephen asked, not taking his stare off of the wrestler.

"I guess not," I said.

I didn't see that guy for a few weeks. When I finally did bump into him in the weight room again, Stephen wasn't there to protect me. Once again I was doing some bench presses. The guy came over to me, like he had last time.

"You need a spot?" he asked kindly.

"Sure," I said, safe in the knowledge that this guy would never dare lay a finger on me.

Stephen protected not only my physical well-being, but my interests as well. As crew became one of my passions, it became something that Stephen paid close attention to. In spite of his two-a-days in the fall, the season, and weight lifting, Stephen always kept abreast of how I was progressing in crew. He knew my erg scores, who I was competing against for seats, and what stroke ratings we had rowed for a particular practice. The minutiae became important to Stephen because it mattered to me.

Stephen was not going to sit idly by and tolerate Vogel stiffing me. He wanted to see to it that Vogel took notice of what I did or didn't have to offer to the program, and deal with me on present merits rather than past performance.

"How many mornings a week did you work out last year?" Stephen asked me, as he threw his Aristotle aside.

"Three."

"Well if you really want it, you're going to have to get in there even more this year. Five days a week, if you can. How badly do you want it, Michael?"

"Very."

"Then it's worth every effort you can make." Stephen got up slowly with a grunt. "I've got to go pick up the mail. Check you later."

"Hey, Stephen?"

"Yo."

"Thanks."

I doubt I'll ever come across a person like Stephen Anderer again. He taught me more by example about what it means, and how important it is, to be a friend.

———————

Junior year I went to the gym for extra work five days a week, starting in the fall. Twice a week in the weight room, and three sessions in the tanks. There was not a shred of doubt in my mind that I could make a top boat if I worked hard enough.

In the fall, most oarsmen don't take practice too seriously. Rowing at Derby is a time to recall the muscle memory required for a stroke. It is also a whole lot of fun, with choose-up races and kegs every Friday. Therefore, I didn't see many people in the gym when I arrived each morning at 7:45.

But there was one face that was a constant at morning workouts. It was Joe Marine's. Joe Marine was his real name, but if it wasn't, it would have been his nickname. He was stocky and strong, with deep set eyes, riveted in a gaze of grim determination. His jaw, square and carved as if from stone, issued forth the same message as his eyes: My effort will be so great that a place in the top boat will not be denied me.

Joe Marine had rowed in Rick's second boat the year before. With a boat full of returning Sprint winners in his class, and Dave's caste system to contend with, Joe's chances of making the JV or varsity seemed as distant as mine.

"Do you think you'll make a boat?" I asked Joe one morning.

"I am counting on it," he said, sticking a pin in the weight blocks of the Nautilus leg extension machine for yet another set.

I wanted to believe that Joe Marine was right. Because if he was going to make it by dint of hard work alone, then, for the same reason, I would too.

Joe Marine toiled longer and harder than anyone in the Yale crew program. As I was leaving the gym one evening after practice, I heard footsteps pounding the stairs. The stairwell was unlit, as the gym was about to close for the night. I waited to see who it was. No surprise, it was Joe, doing extra sets of stairs. The team had completed a grueling stair relay less than an hour earlier, but that hadn't been enough for Joe.

I waved to him as his foot touched the landing and he pivoted to return to the top of Payne Whitney. He nodded back. Joe couldn't wave, because he was cradling a 20 pound medicine ball in his arms.

Sometimes Vogel had us tested with an exercise called bench rows. We would lie face down on a bench that was about four feet off the ground. A 60 pound barbell dangled in our hands. The goal was to pull the weight up to the bench as many times as possible in three minutes. All scores were recorded and closely scrutinized by the team. Anything over 100 was really good; under 80 and people thought you were a wimp. I was in line after Joe. He got up and recorded his score: a 72. Surprisingly disappointing. As I positioned myself on the bench, Joe fiddled with the barbell. He was taking a ten-pound plate off of either side.

"Joe," I asked, "How come you pulled 80 instead of 60? Dave's going to think you suck."

"I don't care what Dave thinks about my score," Joe Marine explained. "He isn't going to pick boats based on bench pulls. This way I'll be that much stronger when it comes time to pull an oar in Florida."

What I liked about Joe was that he didn't make a big deal about all the extra work he did. Some guys, like Josh Chernoff, would saunter into the locker room and say, "Whoa, those stairs were a bitch. I practically had to drag myself up the last set."

"But Josh," someone would point out, "we didn't even have stairs today."

"We didn't?" Josh would say, with a look of counterfeit confusion. Translated, that meant, "Gee, I guess I'm just more gung ho than the rest of you." Everyone did some amount of extra work; it just wasn't cool to advertise it.

No one was surprised, least of all Josh, when Joe Marine took his seat in the JV boat for the racing season.

The official spring racing season was still many months off. What was around the corner were the Head Races—The Head of The Connecticut and The Head of The Charles. Both races, slightly more than three miles, were what we looked forward to most in the fall. The races were more a celebration of the sport than dire competition. Both races attracted hundreds of teams from all over the world. At The Head of The Charles, over 300,000 spectators lined the winding banks of the Charles River celebrating the spectacle as much as cheering for a particular boat. It was glorious and I wanted so badly to be a part of it.

As I had done the year before, I made my way over to the AYA and walked downstairs into Dave's office. I glanced at the pictures of his best teams, paid passing homage to the dozens of rowing shirts on the shelf, and then looked at Dave, who gave me a bemused smile as I walked in. Though he didn't recognize a shred of talent in me as a rower, I think he kind of liked the fact that I wasn't cowed by him and took his utter lack of encouragement as a personal challenge.

"What is it, Zig?" he asked with a wide smile and wider eyes.

"Well, Dave, the head races are coming up and I was really hoping that you might let me row in them." With Dave, it was always best to dispense with nuance, as he would surely do the same.

"No way you are rowing in the Charles," he stated flatly, dashing my hopes in an instant. "Not going to happen." At least he tore the Band-Aid off quickly. Hurt like hell, but over with. Then he added, "But if you are interested, I can get you into a boat at the Connecticut."

I was shocked, exhilarated, and vindicated at all at once. All the clichés about hard work paying off in the end were true after all. Though I was far from being in one of the top two boats, my mettle had proved my worth and I was part of the team. But then…

"I think I will have you and McManus row a pair." Dave Vogel said this with a grin that was truly mean. A pair is the most technically difficult boat of all. It is just two rowers, with one oar each, and no coxswain. The stroke (or the number two oar, depending on how you look at it) steers with a rudder attached to his toe plate.

World class rowers might practice in a pair to sharpen their already legendary skills because any error in set is magnified and sends the tiny vessel slamming this way and that. Even for Faust and Hard, rowing in a pair for the first time would be daunting. To throw the two shittiest guys on the team into one for the first time in a head race was almost creative in its cruelty. I had to hand it to Dave this time. He had given me just what I wanted, and managed to completely demoralize me at the same time.

Mac and I decided that we would call Dave's bluff and row in the race. Word of Yale's entry in the club division of the Head of The Connecticut spread throughout the Cooke Boathouse. Disbelief and laughter were followed with a grudging respect for Mac and me for essentially calling Dave's bluff and making him load and rig a pair for the race.

A week or so later, still having never rowed a pair, Mac and I prepared to launch our tippy craft into the Connecticut. Being a port, Mac stroked and would be responsible for steering the boat over the three-and-a-half mile course. We launched an hour before the race, because we had no idea how long it would take us to get up river to the start.

Like a brand new foal on her legs for the very first time, we wobbled, uncertain what to do, or how to do it. But unlike that foal, who was first trained by its mare and then gently but persistently by a trainer before it was considered for a race, here we were, heading to the gate and certain humiliation.

After discovering that we could keep the craft upright with our oars on the water and all of our muscles motionless, we decided to see how much rowing we could do before we lost all semblance of balance. The answer was, of course, almost none. The boat lurched from one side to another, and Mac and I laughed at the absurdity of it all.

Taking a full stroke was out of the question. With our oars out of the water and our seats moving forward at different speeds, we'd surely tip over, feet tied into the foot stretchers. The Connecticut River would not only turn out to be the spot of my first and only head race, but also of my watery grave. We decided to eliminate the slide altogether. Slower, yes. Safer, way!

In the end, the fact that we managed to finish the race was a miracle. We rowed just as I had rowed the first day in the water freshman year. Almost no pressure, and just using our arms and backs. We didn't dare attempt to slide up for a Catch because that virtually assured that someone would have to dive in after our capsized boat.

Not only were we DFL in our race, but we got passed by several boats in the next race that had started way after ours. We finally crossed the finish line, and a small group of spectators and other rowers cheered us with a combination of grudging respect and pity. I shared their sentiment, except without the grudging respect part. We were pitiful and we knew it. The only joy Mac and I got from our demonstration of rowing ineptitude was knowing that Dave had to live with our result as part of his record at the head race. He tried to enter us as the Housatonic Rowing Club, but couldn't get an entry in that name. So we were Yale Lightweights. His lightweights, and we finished last.

TWENTY-FIVE

As the first semester ended, I edged closer and closer to mathematical elimination from the number of A's it would take to earn me a summa, magna, or pedestrian cum laude. "Sine" would be the only Latin adjective before any "laude" associated with me. Getting B's, I found out, was pretty easy. Show up to most lectures, read at least half of what was required, get in a study group with someone who had read the other half, and rely on the writing skills I had learned at Collegiate. To get A's required going to almost all classes and doing everything that was assigned. I could have done that. The third requirement was what tripped me up. You have to really be interested in the subject matter. You have to be eager to learn more about it. It has to matter to you.

Quite frankly, most of my courses, which were in the history of art, didn't matter at all to me. Once I had come up with my stock comment about the joyous celebration of human endeavor, I cruised. The difference between Manet and Monet, though obvious, was lost on me. So too, what separated the Gothic from the Renaissance. I do remember writing in one essay that a particular artist seemed to have one foot in the Gothic, while saluting the Renaissance with the other. The comment in the margin was: "He must have been quite a contortionist!"

The problem was I never wanted to study the history of art, much less major in it. Of course, I was doing it to please my father. He always considered me an intellectual lightweight, and I figured if I studied what mattered to him, he might change his opinion. He didn't.

———

There were a couple of things I didn't realize. The first was that if I had chosen a course of study based on what excited me intellectually, then I might have wanted to delve into that area, demonstrating to my father that I did indeed have the capacity for critical thinking that was the foundation of scholarship.

The second piece I missed was that there was probably nothing I could do to meet my father's standard of intellectual curiosity and accomplishment, no matter the field. He thought I was a lightweight, and that was that. How disappointing and liberating having that knowledge would've been. I could have accepted that I couldn't please my old man, no matter what, and then have been free to explore what stirred me. As it was, I was stuck slogging though courses taught by the most learned minds in the field, and I didn't give a shit. Just give me my B and leave me alone.

By the time the long grey raw New Haven winter began

to give way to the spring, it was time to start thinking about Florida and whether I would be selected for the trip. In fact, I thought about Florida all the time. A good erg, and I'd think I was Tampa bound. A cross word from Dave as I did a weight circuit and my stomach tightened as thoughts of not making the trip loomed large. I was like a day trader. Up one minute, down the next. I saw each moment as another chance to make up for a previous loss or lose what had been recently gained.

It was so different for me. For most of the rest of the guys, Florida was a given. They dreaded it, because it was so damned hard, and that's where the tough decisions about who would make what boat were made. Of course, a few seats — Faust's, Hard's, Morley's, and Jigger's — were set, but the rest were kind of up for grabs. I yearned to be in a seat race that would determine whether I'd be in the 3v or JV. Two-a-days were my hope, my goal. I had been so crushed when I was left behind the year before, and I wasn't sure I could take the disappointment again. Unlike my studies, I was fully committed to crew. While there was virtue in effort, and that became more clear every time someone quit, or I improved just a bit, I still wanted to be fully part of the team, which meant making the trip to Tampa.

As I struggled with crew, faked my way through the academics, and loved every Saturday with Jaymie, I also grew to appreciate my roommates. Steve, of course, was a constant. Now a starting guard on the varsity football team, a philosopher, a student of history, and a dear friend. After nearly three years of rooming together we had shared many late night talks as I stared at the ceiling and he at the bottom of my mattress on the bunk bed, stories after parties, and cheering one another on at football or crew. It was all great and I felt as though I was getting to know an extraordinary man from many angles, and he knew me the way no one else did. This good man approved of me! I couldn't begin to describe, or maybe even fully realize, how much his approbation meant to me.

Another roommate my junior year was Alan Murchie. Alan, or Murch, was a slight man of just over five-and-a-half feet. He had gone to St. Paul's. Unlike me, Alan was a music major and was utterly devoted to his studies. He was a genius on keyboards; the piano, organ, and harpsichord were all second nature to him.

I loved watching Alan sit down at the piano in the Branford College common room, flip open the black lid that protected the keyboard, and start playing. It didn't matter what he played, it was all so beautiful; his passion poured out of his fingers. Suffused in joy to be playing, his face — his whole body — shimmered. Not only could Alan play anything by ear, but he could play almost subliminally. What I mean is that he could play a piece, and beneath the piece, almost inaudible, unless you were listening for it, would be another tune, woven beneath the first. He could play Mozart's *Eine Kleine Nachtmusik* with the Brady Bunch theme running underneath it. It was hilarious, amazing, and a tour de force.

To say I didn't know much about classical music was to exaggerate my acquaintance with the form. But I did know what it looked and sounded like when a talent like Alan sat at a piano and interpreted it. It was emotional, pulled at a part of me I didn't know I had, and had almost not wanted to have. I waited for the crescendo, only to be lured back to the original melody. The piece would soothe and surprise. Teased and took me with it. The pacing, now quick, here creeping along almost lazily before galloping off again. The piano, or pianoforte, as it was called, was well named with Alan at the keys. It was soft, cooing to me, and then loud and harsh. Alan's face, like Itzhak Perlman's when he pulled his bow across the strings of his violin, fully illustrated what he was feeling at the moment, and perhaps what the composer intended, so many years earlier.

How fucking lucky was I to live with a guy like Alan? How glad was I to realize just how fortunate I was!

About a week before Tampa, Dave called me aside after practice.

"Zig," he said with a smile. I didn't know if the smile meant good or bad news. His smile usually just meant he's sure of his decision and had nothing to do with whether it will make me happy or sad.

"Yeah, Dave?" I asked, as I pressed the giant safety pin through my socks, shorts and t-shirt, readying them for the Payne Whitney laundry service.

"I've decided to take you and a few other 4v types down to Florida. I'm not sure if you'll stay one or two weeks, but anyway I want you to come for part of it. You've earned at least that."

This was fabulous news! No matter that he referred to me as a "4v type" which meant I probably wouldn't even have a shot at the 3v, usually the lowest boat on the team. What mattered a lot, what meant everything, was that I was going. I was on the team and would be part of this bonding experience that I missed last year.

Knowing Dave wasn't one for small talk, I just thanked him and moved on. I don't think he saw me punch the air in exaltation as I left the tanks and turned the corner towards the stairs. I'd made it.

Tampa was glorious. Sure the predawn wake ups by the coxswains were brutal, and yes my hands turned to hamburger meat from the two-a-days and burned like hell when the salt water splashed into the open sores. And yeah it kind of sucked that Dave sent me and the other 4v types off on our own while he paid attention to those vying for seats in the first three boats. But I was where I had been aiming to be all year. The same was true for Rob Wiznovski, Peter Cooley, and Eric Brende. We'd all worked our asses off, and none of us were sure we'd be here, so we all appreciated it.

Dave had us rowing in a four, and told us what our workout would be before each session. Rob Wilen, our cox, was also the coach for our boat. He timed the pieces, critiqued us, and every now and then would get us near a boat from another college that shared the water with us, and we'd "race" them. They wouldn't know we were racing, but it felt like the sprints to us. Up a seat off the start fellas.....power 10....settle down......early at the catch Eric...they are making a move...stay cool..... now it's our turn...gimme ten.....that's it....I've got their bow ball and we just crossed the finish line!"

We'd collapse over our oars, chests heaving, patting the guy in front of us on the back. We'd done it.

True to his word, Dave told us to beat it after a week. Something about the second week not being in the budget, which sounded like bullshit to me, because the team slept in a barracks room, not hotel rooms, and our boats were already down there. Whatever. I think he just wanted us out of there so he could concentrate on the V and JV without having to worry about us. We all got it, headed to the airport and went back north.

But rather than take the second week off, we all agreed to go back to Yale, meet at the Boathouse each afternoon, and practice. A few calls and Darius Teeter, Jim McManus, Kendall Willets, and Pete Calabrese, all of whom had quit earlier in the year, joined our boat and met each afternoon for practice. Coit Lyle, a coxswain from the 1970s whose main job, I heard, was being the alumni presence at Skull and Bones so that the new groups could learn the traditions (did he have to show them how to jerk off in a coffin, if that's what they did?), signed on to be our coach.

We commandeered a decent boat, and Coit put us in the seats he thought would work out best. Pete stroked, and I was in the four seat, part of the engine room, a step up from the three seat, Ben Norris' "black hole" of rowing.

For six days we worked on our starts, did long pieces to lengthen our strokes and get the boat to run out from under us on recovery, and cranked out two minute pieces to work on sprinting for the finish.

"You're a team," Coit announced after our last practice. "I don't know if we are going to get you any races, but you are indeed a team."

We were proud of it and one another.

To recognize our team and the special, if separate, status we had from the rest of the lightweight rowers, we decided to get our own special shirts. If the Varsity and JV had sashes, we'd have our own cool shirts. Brende came up with the design, and they were awesome. Blue shirts with a white Henley tab going down from the center of the white trim. A "Y" on the left breast, just like on all the other boats' shirts. But here's where our shirts got super cool: We had a 4 and a V on either side of the Y, and golden oars crossed through the Y.

When the shirts came back from the embroiderer, they looked fantastic. We wore them out to the first practice on the

Housatonic once everyone else returned. The nine of us strutted into the boathouse. Dave smiled in begrudging respect, and Hard asked me how he could get a shirt like that.

"Simple," I explained, "have what it takes to make the fourth varsity lightweight crew at Yale. Very few do."

"Zig," he said, "you're right. You guys look great in those shirts and I bet you don't lose one of them."

There wasn't much chance of us losing our shirts for the first several weeks of the season. This wasn't because we scheduled weak crews in the beginning of the season, like some big-time college football teams do before facing conference foes. No, we were going to keep our nifty new shirts, because there were no other 4v's to race and Dave didn't bother scheduling Coast Guard and Trinity like he had the year before. We raced with the 3v, finishing third each time, but sometimes within hailing distance of second place.

Our season would come down to one Saturday afternoon on the Charles River. Harvard had a 4v four, and we heard that they would cobble together an eight made up of their four and some freshman heavies too shitty to make the first or second boat.

We practiced hard each day. Coit drove us hard, but had a totally different manner than Dave. He was gentle, praised us, told us what we could do to be better rather than what we did that wasn't good enough, and kept us focused on Harvard.

Meanwhile, our varsity boat was awesome. With Faust stroking, Hard, Morley and Jigger in the engine room, and Chip, the sophomore from Iowa, the boat was just faster than any other boat. They rowed away from fabulous crews off the start and only lengthened their lead from there. I was awed and proud to watch these guys — my teammates — literally leave every other boat in their wake. They were stronger than anyone else, rowed together as no other boat did, and I couldn't imagine any nine men working harder towards a common goal.

When they won, and they won every time, did they return to the dock with the giddy excitement of someone who had done something new and exciting or unexpected? No. They were certain that if they rowed their best, that they would win. But that didn't diminish from their joy and satisfaction. In most races, they competed against themselves, their own expectations. And they were so damned good that they were able to clear the ridiculously high bar they set for themselves each Saturday that spring.

While the fourth boat prepped for our duel with Harvard, the spring of junior year was also "tap season" for secret societies. This meant a great deal to some of my classmates, not much to many more, and held a distant and vague interest for me.

TWENTY-SIX

S ecret Societies. What are they? Before my freshman year, a friend of mine told me of a club at Yale called Skull and Bones that was so secretive that no one was supposed to know who the members were, or what they did when they were in the club. All my friend told me was that if you were tapped for Skull and Bones, you were guaranteed a job for life, $25,000 upon acceptance to the club, and entrée into the world of power and privilege. They had their own island in upstate New York, I'd been told, and even had a swimming pool in their clubhouse on campus. My interest was piqued, but only for the length of the conversation. Skull and Bones held about as much of my interest as Neptune or Jupiter. I'd never go to either and would likely not know anyone who had been; there wasn't a whole lot to care about.

Skull and Bones, the oldest and most secretive and prestigious of the dozen or so senior societies at Yale, was founded in 1832 by a group of students who didn't think Phi Beta Kappa was selective enough, and wanted to convene a group of the senior classes' most talented and distinguished men to meet privately twice a week. So was born Skull and Bones. The list of those who were in Skull and Bones was impressive: Taft, the Bushes, Payne Whitney himself, Henry Luce, to name a few. Most football captains, publishers of the Yale Daily News, and other class luminaries would be tapped by Bones, as it was known. How you got tapped or what happened when you were in there was a mystery, which, of course, made it all the more alluring.

Every now and then, I'd see someone approach the sandstone, windowless building on High Street that was Skull and Bones and wonder, for a moment, who that was and what he was up to. Or if I was coming out of Naples Pizzeria on Wall Street, and I crossed over College Street, a couple of guys approaching the gates of the windowless marble home of Scroll and Key, another prestigious society, might capture my curiosity for a moment. But the moments were fleeting, and of no consequence. As I was neither the star of a sport, editor of the paper, or a leading scholar in the class, I would have to find another way to pass time on Thursday and Sunday evenings next year. I sure wouldn't be spending them in a spooky building with the elite of my class. Did I want to get tapped? Sure. But I also wanted to date Joannie Dea, Mandy Silver, and Chris Wolfe, but that wasn't going to happen either, so why waste time obsessing over it?

Actually, I wasted plenty of time wondering what it would be like to be with these women, but I didn't worry so much about my chances at a secret society. I guess some things that you can't control were worth worrying about and others weren't. Women were; Bones wasn't.

In the early-to-mid 20th Century, Tap Day was a very big deal. Juniors sat on the fences that lined the Old Campus waiting to be tapped. It was a public spectacle, covered on the front page of The New York Times, and those tapped were feted as they took their place amongst the sons of Eli who mattered most. As we neared the end of the new millenium, the primacy of the societies had lessened, but there was still some feeling that the few guys in Bones and Keys were special somehow, and they would share a bond with one another forever.

By April, talk of Tap Day sprang up during meals. Who, exactly, were the members of the societies, and what was the selection process? I wasn't sure who was in which society, but I had heard rumors. I hadn't been taken out to lunch by a group of seniors for an "interview," if that was how they did it, so my limited attention span had to find something else to focus on for a moment or two.

———————•

Late on a Wednesday night, our phone rang. It was Adam, a senior who lived downstairs from us.

"Hey Zig," he said cheerfully, "I've got some boxes I need to move, and I was wondering if you could help me."

"No problem. But Steve's here and he's like 90 times stronger than I am. Want him to help you? It'll get done faster."

"Nope," Adam said, "why don't you meet me outside the entryway in five minutes." And he hung up.

"Adam is in Bones. I think you're about to be tapped," Steve said. "Get going."

I just couldn't believe it. I was about to be tapped for Skull and Bones?!? I didn't bother to wonder why. I was thrilled! It was something I had never imagined, never aimed for, but I guess on some level had always wanted. I sure wanted it now.

I sped down the stairs as casually as I could, and met Adam (box-less) at the appointed spot. I reached out to shake his hand, smiling as broadly as I ever had. Adam was stone-faced. "Follow me and speak to no one," he intoned. And then he took off running down the sidewalk.

He wasn't sprinting, so I kept up, all the while wondering where we were going, and what would happen when we got there. Left on Elm, past Educated Burgher, and then past the Co-op. We were heading towards Paine Whitney. I had made the trip from Branford to Paine Whitney over a hundred times, but never like this.

When we arrived at the rear of the gym, Adam stopped and knocked on a door I didn't even know existed. The door swung open and I followed Adam through the bowels of the gym in pitch-black darkness. He held a candle to light the way. It was dark, silent and very eerie. But I was about to be tapped by Skull and Bones. How cool was that!

Finally, we arrived at the entrance to the tanks. The doors swung open, and Adam left my side to join the 14 others who stood around the tank, holding candles, with hoods over their heads. If I had ever imagined what it might be liked to be asked to join Bones, this was it.

A hooded figured stepped forward and informed me I had been selected by "the society known to the world as Skull and Bones." I was told to meet them at a certain place in a week with my decision. The man then said, "Speak to no one." He put a piece of rolled up paper in my hand. They all blew out their candles, and I was firmly pushed out of the room.

When I got back onto the street, I looked at the scroll in my hand and saw it had a black wax seal on it. The mark was in the shape of a skull and crossbones, proof of the surreal experience.

I looked around. It was well after midnight, and the streets were empty, save a few people coming back from Rudy's or heading to Park Street for a sub. What had just happened to me? What did it mean? I wasn't sure at all. But I did know one thing: I was exhilarated. Happier and prouder then I had ever been in my life. Through some unknown process that had gone on for over 150 years at Yale, I had been chosen as one of only 15 men to have a very special experience. I literally couldn't believe what had just happened. But as surely as I couldn't grasp it, there was a piece of paper in my hand to prove that it had.

I got back to my room and Steve got up from the couch. "Well?" he asked.

"Yup." I nodded.

Just then, the phone rang. It was Mike Hard.

"Zig, do you have the notes for the ancient Greek class? I blew off the last couple of classes and I need the credit to graduate." Hang on a sec. This was Mike Hard. The Mike Hard. The god. The Mike Hard as in Morley and Hard. And he was calling me.

It was too much. I had heard that he was in Scroll and Key, a society second to Bones in age and prestige. I really didn't care what society he represented; Mike Hard wanted me!

"Sure do," I said, playing along and only sort of hiding my excitement. "How can I get them to you?"

Hard told me to meet him outside the dorm in the same spot Adam had met me less than an hour ago.

When I got there, Mike shook my hand, smiled warmly and said, "Zig, this may sound weird, but follow me and speak to no one."

He walked briskly and I followed. Right on Elm, left on College and up the stairs of Woolsey Hall, a concert hall I passed countless times but had never considered entering. Now I couldn't wait to get in.

Mike joined 14 other guys, all dressed in coat and tie, in a semi-circle on the stage. One of the guys was Morley. Andrew Morley. The god. As in Morley and Hard. Steve Gavin had been in Keys. Morley and Hard were in Keys. And they wanted me!

One of the guys stepped forward and told me that I would be asked to join "the society known to the world as Scroll and Key." Then, each of them shook my hand and introduced himself. Finally, Mike walked me out and we started to talk as he walked across Cross Campus.

"Congratulations, Zig," he said. Hard has the nicest, most sincere smile. "This must be a bit of a surprise."

"I don't know what to say," I stammered. "This is all such a surprise. And believe it or not, I went through the same thing with Skull and Bones just before you called."

Mike stopped and looked at me. "You just got tapped by Bones?" He seemed speechless for a moment. Then he put his hand on my shoulder. "You know something, Zig, that doesn't surprise me a bit. You are something else. Of course Bones would want you, and Scroll and Key would be lucky to get you. Enjoy the moment. And if you want to talk about your decision, give me a call or we can talk at the boathouse."

I was the only one in my class who went to both the tanks and Woolsey Hall that night. I had been tapped by both Skull and Bones and Scroll and Key. Paul Mellon was the first person at Yale to be in my position and I don't know how he felt (he probably expected it) but I was completely overwhelmed and very happy. Perhaps I was Gavinish after all.

Over the next week, I met with captains of teams, editors of papers, top scholars in the class above me, each of whom was trying to convince me, a shitty rower, with fewer vowels on my transcript than the word vowel itself, a member of no clubs, practically an imposter, to join either Skull and Bones or Scroll and Key.

Coit Lyle pulled me aside at the boathouse before the 4v launched and told me that he knew I'd make the right decision.

In the end, I chose Scroll and Key. I knew a few of the other guys who had been tapped by Bones and figured I would still be friends with the ones I liked no matter my decision. There was one guy I thought was a complete douchebag, and spending a year sharing my deepest secrets (or whatever it was they did in there) with him wasn't too appealing. Most of all, I joined Keys because Mike Hard asked me to. Not only did I idolize him as a rower, but I admired and respected him off the water. He was kind, smart, and sincere. How could I say no to him? I couldn't and I didn't.

A week after that surprising Wednesday evening, 14 other guys from the junior class and I entered the windowless building on the corner of Wall and College Streets. We were Keysmen now, and had no idea what the next year held for us. but we were excited to find out.

———————

On April 20, 1985, the Yale Lightweight fourth varsity four was lowered into the Charles River at the Weld Boathouse. Moments earlier, Coit Lyle addressed us. He told us how prepared we were and how proud he was of us. In his soft Southern drawl he said, "Gentlemen, you are as prepared for this race as any crew I have been associated with in nearly two decades. This fourth varsity has brought honor to the tradition of Yale rowing, because you have given more than has been asked of you, have persevered where many others would not have, and I am quite certain you will acquit yourselves on the water. Now go out there and do what you have prepared to do." He never raised his voice, and he looked at each one of us as he spoke.

For the first time in my life I had given everything I had. If we didn't win, I couldn't use the familiar crutch of lack of effort; rather, I would have to face the fact that we weren't good enough, that all that work didn't make up for a relative lack of talent. What I didn't realize until that moment is that lack of talent is fine; it's lack of will and effort that is a shame. This is starting to sound soft, like a little league there-are-no-losers-if-you-try-your-best attitude. Make no mistake. I, and the other four men in that boat, wanted, with all our hearts, to beat Harvard. And if we did row back to the boathouse without our 4v rowing shirts with the golden oars, we'd be heartbroken, and the disappointment wouldn't go away just because we knew we had left it all on the water.

After our warm-up, we paddled to the starting line. Rob Wilen had Cooley take a couple of small strokes to get us straightened out. The four of us buried our blades in the water, our seats half way up the slide, as we listened for the starters words. "Êtes-vous prête? Partez!"

And we were off! Half slide, half slide, three quarters slide, full. Cooley took the cadence up to 42 strokes a minute and Rob called a ten to get us to focus on the start. Six strokes into the race, he said, "I've got their stroke!" which meant we'd gained a seat right off the bat. Since we'd never raced another 4v, we had no idea how good we were. As we'd rowed in a vacuum, there was a fear we'd get blown away. Now at least we knew that wasn't going to happen.

Everything was in the boat. We trusted one another utterly. No sneaking a peak to see where the other boat was. Rob handled everything as well as any coxswain could. Encouraging us, letting us know where we were without distracting us. My legs burned with lactic acid, my lungs ached as they struggled for enough oxygen to fuel my effort. I'd felt this way before. On every erg in fact, and in every race. And in most pieces in practice. But this was a different burn, a different ache. It was the ache of a man fully prepared for the moment, and the pain urged me on, rather than made me wonder how much longer I could take it.

We led by half a length at the 500-meter mark of the 2,000-meter race. As we approached the Mass Ave bridge, we took a power ten. Our boats were on opposite sides of the bridge pillars, and when we emerged, we had open water with 500 meters to go. There was no letting up, no lack of focus, no premature celebration. We had come to race our best 2,000 meters and Rob made sure we stayed on it until we crossed the finish line.

As we crested the buoy marking the end of the race, Rob told us to paddle and then weigh enough. We'd won!

We'd beaten Harvard at crew. Harvard and Yale had been rowing against one another since 1852, 23 years before the two football teams squared off on the gridiron. It was the longest intercollegiate rivalry, and I was now on the winning side of it.

There was no splashing of water, hollering, or any of that. None of us really thought about what would happen if we won. We prepared diligently, rowed well, executed our race plan and here we were. I patted Eric on the shoulder and between breaths told him what a good row it had been. This was the feeling I had been waiting for without even knowing it: the deep satisfaction of a job well done.

The Harvard four paddled up next to our boat and we grabbed their blades and pulled their shell towards ours. "Nice race," they told us. They were as tired as we were, and for all I knew they had worked as hard. They were in the fourth boat, too. The bottom of the Harvard program. But I admired them. I am sure they all had stories as well.

Discouraged and wanting to quit, but not quitting. In many ways, the five men in our boat were the only five people who knew how they felt, and vice versa.

Then the guys in the Harvard boat peeled their sweat-soaked fourth varsity rowing shirts off and handed them to us. I accepted mine gratefully and shook the hand of the man in their three seat. Then our boats pushed away from one another and we paddled back to the boathouse, our Harvard shirts in our laps, and our shirts still on our backs.

Coit greeted us with a big smile as we got back to the dock. "You did it! You rowed your best piece of the year when it mattered most and you beat Harvard! Well done, gentlemen."

When the boat was out of the water, we shook each other's hands and smiled broadly. I saw Coit standing off to the side, and I went up to him. "Coit," I said. "We never could have done this without you. You cared when no one else did. What's more, you're a great coach. You got us rowing together, helped with technique, and somehow knew what buttons to push with each of us. Great job." I reached out to shake his hand and he took it in his. In my left hand was the Harvard shirt I'd just won.

"This is for you, Coit," I said, handing it to him. "You earned it and deserve it."

Coit took the shirt and smiled. "Thank you, Zig," he said simply.

——————

45 minutes later, the fourth varsity four, plus Mac, Calabrese, Teeter, and Kendall became the fourth varsity eight. We put our boat in the water and got ready to race a smorgasbord of crappy Harvard oarsmen. Some lightweights, some heavies, and some freshman.

The race was over almost as soon as it began. We blew their boat off the start, and by the time we had settled to our 36 stroke a minute cadence, we were half a boat length ahead. The wind picked up and our boat — our crew — handled the conditions better than the other group who hadn't trained together for this moment. As Rob called our final strokes, there was open water between our boats.

We'd beaten Harvard twice in a day, and I rowed back to the boathouse with another shirt in my lap. This one I'd keep. Coit came up to me later on.

"Zig, I'm not sure I have a rowing shirt that means as much to me as the one you gave me today. Thank you, my friend."

"Coit," I said, with the assuredness of a man who'd done what very few Yale oarsmen had ever done, "I won two, and still got to keep one."

"True," he replied. "But you didn't give me your shirt after you'd won two. You gave me what could just as easily been the only Harvard rowing shirt you'd ever win. There's a difference."

"You gave me more," I said.

"Not even close," he said.

"Let's call it even," I offered, and I gave him a hug.

On that Saturday, there was nothing separating the 4v from any Varsity crew that had ever rowed at Yale, aside from the speed of our boats, which didn't seem to be the point after all. Sacrifice, determination, singular focus, and really hard work. All clichés until they aren't. I went to sleep that night knowing I was an oarsman and had been all along.

TWENTY-SEVEN

The summer between junior and senior years I taught at Hotchkiss summer school and decided I wanted to become a teacher. Actually, I had wanted to be a teacher since I was a third grader at Collegiate School. My teachers were my heroes and I never wanted to be a firefighter, astronaut, or even a major league baseball player. Thanks to the likes of Mildred Keithline, Martha Eckfelt, and Joe D'Angelo, teaching loomed so much larger than the careers that most kids dream of having.

I didn't miss a day of school from October of 1973 until I graduated in June of 1981. And it wasn't because I never got sick. Whereas some kids pretended to be sick to stay home from school, I often pretended I was healthy just so I could be at school. It was sanctuary from a home in which I didn't always feel safe. And it was a place where I dared to take what seemed to be huge risks, often failing, but certain that my teachers would be there to help me up, comfort me, and urge me to try again. God, I wanted to be a teacher.

My summer at Hotchkiss didn't so much confirm that I wanted to teach as it showed me how much I loved being in the classroom (which was different from being a teacher; that title only comes with years of experience). I truly enjoyed the daily challenges of making a scene in literature come to life and have meaning; getting a student to go from describing almost what he meant to exactly what he meant; and all the moments out of the classroom that helped me connect with students and nudge them towards the point where they could think for themselves, express themselves, and leave each class looking forward to the next one as I sure did.

———————

I learned something else that summer, and the second thing I learned would make the first thing possible. I learned that I was rich. Or at least that my family had a big fortune and that wealth would be part of my life. Just before I turned 21, my father asked me to meet with him. I replayed the last few days of my life, at least what he could possibly know about my activities over that time, and was relieved to discover no malfeasance. So I walked into the den knowing I wasn't going to get ripped.

Dad looked up and smiled when I walked into the room.

"Well?" I asked him.

"You're rich." he said.

"What?" I asked.

"You're loaded. Or will be."

"Back up," I said. "Start over. What'd I win?"

"You didn't win anything?" my dad explained. "Didn't do

a thing, except choose the right grandparents." He smiled again

This seemed to be a big topic, and I was getting codes and jokes I didn't get.

"Look," he explained, now knowing that I really didn't know what he was driving at. "You know Block Drug Company, the company Pops works at?"

"Sure," I said. "I worked there after freshman year."

Early in the 20th Century, my great grandfather Alexander Block, a recent immigrant, opened a drug store in Brooklyn. A few years later, he decided he could make more money if he supplied the drug stores, so he went into manufacturing. Eventually, the company developed its own products, mostly in the dental category, and by the time I went to work there for a summer, it did nearly a billion dollars a year in sales and had operations around the world. When I asked my grandfather how many people worked at Block Drug, he said, raising one eyebrow, which was his signature move, "About half of them."

My grandfather, though a stern disciplinarian, was also a very funny man, though he had such an effective deadpan delivery that he would have to say, "that was funny" after cracking one of his doozies. I think the funniest thing my grandfather ever did was name my mother. She was due to be born at the end of March, and had she been born on Easter Sunday, he was determined to name her Bunny. If, on the other hand, she was born on St. Patrick's Day, well then they would call her Patty. But she wasn't born on either of those days. She was born on the day one of my grandfather's relatives had his leg amputated. So he named his daughter Peggy. Not Margaret. Peggy.

My summer at Block Drug was kind of a joke. I had little interest in figuring out new ways to sell denture cleansers. But everyone treated me very well. I was, after all, Leonard Block's grandson. After eight weeks I heard, "where would we be without you, Mike....I wish I'd thought of that...you have a feel for marketing, just like your grand dad...."

When I returned to Yale, where I didn't receive quite the flattery, at least folks were honest with me.

Dad continued, "Well, the company is very valuable, and the Block family, which includes Mom and eventually you, owns a bunch of it."

"I thought Pops was rich because he made a lot of money every year running the company," I said.

"He is," dad explained. "Actually, that isn't wealth; it's income. And a lot of income. The real wealth is in the value of the company. So Pops might make a few hundred thousand dollars a year, which funds his lifestyle, but what makes him—us — wealthy is the value of the company."

"How do you know how much a company is worth?"

"It's hard to tell if it's a private company, but if it's a public company, like Block Drug is, you multiply the number of outstanding shares by the price of each share."

"What's it worth?" I asked.

"Today, nearly a billion dollars."

"We're billionaires? Yipee!"

"Nope, we aren't," Dad said. "Other people and institutions own stock. But the family owns most of the company. And you, now that you're turning 21 years old, get a small sliver of that. As you get older, Pops has planned for you and Katie and the other grandkids to get more."

"I see," I said. "This doesn't change anything, does it?"

"It does and it doesn't. It doesn't because you have always lived with wealth, whether you realized it or not, and you will continue to. It does because now you know. By the way, I've set up trusts, for tax reasons, and the money will be held in accounts for you until you reach certain ages, at which time it will be distributed to you. That way you don't piss it all away."

What Dad did there was clever. By telling me that he had set up the trusts, and the timing of the distributions, and since he was the one telling me how wealthy the family was, it made it seem like he had created the wealth, and I should be grateful to him for the thoughtful way he had devised to get me funds as I got older. The truth was that it was my mother's father who had built the business. My father, in fact, had a small fraction of the money that his wife had, but had somehow assumed control of the future of her family's fortune, at least as it related to me.

The dynamic of a man, especially one with a fragile ego, marrying a wealthy woman, must be a tricky one. After all, my mom wore the financial pants in the family, and though my father enjoyed the benefits that came from the wallet she pulled from the back pocket of those pants, they weren't his pants, and this had to pain him. With me, at least, he could be in control and I would be the grateful recipient — which I was.

"Where do I sign," I said, rubbing my hands together in mock greed. "Gimme gimme."

"I'll get you the documents soon. Get out of here," dad said, motioning to his door.

My immediate reaction as I left the room, was, "Wow! That's a shit load of money." I had as much to do with earning it as I did my height. I inherited both. So I could neither take credit nor apologize for either. But to deny the existence would be foolish. It seemed pretty abstract but kind of cool at the same time. Sort of a shocker.

It turns out that not only couldn't I really tell which of my classmates was wealthy and which weren't, I didn't even know that about myself. I guess I should have figured out that my family was rich, but I didn't focus on it. The evidence abounded, had I cared to think about it. A duplex on Fifth Avenue designed by an architect discussed in a course I took sophomore year, a country house, trips to Europe, Africa, Egypt. The walls of our apartment had art by Rothko, Lichtenstein, Oldenburg, and Dubuffet. The trappings of wealth were everywhere, yet to me they went as noticed as the purloined letter. Did I not think these things, this lifestyle, cost money? I truly didn't think of it, which could either be chalked up to a troublesome sense of entitlement, a blasé attitude of those who work for nothing, or it could be a sign of a wonderful naiveté born from the fact that I didn't notice these things because they really didn't matter to me. Perhaps it was typical puerile self-centeredness. I hardly cared or took much notice of what my parents had. What mattered most to me were the things that directly affected me, and my life seemed roughly the same as that of my friends. It was a mix of these three, and maybe some other factors, that shielded me from the fact that the Blocks, and therefore the Danzigers, were very very wealthy indeed.

I came to the realization that unless people stopped brushing their teeth, cleaning their toilets, and shampooing their hair, money would not be a worry for me and that I'd likely be a very rich man someday. I wondered if my wealth would be an identifying characteristic. What is the purpose of wealth? Would I be a good steward of whatever I was lucky (and I knew it was luck, not skill) enough to get (not earn)? Would people identify me by my wealth? If so, how would that change how they treated me? I remembered the words of the song "If I Were a Rich Man" from *Fiddler on the Roof*, "And it won't make one bit of difference if I answer right or wrong. When you're rich, they think you really know!" Or would my whole life be like the pleasantly bullshit existence I had that summer at Block Drug, where everyone kissed my ass, and then, I am certain, turned around and either talked, or thought, about what a spoiled punk I really was. The truth is, I wasn't as great as they told me, nor as awful as what they told one another. Money is a lens that distorts both ways.

Ultimately, I decided that these issues, while they might loom large someday, would play no role in my life for at least the next few years. What I also began to have was a deeper appreciation for crew. Crew was a meritocracy.

Ergs didn't care whether you were rich or poor, the distance from the bottom of the Payne Whitney staircase to the top was the same for everyone, and the timer ran at the same pace, regardless. Coaches only cared who made boats move fast, not how rich their grandparents were. In short, with crew, I knew where I stood, and I liked it, come what may.

TWENTY-EIGHT

Our suite senior year was glorious. It had been an apartment for the Dean years ago and was the most coveted housing in Branford College. The living room was huge, big enough for the giant waterbed we put in the middle of it, and a fireplace, which we were forbidden to use. I suggested we could just puncture the waterbed if any of our fires got out of control, but none of the roomies thought this was such a swell idea.

In fact, our apartment was right over the Dean's office. The Dean had said of our waterbed, "The first one you are ok, but the second drop that hits my desk, you will all be expelled."

There were two bathrooms for the four of us, and even a kitchen, which we never used. Alan and Lincoln had single rooms, and Stephen and I shared a room with bunk beds. It was quite a set up and I couldn't imagine a better way to spend my final year at Yale.

I was finally beginning to grow into my body. When I stepped on the scale in Payne Whitney, the needle zoomed past the 150 and 160 marks and settled a shade over 170 lbs. There was no way I could lose 15 pounds. I was filling out and would only be getting heavier. I had to break the news to Vogel that he would have to make do without me. Somehow, I didn't think he'd care.

I popped over to York Street to the Association of Yale Alumni offices to let Dave know he'd have to find a way to survive without me. This wasn't like my other visits with Dave, where I was going to find out if I was going to Florida or rowing in a Head race. This time, I'd be delivering the news.

His door was open and I peeked in to see him sitting at the desk, jotting something down. He looked up and smiled. "Hey, Zig." Even though I was a shitty rower and life would have been easier for him if I had just quit in the middle of sophomore year like any normal person would've done, Dave liked me and I knew it. He liked me because he knew I loved crew and worked really hard to be as bad as I was. He had no respect for my talent and I was no use for any of his top boats, but I think he did have respect for my approach to the sport. In the same way, while I kind of hated him for never really giving me a chance, and treating me and the other lousy rowers like third—-in our case, fourth—class citizens, I totally respected his commitment to the sport and his ability to put together fast boats that won in the spring.

He was, quite simply, great at what he did.

"Hey Dave," I said. "I won't be in the last lightweight boat this year."

"Oh no?" he asked. "You work out over the summer? Going to crack the 3v at last?" He grinned. Making the 3v was never anyone's goal. Most felt relegated to the 3v; for me it would be an accomplishment.

"I did work out this summer. But I also gained some weight which I don't feel like losing just to have a shot at the 3v. I'm 170 now and think I should row with the heavies this year."

"Well Zig," Dave said, leaning back in his chair and lacing his hands behind his head. "You can do what you want, and we are going to miss you this year. But let me tell you this: you are going to have a really hard time as a heavy. They are all bigger and stronger than you, and you don't have a lot of skill to fall back on, as you've proved the last few years. I don't think you have a prayer of making a boat there, but I am sure you'll try."

"You might be right, Dave," I said, "But I am going to give it a try. They graduated a bunch of guys last year, our class is pretty thin, and who knows, maybe the sophomores really suck."

Dave shrugged. "Whatever. We'll miss you but it'll be good seeing you in the tanks and on the river." He picked up his pencil and returned to his notes, a sign the meeting was over.

Dave's counterpart on the Heavyweights was Tony Johnson. Like Dave, Tony had been with Yale Rowing for years and had had real success, especially in recent years when he had superb crews. But his demeanor was the opposite of Dave's. Where Dave was bombastic, Tony was calm, avuncular.

Along with being tapped for Skull and Bones and Scroll and Key, which were very private honors, I was selected to represent Yale in the most public way. Jim Azzizi, a guy a year ahead of me, asked me to be Handsome Dan the Bulldog, Yale's mascot. Unbeknownst to me, Jim, an earnest mechanical engineering major, had worn the blue bulldog suit during the 1983 football season, and as Bulldog, he got to choose his successor. He knew I had roomed with guys on the team, had been to most of the games, home and away, and wasn't afraid of attention.

I accepted immediately, and just before leaving for summer break after junior year, he handed over the blue furry body with a little tail and four buttons up the back, two matching gloves with four fingers each, and giant blue head, made out of papier-mâché and covered with blue fur, except for around the left eye, which was white. The outfit also came with a varsity letter sweater. Even though it wasn't really my letter sweater, it felt great to pull it on.

Maybe one day I'd have my own. Until then, this was mighty nice. I was about to become the symbol, the dogification of Yale University, and I took the role very seriously.

I decided that Handsome Dan needed to be more of a presence, more of an Ambassador than he had been in the past, when he just roamed the sidelines, ran on the field with the band at halftime, and maybe ventured into the stands a time or two to work the crowd. I decided to take the dog on the town. I would visit Yale New Haven Hospital and amble into the pediatric ward. I'd walk the hallways, and stop to cheer a sick child in a wheelchair, or pat the head of a little boy or girl in the waiting room. Problem was, a 6'5" bulldog terrified most kids, and often they would cry. I'd get upset, take my head off and say, "Don't worry, it's not really a giant dog, it's just me." This would further confuse the ailing child, and eventually I was asked by the hospital staff to stop coming by.

Of course, one child who loved the fact that I was Handsome Dan was Jaymie. I picked him up at his home on Dixwell Avenue one Saturday before the season started. I was driving my VW Rabbit and wearing my mascot suit. He thought it was a riot, and when I let him wear the hat, well that was just the best! The sight of a tiny child with a huge blue bulldog head wobbling on his shoulders as he waved and blew kisses to the imaginary adoring throngs was too much. Jaymie even came up with a new and very clever name for me: Michael Hand-some Danziger. I loved it and so did he.

Aside from clowning around with Jaymie, most of my bulldog work was done on the gridiron, as I had been banned from the hospital. Problem was, I wasn't the only bulldog on the sidelines. There was the real bulldog, Handsome Dan VII, who was in his rookie season, too. It seems Handsome Dan VI had gone paws up the summer before, and they were breaking in a new English bulldog.

This bulldog didn't cotton to his gigantic blue counter-part. In fact, every time we got near one another, he growled, strained at his leash, and lunged at me. I had never been around dogs before, and was scared shitless of Handsome Dan. I want-ed nothing to do with him. So we reached an unspoken agree-ment. We would stay on our own sides of the sideline. He would run on the field with his handler before the game, and I'd have halftime. The agreement was amicable, like a good divorce. No overt hostility, but those looking could see a chill between us.

We kept it together for the fans.

It all fell apart and went horribly wrong at the Princeton game, which was the final home game of the year. The Thursday before the game, I got a message to call the Sports Information Director about some special plans for the game.

"Michael," he said and then added with a chuckle "Or

should I call you Handsome Dan?"

"Either is good," I said.

"Well, we've got something cooking for halftime at the Princeton game and you are going to play a part."

"Sounds great, what is it?"

"Well, as you know, this is Handsome Dan VII's inaugural season and I thought we'd do something special, a little different. At halftime, after the Band does its thing, I've arranged to have Handsome Dan, his handler, you, and the President of the Westminster Kennel Club meet at midfield for an official anointing ceremony. Handsome Dan will formally become the school mascot."

I hated the idea. "It'll never work." I stated flatly.

"Why?" he said. "It's perfect."

"Perfect except that dog hates my guts and I hate him right back. We don't get along and it could get ugly."

"C'mon, Michael," he said. "Believe me, it'll be fine,"

"Believe me, it won't," I countered. "Trust me, it'll blow up in your face, big time."

Then he began to play hardball. "Look, it's all set. If you don't want to do it, we'll find someone else to wear the damned suit. That's all."

I was the bulldog, and no one else was going to do it but me. "Alright, I'll do it," I agreed without enthusiasm.

"Great! Let's talk before the game on Saturday."

The ceremony was one of the great I-told-you-sos of all time. And it would have been funny if it hadn't turned near tragic.

After the band cleared the field, the PA announcer said, "I'd like to direct your attention to midfield. On hand today is Bill Pickering, President of The Westminster Kennel Association, Handsome Dan VII, and his handler Scott McManus. Joining them is our very own Handsome Dan!"

With that, I trotted out towards the small assemblage on the Y at the 50-yard line. As I got to my spot, I looked at Handsome Dan VII and he looked at me. This was his moment, and he didn't want me anywhere near him. But I was. He glared at me and our eyes met. And then he somehow slipped his leash and all hell broke loose.

He lunged at me and off I went, heading for the safety of the sidelines. The crowd cheered as I ran with the bulldog in hot pursuit. I made it to the sidelines where I thought I would be safe. But I wasn't safe at all. In fact, I was quite possibly in mortal danger. He was right there with me. I backed up, keeping my eye on this squat beast.

After a couple of steps in retreat I tripped over a bench and landed on my back. Handsome Dan VII pounced. He was on top of me, tearing at the blue fur of my costume. As the fur, fake though it was, served as a good insulation, I only wore a t-shirt under the outfit. He was digging in to me. I had one furry blue paw at his neck, trying to push him away and maybe strangle him a bit. With the other hand, I lamely smacked at his face, which only ticked him off more.

Tens of thousands of spectators roared, thinking this was choreographed. It wasn't and I was quite sure that this was how I would die; a blue furry gladiator. I could feel the dog's teeth breaking the skin around my shoulder, and warm blood trickled down my side. I was truly panicked, and didn't know how I'd survive the fight that had been brewing all season and had finally come to this.

Just then, a security guard in an orange vest pulled the dog off of me as an assistant coach helped me to my feet.

Handsome Dan VII was corralled away from me, and I

stumbled towards to the locker room as the PA announcer said, "Well, we see that Handsome Dan has the spirit we are looking for. We can only hope our teams will be as tough!"

My wounds turned out to be quite superficial. A few stitches to the fur and I was ready to go for the second half, though I was in a sour mood.

Here's the thing about Bulldog mascots: Sick kids and toddlers were scared of you. Five to eleven-year-olds were the sweet spot. They were amused, delighted, wanted to high five you, get a picture taken, and maybe even an autograph. I love that age. The next age, young teenagers up till about fourteen, were the worst. They knew I wasn't a real giant blue dog, but just some poor sucker chosen to wear the suit. They also knew that the mascot is loveable and can't really fight back, bringing out some pretty nasty behavior. They turned into name-calling, butt-grabbing, tail-pulling assholes.

Kids in their upper teens get the joke, and either ignore you or give you half-hearted recognition. I kind of hated that middle group and this particular day, I just wanted the game to be over.

But there was no way I was going to be on the sideline again with Handsome Dan VII. He had the taste of blood and knew he could whip me. So I made for the stands, where I might get heckled, but at least I would be safe.

I was in a shitty mood after almost getting mauled, and this one kid got on my bad side. He was a wisenheimer 13 or 14-year-old who kept calling me a pussy and telling me his bichon frise could kick my ass. I tried to ignore him, really I did, but when he yelled, "Hey bitch, come over here!" I decided to oblige him.

A few of his friends were egging him on and he was loving it. So I made my way up to say "hi" to him. As a mascot, I was never to speak, just wave, blow kisses and prance around. I made an exception this time.

As I got next to this kid, he called me a pussy a few more times and laughed a bully laugh. I extended a hand to him and he took it. He shouldn't have. Had I not almost been treated like a giant snausage just half an hour earlier, things may have been different. I might have ignored this boy. But it had been a rough day and you can only push a guy inside a bulldog suit so far.

As I waved to the crowd around me, I grabbed his hand and squeezed it as hard as I could, and I could see the pain register in his eyes as this kid's knees buckled.

I brought my blue head close to his. "Listen to me, you little motherfucker," I growled as I tightened my grip. "I am sick and tired of your fucking shit and I am not going to take another second of it." More waving to fans who smiled and waved back. I continued. "I am going to break every fucking bone in your chicken shit cowardly hand if you don't give me a big hug right now." The kid was nearly in tears. He put his free hand around me and gave me a hug.

"'Attaboy!" I said. "Now you make sure to keep your mouth shut for the rest of the game. Another syllable out of you and I will be back. That's a promise" I had turned into a monster. He nodded, utterly defeated. I let go of his hand, rubbed his head playfully, and walked up the stairs of the Yale Bowl to an eight-year-old who had a big smile on his face.

Lost to a dog, whipped a kid. All in a day's work.

I returned to Yale ready and determined to earn my spot

on one of the top three heavyweight boats. I wanted finish my career as an oarsman on a high note. Throughout the fall training season I kept constant track of where I stood against the others competing for a seat in the varsity three: a field that included a number of sophomores who were game for the challenge.

At the end of football season, my roommate and dear friend Stephen Anderer decided that with no more off-season and spring practices, he would join me and sample the Yale Crew experience just for the fun of it. I thought it was great, because he and I could share something I had developed a passion for, and in which he had always shown genuine interest in lending me his support.

And I suppose it should have come as no surprise that he would do well. He was strong as a bull and had a maniacal work ethic, two major plus factors as an oarsman.

My annual anxiety over making the Florida trip was palpable. Finally, a few weeks before the trip, Tony Johnson called me in to speak to him. A bad case of déjà vu washed over me as I made my way down the stairs to his office. I'd had this talk with Dave Vogel twice and wasn't relishing the thought of another kick in the groin. But they had to take me. I worked my ass off! I earned this!

I'm barely in my chair when Tony says, 'Mike, we're choosing our Florida team, and you worked really hard, and you're a senior, but I just can't take you."

Vogel would stab you in the chest, and he wore his heart on his sleeve. Tony Johnson had his heart hidden, I never saw it coming.

"Why not?" I gasped.

Tony didn't blink. "There are a lot of Sophomores on the team, who if I don't take them, they'd quit."

'Tony, I didn't get taken as a sophomore, and I'm standing here as a senior asking you to take me."

Tony did his best to muster some form of empathy. "Zig, you're not like anyone else. Everybody else would have quit. We'll see what happens when we get back.

His words were akin to tearing the heart out of my chest and showing it to me.

It was a somber walk back to my room, where I found Steve sitting on the waterbed in our suite.

He takes one look at me and says, "What's the matter?' He's smiling. So I ignored his question and countered, "What's the good news?'

"I made the Florida trip, I'm the last guy he picked."

"Congratulations!" I offered weakly but with sincerity.

"What's yours?'

I paused, "I didn't make the trip." And Steven burst into tears.

"Nobody wanted it more than you did, I'm going for you." And that was that.

I didn't row in a single race at Yale during my senior year.

———————

In part to salve my wounded spirit, and also to do some "research" for my senior essay I decided that to use the week when I would otherwise be in Florida to return to Florence.

I made it a point to see the boys from the Società Canottieri Firenze: I hung out with them and also went to a couple of libraries, took out a few books, and did a half-assed job gathering research for my senior essay on San Michele, which is a grain refinery from the Renaissance in Florence.

I wanted to talk about the statues and how they represented the progression from gothic to renaissance art. I interviewed such people as the guy who sold the postcards outside of the building. As I pointed out, mine was a very unique and scholarly approach to my senior essay.

Meanwhile Stephen and the boys went down to Florida for training. When they came back, the first race of the year was against Syracuse. When they returned to campus, Stephen walked in the room. He had a Syracuse shirt on his shoulder. He took it off, threw it at me and said "That's yours, buddy. I hung your weight on the end of that oar, every bit as much as I did mine." It was the only shirt he ever won.

While my shirt collection included a coveted crimson jersey with a white H on the left breast, it was meager indeed. But the small quantity of cotton in my dresser drawer would be rendered meaningless when I received the sartorial symbol of athletic success at Yale. The Yale Letter Sweater, a thick cream white woolen sweater with a large felt Y sewn on the center, was awarded to athletes who had made meaningful contributions to their teams. The first Letter Sweater was awarded to Harvard football players in 1875. Yale followed a few years later, and ever since those sweaters have been prized possessions and maintained places of honor in closets around the world. They are worn with pride on chilly fall afternoons at the Yale Bowl by recent grads and nonagenarians alike. All who see a man or woman with a letter sweater knew they were in the presence of someone whose athletic accomplishments met the exacting standard of varsity coaches. Each sport had its own requirements for a Y. Not every member of a team received a letter. In some sports, letters were awarded to players who reached certain milestones such as games played or points scored.

In crew, there are three ways to receive a Varsity Letter. The first was to row in the Varsity eight. The second way to get a sweater was to row in a JV, or second varsity boat, that beats Harvard. The third way to earn a letter was the hardest of all. The ten percent of oarsmen who rowed all four years were honored with the same Letter Sweater given to the most talented oarsmen. Of the more than 200 men and women who took tentative strokes in tanks as freshman in 1981, 17 attended the Varsity Athletic Dinner in the spring of 1985. Most of that group were in the top boats. Not quitting, especially for those who toiled in lower boards, wasn't as simple as just showing up.

When, on Old Campus after attending the informational meeting, I committed to not quitting, I could not have imagined what it would take to fulfill that seemingly simple goal. There was nothing tangible, or even explicable, that captures just what a commitment it would take to meet the third letter standard. The time alone that crew required proved too much for scores of would be rowers. The physical and mental strain was never ending. We were routinely dared to push harder than we thought—than we KNEW!—we could. Many quit because they watched guys like Faust leave all in the tanks, or the ergs, on the stairs, on the water and knew they couldn't give as much of themselves as the sport demanded. For some though, watching the top guys give the cliched 110% each day inspired similar effort.

As much as any sport at Yale, Crew was a year round endeavor. It was relentless, and those who earned letters had to be relentless too.

The day after the Sprints, Vogel and Tony handed Letter Sweaters those who met one of the three requirements. But there would be no sweater for me. Even though I hadn't rowed in the spring race, I was at the docks each day and filled in if a boat was missing someone. But I hadn't quit. I had earned that Y. Or had I? Though Vogel lobbied hard for me, Tony decided that I actually rowed three years as a Lightweight and one as a Heavy. Since they were technically separate teams, I hadn't rowed all for years for one team. Tony wasn't being a heartless dick about it. For starters, he wasn't heartless at all. He was kind and thoughtful and had been part of Yale crew for over a decade. He decided to go by the book. I didn't really blame him. Once you start making judgement calls, it gets tricky. Therefore I became perhaps the only oarsman to row four years and not receive a letter. A singular accomplishment.

———

At the end of my rowing career, Vogel called me to his office. One last time I made the walk over to the alumni offices, down the spiral stairs and past all the shirts hanging on the walls.

"I've coached close to a thousand oarsmen, and I think I am a pretty good judge of talent."

Where's he going with this?

Then, he declared, "You are by orders of magnitude the worst oarsman I've ever coached."

I couldn't believe he had called me here simply to nullify my four years of toil and sacrifice. But I had a sense that Dave wasn't finished. I just hoped it wouldn't get worse, if that was even possible.

"But I really want you to understand what I am about to

say." Dave continued before taking a pause. I saw an expression on his face that I'd never seen before.

"You're better than every motherfucker who ever quit"

"That's it?" I asked.

"That's everything." Dave replied.

Dave Vogel's words validated my entire experience as an oarsman. It had all been worth the effort.

Even though Steve Anderer and I roomed together four years, three of them sharing a bunk bed, I didn't know everything about my dear friend. I knew that his family wasn't nearly as wealthy as I now knew mine to be, and that since his father died, his mother was in dire financial straits, sometimes choosing between heat and electricity because she couldn't afford both. What I didn't realize was that Steve was diverting money he had planned on using for tuition to help his mom with her bills. What he did was noble and private and the fact that I didn't know about it made it more so. What is it they say about character? It's doing the right thing when nobody's watching. That was Stephen Anderer.

I guess I was wrong about Yale being a place where class didn't matter. Though it's true that we all ate the same food and slept in the same accommodations and dressed roughly alike, some students and their families made huge sacrifices for a Yale education, while for others Yale was a large but manageable line item on a family budget that was always in the black. While you might not be able to distinguish between those with money and those who struggled financially by looking at the students on Old Campus or Cross Campus Library, it was there and it mattered, unspoken as it may have been.

Perhaps, no not perhaps, indeed yes, those who either paid for college themselves or for whom loans, grants and parental sacrifice made college possible, got more out of the experience. I've found that the value of something is enhanced when the cost involves sacrifice.

I found out about Steve's circumstance when he came back to our suite in early May, clearly not happy at all.

"Sup?" I asked.

"Nothing," he lied.

"What?" I asked, neither wanting to pry nor ignore.

"The Dean told me I had to go to the Bursar's office," he explained.

"The what?" I asked.

"Bursar," Steve explained. "It's the business office. They keep track of tuition payments, stuff like that. Turns out they won't let me graduate unless I come up with the $11,000 I've been sending my mom to help her with the bills."

"So they are going to fail you out?" I asked.

"No, Michael," he answered as patiently as he could, "it's not an academic issue. I'm set there. It's a financial issue. No money, no diploma. When I come up with the money, they'll send it to me. But on graduation day, I'll get a folder with a blank piece of paper in it, not a certificate suitable for framing." He punctuated the last three words with a thin smile and air quotes.

"Damn," I said, "Wish I could help."

"It's my own fault," he said. "My mom needed help and I kinda got sideways with it all." He turned and lumbered to-wards our room.

Stephen Anderer had earned his degree from Yale, and I

knew this as well as anyone. Not only did he technically complete all his academic requirements, he was a true scholar, with genuine intellectual curiosity. Unlike too many others, including me, Stephen realized the unique opportunity he had at Yale to learn from and with some of the smartest people in the world, and he took full advantage. Stephen took nothing for granted and I was jealous of that quality.

A day or so later, I walked over to the Bursar's Office, a place I'd never heard of before Steve mentioned it, and would never think of again. I walked in and was greeted by the receptionist.

"May I help you?" she asked.

"Yes, I'd like to clear a debt with the college before graduation," I replied.

"Student ID number?" she asked, poised to type it into her computer.

"I'm not sure," I replied. "I don't know it."

"You don't know your ID?" she looked up at me. "And you're a senior? What's your name? You know that, don't you?" And she smiled so it wasn't so mean a question.

"My name is Michael Danziger, but I am not here about my account," I explained. "I am here about Stephen Anderer's account."

"Well, Michael Danziger," she said, "Stephen Anderer will have to come here for his account."

"Here's the story. He's my roommate and he has worked awfully hard for his diploma and is due to graduate magna cum laude in a couple of weeks."

"He won't graduate magna cum anything if he doesn't pay what he owes."

"I understand. He told me that. Would it be ok if I paid the $11,000 for him? The money doesn't have to come from him, it just has to be paid, right?"

"So you want to pay off your roommate's school debt?"

"That's right. I have a check here. Please don't tell him I did this. I just think he deserves his diploma."

She looked at me with kindness and surprise. "Michael Danziger, this is a first. He's got one hell of a roommate, and I promise not to tell."

"So do I," I said, writing a check to Yale University, the biggest check I'd ever written.

A few days later, Stephen joined me at dinner. "Damnedest thing," he said.

"What's that?" I asked.

"Got a message from the Bursar's Office that my account is good to go, and I'm getting my diploma after all."

"Well, that's a relief," I said. "How 'bout we celebrate with a few at Rudy's later on."

"Sounds good. It's funny though," Stephen said, reaching for some meat loaf on my plate. "I asked if there had been a clerical error or something, and the woman just said it was taken care of. I asked her for details, and she just repeated that it had been taken care of. What's up with that?"

I took a swallow of my fruit punch from one of the three small glasses I had filled. "Sounds like they fucked up and then fixed it to me."

Stephen fixed me with a look, kind of curious. There were precious few secrets between us and I had a shitty poker face anyhow. "Was this you?"

What could I do, lie? Plus, I hadn't done anything wrong. I thought.

"Here's how I see it, Steve," I started. "You earned your degree and then some. And you've worked your ass off to pay for most of it. And you got caught short because you were help-ing your mom. And she will be so proud of you at graduation. And I have money I didn't earn and that's doing nobody any good sitting in a checking account. So I helped clear the way for something that was yours already."

"You did this?" he asked.

"Uh-huh."

"I don't know when I can pay you back."

"I'm not asking you to."

"I can't accept this gift," he said firmly.

"It's not a gift, It's not like I gave you money, or paid for you to take a vacation. I simply helped make it possible for you to receive what's yours already."

"Michael," Stephen said reaching out to shake my hand, which I took. "That is one of the kindest, most generous acts I can imagine."

"Please," I said, "Don't mention it. What are friends for?"

"And now," Stephen Anderer told me, "our friendship is changed forever."

"What?"

"Your action, while kind, has forever changed the dynamic of our relationship. I am very grateful, but you are now the do-nor and I am the recipient. That's not a friendship. That makes you my benefactor."

I was familiar with Polonius' warning to Laertes about lending and borrowing, "For loan oft loses both itself and friend." But this wasn't a loan, no one was borrowing, and I thought my action defined friendship, not threatened it.

"Steve," I reasoned, "You've given me so much more than I could ever give you. Friendship, loyalty, your Syracuse shirt, the example you've set. What I gave pales."

"All the same, it changed everything."

We finished our dinner, and talked of drinks at Rudy's. And I knew he was right.

That was his pride talking. Looking back, I should have known that what I had done would bother Stephen. Knowing how he reacted, would I have done it again? Every time.

———————•

Three weeks before graduation, I walked into the Art History building on High Street and knocked on a door that I'd never knocked on before. A professor came to the door. "Can I help you?"

"My name is Michael Danziger. Here's my senior essay."

"Michael Danziger?"

"Yes", I replied.

"I'm your advisor, why haven't I met you?'

"Because I didn't need any advice, I suppose. Here's my essay."

A week later, I received the essay back with a big red F on it. Her comment read, "Your "research", which was little more than the information that anybody could have gleamed from the backs of the postcards you purchased - sold by your primary source, Bertaldo - is a joke. If you receive a degree from Yale in two weeks, your degree, all by itself, will cheapen every other degree handed out that day."

Luckily, sort of, every essay is read by the advisor, and then a blind reader: someone who doesn't know you at all. My blind reader described reading my essay like "Watching a clown skier trying to get down a slope, and wondering whether or not this is the worst skier he's ever seen or the best skier, who is so phenomenal at what he does, that he can make fun of his amazing talent and look like he's on the ragged edge. In terms of scholarship, I don't know where to go with this, but I'm going to give you the benefit of the doubt. You're a clown-skier-scholar. Also, you spelled renaissance three different ways."

He gave me a B+, which averaged out to a D: D for diploma.

A week later, the lightweight crew held their annual banquet. I got a call from John Leone, asking me if I could attend, even though I was technically a heavyweight.

"I'd love to", I confirmed.

At the banquet, they handed out all the usual awards, and then Leone, a junior, announced, "We've got something we'd like to give all the seniors." As Leone called out the names, they started handing out pewter mugs with a Y with crossed oars and a 150 underneath them, with the persons' name engraved on the other side.

Finally, after the mugs had been handed out, John called my name. The guys I'd rowed with, who helped me become who I was, rose to their feet. I looked at the mug, the pewter culmination of four years of toil.

Upon closer inspection, they spelled my name wrong. D-A-N-Z-I-G-G-E-R. But it didn't matter. I was part of the team. Then they said "Here's to the crew", and we all drank. I belonged.

EPILOGUE

STEPHEN

After graduation, Stephen Anderer moved to Philadelphia, where he earned a law degree at Villanova and a psychology degree at Hahnemann University. In an age before email, cell phones and social media, our friendship simply drifted away. Our relationship didn't fall apart, it simply never matured beyond what it was,. We'd see each other at reunions, and exchange holiday cards. He met a wonderful woman and had three daughters. Life went on.

Once, at our 30th reunion, he approached me.

"Michael", he said as he reached out his hand to shake mine (unlike everybody else, Stephen never called me Zig), "There's something I've been meaning to tell you. Thank you."

On August 28, 2016, just weeks before I started penning this Epilogue, Stephen died tragically while swimming as part of a triathlon in Philadelphia. At his memorial service, as I passed through the line, I paid my respects to his widow, Susan. I doubted she knew who I was as I introduced myself and expressed my condolences. Her face lit up as she turned and summoned her daughters, Arielle, Meredith and Samantha, to her side.

"This is the man who helped your father get his degree. Without him I never would have met him at law school. Our family wouldn't exist." It meant the world to me to hear these words. It not only validated what I did 31 years earlier, it salved an open wound over the loss of such a good man far too soon.

MAC

The son of Irish immigrants, Jim McManus grew up in very modest circumstances in New Haven. The fact that he got himself into Yale was a minor miracle. My partner in finishing fifth against the women's four in a 2-man shell at the Head of the Connecticut would go on to be a CEO of several firms, including several years at the Hinckley Yacht Company. In 2013, he was diagnosed with what seemed a beatable cancer, and he went into this fight fully confident that he would emerge victorious, though the treatment was torture.

Two weeks after hosting a party at the 2014 Harvard-Yale game Jim found out that his cancer had spread throughout his body. I spent time with him in his last months reading sections of this book, to his great amusement. I will miss him.

VOGEL

Like me, Dave Vogel moved from Lightweights to Heavyweights, taking over the head coaching position for the Yale heavies for many years. Unfortunately for Dave, his tenure coincided with that of legendary coach Harry Parker at Harvard. He eventually moved to Trinity College in Hartford, coaching the women's crew. Under his tutelage, that program won an NCAA championship. He told me that what he loved most about it was the fact that, at the Division III level, he could bring race strategy into the equation, and really coach, as opposed to throwing eight incredible oarsmen into a boat. He embraced the role of being a coach and mentor to these young women.

RICK

Rick Elser coached the lightweights for a couple more years after I left and then opened a bar in New Haven, naming it Richter's (his actual name was Richter, not Richard or Rick). He got involved in local politics and made an unsuccessful run for Congress.

MIKE

Mike Hard went to work on Wall Street after Yale, then moved to Philadelphia, where he rowed at the Vesper Boat Club. Mike tried out for the U.S. National Team, where he was told by coach Korzeniowski, "Your technique isn't quite strong enough. Thanks for trying out. But there is an erg test tomorrow if you want to stick around for that."

Mike's erg test was a Bob Beamon-esque performance in terms of shattering all previous records. After he was done, coach Korzeniowski said, "I can teach you to improve your stroke, but I can't teach you to do what you just did. Welcome to the team." Mike would row for several years for the U.S. team.

Also, he is godfather to my youngest son, Teddy, who just began his rowing career at Belmont Hill as a freshman.

TONY

Tony Johnson left Yale for Georgetown, where he coached for several years. In fact, his last two years at Georgetown was the first for my son, Robbie. Ironic that the guy he saw as not worth taking to Florida would one day send a son into his program who, according to Tony, is "the kind of oarsman you build programs around." Robbie is now captain of the Georgetown Heavyweight Crew.

JAYMIE

In an era without social media, or even cell phones, I lost contact with Jaymie a few years after I left New Haven. But on my 40th birthday, my mother — who has unique skills for research and genealogy, managed to track him down in South Carolina, where he was working as a tradesman. Also, he was married, and was a father. His experience growing up without one must have taught him the importance of sticking around. We had a great talk that day, and I was truly proud of him.

MY LIFE

The lessons learned from my crew experience at Yale – about perseverance, and how the reward is in the work – served me well over the years since I left New Haven. I think my time with Jaymie also opened my eyes.

My greatest accomplishment in life is raising four sons – James, Robbie, Charlie and Teddy – who are the reason I get up out of bed in the morning. But I am also proud of the fact that I co-founded a college access program that has served more than 2500 underprivileged kids from some of Boston's poorest neighborhoods.

Just like rowing crew at Yale, I had absolutely no experience or skill, but I worked hard and I never gave up. But unlike at Yale, where my effort and dedication did not produce much in the way of results, The Steppingstone Foundation has been a tremendous success and continues to thrive today.

Nearly two years ago I was diagnosed with advanced renal failure. As the word got around about my condition, I was moved by the messages of support I received from my fellow oarsmen. One of these was Jim Faust, who wrote, "I'm sure you know there are four boats worth of friends you can count on always, and know that I sit in those boats among others who would do anything to help anyone rowing in front or behind." So many others wrote similar messages of support.

The same voices that were there to encourage me on the erg, pick me up after I was down, and urge me to get up the stairs during winter training, were there to give me the will to survive.

I am currently waiting to receive a new kidney. There is no telling how long it will take, so in the meantime, I go back to the lessons I learned as Yale's Worst Oarsman...Ever. Never quit. Work hard every day to be your best. That's what I will do now. Thanks for reading my book.

MICHAEL P. DANZIGER

SAY HELLO AT:

FACEBOOK.COM/SMALLPUDDLES

CPSIA information can be obtained
at www.ICGtesting.com
Printed in the USA
LVOW13s1546241217
560725LV00018B/280/P